6/9/14

In Praise of *Willard Garvey: An Epic Life*

"*Willard Garvey* is, yes, great fun to read! What a saga; Garvey defines the term 'larger than life.' It is a wonderful story of a tireless pioneer and entrepreneur who carried the torch for free markets and freedom to innovate all around the world—overcoming obstacles which would have made any reasonable person turn tail and run like hell. In these confusing times, it is a tale that will both entertain and, better yet, inspire. *Willard Garvey* has renewed my spirits."

—**Tom Peters**, bestselling author of *Thriving on Chaos, Liberation Management, In Search of Excellence* (with Robert Waterman, Jr.), *The Circle of Innovation* and other books

"Willard Garvey was a long-time friend and supporter. As the wonderful book *Willard Garvey* shows, he was a man of action who could never sit still very long because he had so many projects that required his attention. As his friends and family will attest, men like Willard don't come along very often. I was honored to play a small part in his life."

—**Robert J. Dole**, former Majority Leader, United States Senate

"Willard Garvey liked to say that 'life is a project.' His own life, however, was not simply a project, but an amazing series of diverse projects, each the realization of his penchant for viewing every problem, whether private or public, as a beckoning opportunity. Living his long life at a breakneck pace till almost the very end, he left a visible legacy that included changing the skyline of his beloved Wichita, building improved housing for people in slum-ridden cities around the world, and hugely expanding the business empire he inherited from his pioneering father. For Willard, government was an intrusive problem and private enterprise a reliable solution, and his initiative never slackened as he advanced an endless stream of ideas and devoted his wealth and energies to the realization of his dreams for improving human welfare. Readers will find Maura McEnaney's book *Willard Garvey: An Epic Life* to be a fascinating and well-rounded account of this remarkable man's life and accomplishments."

—**Robert Higgs**, Senior Fellow in Political Economy, The Independent Institute; Founding Editor and Editor at Large, *The Independent Review*; author, *Crisis and Leviathan, Competition and Coercion, Delusions of Power*, and other books

Louisburg Library
Bringing People and Information Together

"*Willard Garvey* is an engaging and motivating story about a leader who made a real difference!"

—**Steven S. Reinemund**, Dean, Wake Forest University School of Business; Retired Chairman and Chief Executive Officer, PepsiCo, Inc.

"*Willard Garvey* is a business biography of the first order. Pulitzer Prize-winning author Maura McEnaney crafts an impeccably researched but fast-moving story driven by the dynamic life of a visionary entrepreneur. Quintessentially American, Willard Garvey was one of the truly great advocates of free enterprise—in the USA and abroad."

—**Jonathan J. Bean**, Professor of History, Southern Illinois University

"Willard and Jean Garvey were a joy to be around, lots of laughs during the many Chief Executives Organization trips my wife Stevie and I traveled with them. As so well discussed in the fabulous book *Willard Garvey*, Willard was a clever, astute businessman who enjoyed the interaction with the various businesses and entities in which he was involved. His work ethic and integrity earned him a well-deserved reputation for fairness. He was a generous and caring man, and we were proud to be counted among his friends. Spending time with the Garveys was something we looked forward to at every opportunity. I feel especially complimented to have known them and I strongly encourage others to read this inspiring book."

—**Karl Eller**, Chairman and Chief Executive Officer, The Eller Companies; former Chairman and Chief Executive Officer, Circle K Corporation

"As superbly presented in the book *Willard Garvey*, Willard was an innovator and a risk-taker, unafraid of failure or the lessons it could teach. As this compelling biography demonstrates, he was a man with the courage of his convictions—a trait our country so desperately needs at the present hour."

—**Charles G. Koch**, Chairman and Chief Executive Officer, Koch Industries

"Author Maura McEnaney's fascinating biography *Willard Garvey* illustrates how a larger-than-life American original manifested one of his favorite aphorisms, 'patriotism and government are two unrelated subjects.' Born a veritable 'dust-devil' from Kansas soil Garvey whirled through life with passion and purpose leaving a trail of high accomplishments and perplexed bureaucrats."

—**John W. Sommer**, Knight Distinguished Professor Emeritus, Univ. of North Carolina, Charlotte; former Dean, School of Social Sciences, Univ. of Texas, Dallas business, community, and country. Like Teddy Roosevelt's 'man in the arena,' Willard could be and sometimes was, knocked around or even occasionally down, but no one could keep him there. One of his final projects was the remodeling of the old Holiday Inn where the sniper murders of 1976 had occurred. He turned this defunct hotel into the most successful downtown apartment projects completed by his son Jim and grandson Michael. I also recall the very first project I worked with Willard concerning the elimination of the city government's trash service. I wrote an article for *Reason* a couple of decades ago describing that transformation. I am delighted to have known him and happy to call him my friend."

—**Karl Peterjohn**, Member, Board of Sedgwick County Commissioners; former Executive Director, Kansas Taxpayers Network

"The superb book ***Willard Garvey*** vividly shows that Willard was a man of many hats – involvements. He was a man who made a difference in the world, and he was a family man to both his family and his employees."

—**Gary L. Bengochea**, President, Nevada First Corporation

"As shown in the wonderful biography ***Willard Garvey***, Willard charged through life the way he drove his lovable old cars. Fast, faster, and zoom."

—**Jay C. Nichols III**, former Chief Executive Officer, Nichols Industries

"***Willard Garvey*** is a book well written, stimulating and very interesting. I wish to congratulate Maura McEnaney and all the Garvey family for such an accomplishment. Written with amenity and dexterity, the book includes an endnotes section with many references that assure the reader that the research has been serious and that what they read has a solid base. For myself, I worked in 'Hogares Peruanos' (Peruvian Homes) with Willard, and I admired his leadership and dynamism. I met with him personally during working activities, and also had the pleasure to meet his family in Wichita, from all of which I have fond memories. Now, after reading his biography I have learned so many other things of his 'epic' life that I admire him and the whole family, even much more. A book like this is not only a well-deserved homage to Willard, but also a very stimulating reading for other people, particularly the young who are going to shape the world through their doings."

—**Rodolfo Salinas**, former President, Hogares Peruanos, Lima, Peru from this project enabled me to go to law school and become a member of the Colorado Bar. Willard and the Garvey family have done so much for so many people through so long a period of time and I am one of the beneficiaries."

—**Tom Jordan**, President, The Jordan Companies

" *Willard Garvey* is a wonderful book about a man who was a gentleman and dear friend. I cannot recommend it more highly for others to understand why this insightful biography of Willard is so important and well-deserved."

—**Fran D. Jabara**, Founder and Principal, Jabara Ventures Group, Inc.

"In *Willard Garvey*, Maura McEnaney has truly portrayed Willard as a man of the world, always at the forefront, participating, engaging, and taking on whatever life had to offer, at all levels of business, government, sports, arts, charities, philanthropy—rooted in and guided by Christian principles. I was honored to be a daily witness to his life for over 40 years."

—**J. Harvey Childers**, Retired Executive Vice President, Garvey Industries, Inc.

"*Willard Garvey* does a great job of capturing the 'spirit' of the man. I started reading the book this afternoon and could not step away until I had finished it. It was very moving for me as I had experienced many of the projects it covered. It is apparent that his belief system was human independence and privatization, 'Everyman a Homeowner,' and this was deep seeded in family experience and wartime observation. I am so fortunate to have worked for a true entrepreneur with global aspirations, an education beyond compare. I have never met anyone, anywhere, more principled and with more innovative ideas. Willard Garvey was demanding, but he was fair, and his employees and associates were always reminded of his policy of 'less government is better.' Obviously, we could use that in our current political scene. I highly recommend this book for anyone."

—**Bob M. White**, former President and Chief Executive Officer, White International (formerly Garvey International, Inc.)

"*Willard Garvey* includes great stories and I especially enjoyed the early family history including the incredible entrepreneur Ray Garvey, Willard Garvey's father. Willard himself was a man of many passions: family,

"*Willard Garvey* is a well-researched and well-written biography of a truly unique man. Maura McEnaney offers details that even close friends did not know about this multifaceted, energetic, and irrepressibly enthusiastic entrepreneur."

—**Martin K. Eby, Jr.**, former Chairman of the Board and Chief Executive Officer, The Eby Corporation

"As the marvelous book *Willard Garvey* reveals, Willard was a man of extraordinary courage, conviction, and independence with respect to his life's passions and goals, which he doggedly pursued with or without the backing of others. Inspired by and based on his conviction that a legally-educated workforce was vital to the economic growth of Kansas, and with the loving support of his wife Jean, Friends University has provided a master's level legal education program to business professionals since 2004. It has been my pleasure and honor to chair the manifestation and continuation of this dream."

Dixie F. Madden, Willard W. Garvey Distinguished Chair in Law and Director of the Garvey Institute of Law and Master of Business Law Program, Friends University

"Anyone who either knew Willard or wants to know him, as well as everyone else, should read *Willard Garvey*. Author Maura McEnaney absolutely 'nails' him in this great book. It touches on his excitability, sensitiveness, irascibility, creativity, initiative, good will, and continuing evolvement. The world is a far better place because of Willard Garvey."

—**Richard A. DeVore**, Founding Partner, DeVore Enterprises

and laying the foundation for today's conservative movement and Tea Parties. All who love liberty and freedom under God's laws are deeply in his debt."

—**Richard A. Viguerie**, Chairman, ConservativeHQ.com; Chairman, American Target Advertising, Inc.; Founder and Publisher, *Conservative Digest*

"*Willard Garvey* is an incredibly insightful biography of a true visionary and champion of private enterprise who not only talked the talk but walked the walk."

—**Harold Dick**, President, Summit Group; long-time Director, Garvey Industries and Petroleum Inc.

"Reading *Willard Garvey: An Epic Life* is spiritually rewarding. This biography of Willard Garvey captures the determination, joys, drama and even contradictions in the life of a great entrepreneur. The Kansas state motto *ad astra per aspera* (to the stars through difficulties) summarizes his life and legacy. The book takes you to many lands, from troubled Latin America and the Californian woods, to Asia and the islands of the South Pacific. The vivid and realistic descriptions of those territories and cultures, which I also had the luck to enjoy, suffer and traverse, makes *Willard Garvey* a book that can be enjoyed by readers across the globe. The best of America was built by similar spirits, it is the dream of that America which makes me and other immigrants, feel privileged to be here."

—**Alejandro A. Chafuen**, President, Atlas Economic Research Foundation; Founder and President, Hispanic American Center of Economic Research

"*Willard Garvey: An Epic Life* is a marvelous tribute to an outstanding American! Dillard found in Willard a good and loyal friend of many years beginning in their early Young President's Organization days, both sharing the same conservative beliefs and values. He especially enjoyed the relaxing gatherings of fellow CEOers at the Garvey Nevada ranch and Jean and Willard's visits to us for quail hunting in South Georgia."

—**Danne J. Munford**, widow of Dillard Munford, Founder, Chairman and Chief Executive Officer, Munford Do-It-Yourself Stores

"The splendid biography *Willard Garvey* is of considerable interest. I had the pleasure of working with Willard and his firm Petroleum, Inc., in a very successful deal in the Denver Basin in the 1950s. The revenue

"**Willard Garvey** is an inspiring biography of an iconic figure. Reading this wonderfully educational and insightful volume I recalled how Willard was a lot like Margaret Thatcher; neither one was for a moment idle, always hustling and bustling, and never stopping in their probing questions which challenged your every position. As with Margaret one always prepared hard for meetings with Willard and you knew instinctively where they stood. And just like Margaret he did not care at all what people, especially the media, thought about him as long as he knew in his heart (and mind) that what he was doing was right. Totally right. I just wonder what would have happened had Major Garvey met Oxford undergraduate Margaret Roberts (later Thatcher) when they were close neighbors in WWII. Oh, dear me, what a thought!"

—**John Blundell**, former Director General, Institute of Economic Affairs, London, England; author of *Margaret Thatcher: A Portrait of the Iron Lady* and *Remembering Margaret Thatcher*

"Until my reading the fascinating book **Willard Garvey** and even with my having known Willard for some 60 years, I was not aware of the full range of the numerous areas in which he was involved. He truly lived 'An Epic Life' but in addition, he was great company and fun to be with."

—**Nation Meyer**, former Senior Chairman of the Board, First National Bank of Hutchinson

"Until the book **Willard Garvey**, I did not know of Willard's fabulous successes in real estate, related businesses and foreign investments. I only knew him as a friend and politically in which he was very formidable. He had influence with the administrations of Presidents Nixon and Ford, more than I had, and he used his influence effectively and quite frequently. I knew him as a man who got things done when I was not able to do so. Obviously I knew him very personally and pleasantly, and I recommend the book enthusiastically."

—**Howard H. Callaway**, former U.S. Congressman; former President, Callaway Gardens Resort, Inc.

"My friend Willard Garvey was a major unsung hero of the cause of liberty, the conservative movement and limited government. As accurately revealed in the fabulous book **Willard Garvey**, Willard was a leader who mostly operated under the public's radar quietly helping to change American public policy

WILLARD GARVEY

WILLARD GARVEY: AN EPIC LIFE
Copyright © 2013 by LibertyTree Press

LibertyTree Press
100 Swan Way, Oakland, CA 94621-1428
Telephone: 800-927-8733
Fax: 510-568-6040
Email: info@libertytree.com
Website: www.libertytree.com

ISBN 978-0-9886556-1-4
Library of Congress Cataloging-in-Publication Data Available

Cover Design: Keith Criss
Cover photo of Willard Garvey courtesy of the *Wichita Eagle*
Cover map photo: Leandra Lytton
Interior Design and Composition by Jaad Book Design

WILLARD GARVEY
An Epic Life

MAURA McENANEY

LibertyTree Press

For Julie

CONTENTS

"Determine never to be idle. No person will have occasion to complain of the want of time who never loses any. It is wonderful how much may be done if we are always doing." —Thomas Jefferson

PROLOGUE

"I am happier in the pursuit." –Willard White Garvey

WILLARD GARVEY intimidated me long before I met him.

Fresh out of college in 1979, I landed my first newspaper job in the northern Nevada desert town of Winnemucca, Nevada, a two traffic-light gambling town in the heart of sprawling cattle ranches and active gold mines.

A big chunk of the vast sagebrush-covered lands surrounding Winnemucca—about 200,000 acres in fact—belonged to Garvey's Nevada First Corporation, a subject of much talk in the town of then about 4,000.

At the time, I had no idea that the Wichita, Kansas-based Garvey enterprise stretched into half a dozen industries, which in addition to ranching included oil, grain storage, media, commercial and residential real estate, and education. I didn't know Willard was a privatization pioneer or devoted philanthropist. The Winnemucca locals told me only that he was Nevada's largest private landowner in a state where the federal government controls more than 86 percent of its 71 million acres.

What I did know was that there was a delicious romanticism in Garvey's holdings. Ranches called The Bullhead, Stonehouse, and Home Ranch were located in equally romantic places named Paradise Valley or Rebel Creek, evoking real-life images of bandana-adorned buckaroos and cantankerous ranch managers with weathered faces. A drive to see these and half a dozen other Garvey ranches would take more than a day, I was told, unless like Willard, you traveled by plane.

Garvey's land—including the nearly two million acres he leased from the federal government—fed cattle, reaped potatoes, and sprouted alfalfa hay for feed. Another 2,100 acres went to fill an 11 billion-gallon lake he created by damming a local creek. To a 21-year-old transplanted Bostonian, Nevada in all its dusty, dry, mountainous, yet barren glory, transformed my monochrome life into full-screen Technicolor. And as this movie-script life unfolded, I found a kindred spirit in Garvey's daughter Julie, who for a time made Winnemucca her home. As she and others talked about her father, I envisioned a tall, broad-shouldered, mysterious protagonist in a black hat, parting crowds surrounding him as he strolled through town.

I was wrong, of course. Garvey was a 5-foot-11, trim, and (when he wasn't wearing his toupee) balding, energetic, and loquacious character with deep hazel eyes that saw clear to the horizon. In a conversation, he posed rapid-fire questions about your background or business, and before you could spit out the answers, he zeroed in on some connection he had to a prominent person, landmark, corporation, or industry.

I met him at Julie's wedding that same year. When I told him I was a journalist, he told me he once owned a television network and a newspaper. At the time, I remember wondering if I was on the receiving end of a Nevada-sized tale. Much later, I learned of his 1966 investment in the Mutual Broadcasting Corporation and his five-year effort with *Washington World,* a weekly national newspaper in Washington, D.C. These were just two of dozens of entrepreneurial efforts and causes that Garvey undertook in his lifetime.

The second of four children born to legendary agrarians Ray Hugh ("R.H.") and Olive White Garvey, Willard was a contrarian businessman and developer with futuristic ideas, not all of which were greeted by the public with open arms.

He wanted to abolish government and run "cockroach" politicians out of town. He promoted capitalism to socialist and Third World countries through the proposition of home ownership. He fought any and all kinds of tax increases in Wichita, sometimes with great success. He railed against public education, a new jail expansion project, union membership as a condition of employment, and just about anything he believed thwarted personal freedoms. He served as an Army major in World War II as the United States fought for democracy, but by 1970, he and sympathetic thinkers were so dissatisfied with the government that they attempted to start their own country in the South Pacific. That's right: their own country.

As Ray and Olive Garvey's oldest son, Willard was also born into some big expectations. He sought to meet them by looking for opportunities that tested new concepts—like using ethanol as a fuel substitute—and challenging old ones such as publicly operated jails. Unlike his father, who concentrated on businesses that predominantly served the western Kansas wheat farmer, Willard's work sent him to a world beyond the grain. It sent him to new continents, new battlegrounds, new successes, and, in his own words, some new failures.

Family members, friends, community leaders, and associates all agreed that the persistent, sharp-tongued, quick-moving, athletically and militarily disciplined Garvey was often not an easy man to live with or work with or even tolerate at local functions. But interviews with those who knew him best portrayed a man who cultivated great loyalty, an entrepreneurial spirit, and even admiration.

Former Wichita Mayor Bob Knight caught many of Garvey's arrows during his 24-year administration and today counts himself among Willard's admirers. Even though the two did not agree on fundamental political values, Willard was "an amazing citizen," Knight said.

Garvey's construction and development projects changed the footprint of Wichita and other communities around the world. He built Wichita's Epic Center, the tallest building in Kansas; he helped to start two local new schools, a Wichita YMCA, a community television station, and a law program for business executives. Garvey may have been a tough critic of government, Knight said, but he was also "a doer" who took risks. He could bask in "the triumphs of high achievement" or take comfort in knowing he tried what others wouldn't.

If I met Willard again today, I might not find him so intimidating. Through interviews with more than fifty of his former associates and family members—a mere fraction of the people who called him a friend—I know that in addition to being strong-willed, unshakably argumentative, and ceaseless in his thoughts and actions, he was faithful to his family and friends and always, always true to himself.

Some extraordinary people brought a voice to the conditions and circumstances in Willard's life, not least among them Willard's widow, Jean Garvey, and their six children, especially daughter Julie Sheppard, with whom I have shared a friendship of more than 30 years.

Others are no longer with us. Prolific author and historian Craig Miner, the Willard W. Garvey Distinguished Professor of Business History at Wichita State University, was ever gracious, sharing his perspective and interview notes with this non-Kansan, before he succumbed to cancer in 2011. Ruth Garvey Fink was 89 in August 2006, when she ventured out in a white Cadillac beneath a black Minnesota sky to help guests negotiate a tricky intersection near her summer home. She projected the rapid-fire voice of her brother, the smile, energy, and passion of her mother, and a gentility and confidence all her own during our visit. Ruth gave up her bed and slept in a recliner for two nights, while I dreamt of Willard rushing into my room, clapping his hands to wake me, because there was so much we had yet to accomplish. Ruth died in 2007. Entrepreneur Seth Atwood welcomed me into his home with a kind smile and gladly recounted his plan for a new country with two extraordinary men. Mr. Atwood passed in 2010, and Wichita's Bud Beren, nearly killed by Willard's aviation tactics, died six months after our chat. The dashing architect Sid Platt lived until he was 95, dying in 2012. Sadly, after 90 years of vivacious living, Jean Garvey herself passed away in December 2012. She read or was read this book in various forms prior to its finalization, adding insight along the way.

Tracing Willard's life brought me across the country. Two presidential libraries, the Library of Congress, the National Archives and Records Administration, the Kansas Historical Society, and libraries at Stanford University, the Massachusetts Institute of Technology, and Tufts University all helped provide details about Willard's story. The Jean and Willard Garvey World Homes Collection in the Special Collections Department at Wichita State University was the most comprehensive resource. Its one hundred boxes of documents contain an exceptional insight into Willard's life.

Willard Garvey was a complex character. Whether you loved him, hated him, or met him only once, he was unforgettable. That's because he was never idle and always doing. Thomas Jefferson would have been proud.

EPIC ON THE PLAINS

"Why Kansas? Because it is as far as I can get from both coasts." —WWG

MORE THAN A thousand miles from the salty ocean breezes of both U.S coastlines, Wichita, Kansas, rises skyward from the vast South Central Plains.

A journey there by highway is a venture due west from the Atlantic seaboard across the muddy Mississippi at St. Louis and on to Missouri's Osage Plains to the border town of Kansas City. Once inside the Sunflower State—so named for the bounty of giant yellow blooms that prosper in the late summer's scorching heat—the renowned Kansas flatlands are overshadowed by the contrasting beauty of its Flint Hills; sprawling wheat fields begin about 50 miles northeast of town.

From the Pacific coast, a Wichita trip promises more of an adventure. Out of Los Angeles, drivers must cross California's majestic Mojave Desert and pass through the excesses of Las Vegas before hitting Utah and then the Rocky Mountains. In eastern Colorado, the land begins its descent and greets its Kansas neighbor at the appropriately named town of Kanorado. Further along on Interstate 70, the winds pick up at the town of Goodland, where less than a century ago the "good land" of the High Plains once brought prosperity to just about anybody with a tractor.

Eastward still is Colby, Kansas, a slightly larger farm town where Willard Garvey spent the first eight years of his life. Today, Colby dubs itself "The Oasis on the Plains," perhaps more for the availability of traveler services than for its geographic beauty. Architecturally, the county seat boasts the grand Thomas County Courthouse, a proud Romanesque limestone structure built with a $50,000 bond issue approved by residents in 1906 and listed in the National Register of Historic Places. It is one of the city's top attractions. Another is the Prairie Museum of Art and History, where visitors can see a Kansas sod house replica and get a three-dimensional view of life among prairie pioneers at the turn of the century.

In 1928, Willard's father, Ray Hugh Garvey, a county attorney turned real estate man and service station owner, left Colby's dusty dirt roads as a 35-year-old entrepreneur with a wife and four children and headed east to Wichita. They traveled about 300 miles southeast in a Dodge sedan with the hopes that a bigger community could offer more opportunities for young Ruth, Willard, James, and Olivia.

None of the Garveys would regret that decision. Wichita was good to the family, and they were good for Wichita, too. It became the center of their considerable business empire.

MODERN DAY TRAVELERS from any direction are likely to find a welcome sight in Wichita. Named for the Indian tribe that settled in the area around the junction of the Arkansas and the Little Arkansas rivers, Wichita grew first on the shoulders of the cattle trade and the farming industry before becoming best known as a home to the aircraft industry. Namesake company founders Walter Beech, Clyde Cessna, and Bill Lear all called Wichita home at one time, and the city still prides itself on its "Air Capital of the World" moniker.

Aviation provides major support for the local economy, despite Chicago-based Boeing's 2012 decision to close its Wichita plant. The city is still home to Boeing parts maker Spirit Aerosystems, and by another estimate, Wichita makes nearly half of the world's general aviation airplanes.

The vitality of that business and others provides Wichita's 382,000 residents with access to the commercial conveniences and cultural amenities of most any midsize American enclave. The city is home to three colleges, more than a dozen museums, a ballet, a symphony, a horticultural center, and a zoo.

Against the brilliance of a blue summer sky or the foreboding clouds of a classic Kansas rainstorm, downtown Wichita's white buildings stand out as a collective symbol of Midwestern commerce and activity. Foremost in the group and reaching 325 feet and 22 stories into the air is the pointed copper peak of the Epic Center, the tallest building in Kansas.

To some, it may appear to be an unexceptional office tower, about one-fourth the height of New York's Empire State Building. Yet hundreds of lawyers, administrative assistants, investment bankers, and accountants travel in and out of the doors of the 300,000-square-foot building every day. At night, when the downtown neighborhood around Second and Main streets is all but abandoned, a lighted outline of the building's slanted, triangular roof is transformed into the city's true beacon, a reminder, perhaps, of the spirit of hearty Kansans who stood tall to survive the prairie's pioneering hardships.

It also recalls the impact of the man who built it. While Willard Garvey's accomplishments ranged from farming to real estate and his interests eventually extended to five continents, Wichita was always his hometown. Like the center, Garvey's life merits the term *epic*, with Garvey himself as its larger-than-life hero, and the story of the Epic Center reflects the quintessence of Garvey's sometimes blustery, often headstrong, and endlessly optimistic character.

WHEN SID PLATT looked at the Epic Center he thought of his friend Willard Garvey. It had been about 85 years since the two men first met in the early 1920s, as playmates during summer campouts in western Kansas. They parted ways during the college and war years but came together again as men, with Platt plying a trade in architecture and Willard following in his father's footsteps in land development and housing. During their lifetimes, the two friends joined forces on a half dozen building projects in the Wichita area. Willard even called on his friend to design the family home in 1957.

Platt, who at 90 sported the white curly hair, chiseled face, and lean build of a Roman nobleman, still drove to his appointments and spoke with the powerful and deep intonation of a seasoned radio broadcaster. His age was reflected only by his faulty hearing, which led to his retirement from architecture a decade earlier. An architect's second language is numbers, and when you can't distinguish one from the other, the results can be disastrous, he said.

Willard Garvey began his crusade to make the Epic Center come to life in the mid-1980s, when Ronald Reagan was in his second term as U.S. president and the country was beginning to recover from a devastating recession.

More than 50 years after moving to Wichita with his parents and siblings, Willard—a well-connected homebuilder, oil man, ranch and grain elevator operator, and owner of substantial land in and around Wichita—got word that the city's major aircraft companies were shopping for some new headquarters. At the same time, the city was trying to unload a tract of vacant land just south of City Hall. An opportunity was in the making, Willard thought.

As he so often did when mulling an idea that involved architecture and building, Garvey sought out his long-time friend at Platt, Adams, Braht, Bradley & Associates with hopes of bringing the aircraft firms downtown.

"You know, we ought to build those buildings for them," Willard told Platt.

Like so many of Willard's associates often did, Platt tried to get him to think through the idea. Talk to the aircraft companies, he said. See who might be interested in moving downtown. Secure the tenants first and then build a building; it was good advice. But Willard's mind was already made up.

"Hell, we'll just build the damn thing and then they'll come to us," he told Platt. "And while we're at it, let's do two."

The idea of building the largest single development in downtown Wichita's history at a time of uncertainty in the local and national markets was risky to say the least. But the 65-year-old Willard Garvey knew about risks. He had dodged German V-1 "buzz bombs" in London in World War II. He had co-signed a $50 million personal guarantee loan with his father, whose sudden death left the entire family facing possible financial peril. He had lost plenty of money in his lifetime, and he knew that sometimes, the principle overshadows the risks.

An idea man with a lifelong dream of making Wichita a world-class city, Willard Garvey loved to think big, as long as the government wasn't involved. Attracting new companies to downtown Wichita through private efforts was the only way that could work. The city—or any public entity for that matter—did not belong in the development business, he thought. A giant new office complex in downtown Wichita could help propel a "switch from dependence on government and centralized elites." It could "revitalize individual, competitive action." It could fulfill a dream.

At Builders, Inc., the Garvey Industries real estate and construction subsidiary, managers charged with drumming up commercial development were receptive to the idea of building twin 22-story towers on 6.7 acres of prime downtown land. Under the absolutely right set of circumstances, the project could work, advisers said. Under the wrong set, the Epic Center could permanently jeopardize, or even bankrupt Builders, Inc., the business Willard's father, Ray Garvey, had started at the end of World War II.

As usual, Willard wasn't worried.

"You know, I might regret building it," he said, once board members gave the okay to the project. "But if I don't build it, I'll regret it more."

"He built because he had to build," recalled Platt. "He *had* to build."

Platt would eventually design the Epic Center for his friend. It would be the last project he and the businessman, developer, philanthropist, and gadfly of local renown would ever work on together.

For five years, Willard and his associates, family members, financiers, and trusted advisers endured the ups and downs of building a $28 million commercial office project. First, construction was delayed when the developers were unable to purchase an additional acre of land needed for the original four-building design. That design was later scrapped, and Platt was named architect for a new, two-building project. Project managers scrambled to get new plans and financing approved, as lost time added up to lost money.

Epic threatened the financial stability of Builders, Inc. It also threatened a friendship.

Platt remembers walking to Willard's office carrying his big roll of plans and a telephone book-size set of notes from which he would regularly update Builders' executives on the building's progress. Inevitably, the luncheon meetings erupted in arguments as Willard incessantly questioned the project's costs, design details, and decisions. One day, all that nitpicking was too much for Platt to take.

"He just started saying, 'What are you doing? What are you doing?'" Platt recalls.

"I said, 'Goddamn you Willard!'—and I threw the plans down, and the specs over in the corner. Then I said, 'Besides that, damn it, I'm not coming to any more luncheon meetings. They upset my stomach.'"

Despite the flurry of arguments, Platt and his firm successfully executed Garvey's vision, and the friendship held steady. "What we soul-searched for was Willard's idea: that it be *epic*," Platt told the *Wichita Eagle-Beacon*. "Epic, whatever that is, is a pretty big impetus. How do you make Epic on the Kansas Plains?"

The building schematics called for two identical white structures with pointed peaks, a copper roof, and eyehole windows. A tubular concrete design—borrowed directly from the design of the family's grain elevators—would help sustain the building in the face of fierce Kansas winds, giving prospective tenants a sense of security. In height and style, the modern Epic would far surpass the buildings at the nearby Garvey Center, the downtown landmark erected in the 1960s to honor Willard's parents.

On paper, the Epic Center was a winner. To help make it a reality, the city issued $28.5 million in industrial revenue bonds. It also gave Builders, Inc. a 10-year, 50 percent property tax abatement equal to $1.7 million.

But clashes with the city over the design changes, a simultaneous crash in the oil industry upon which Wichita was heavily dependent, and subsequent high office-vacancy rates all spelled trouble for the speculative development. "Sneers and snickers of skeptics and doubters in government, business, and even John Q. Public," were heard all over town, the local newspaper wrote.

The naysayers were wrong. And they were right, too. There would be an Epic Center. But there would be only one tower, plenty of bad publicity, and a forfeited deed along the way. Willard Garvey lost millions on the Epic Center and still came out a winner. He built the tallest building in Kansas, a structure that changed Wichita's skyline and created a permanent beacon for the eventual revitalization of the city's downtown.

ON NOVEMBER 12, 1987, downtown Wichita and its newest landmark were ablaze with activity as the Epic Center held its grand opening. Crowds of dignitaries and tuxedo-clad employees of Garvey's Builders, Inc., mingled as they moved between floors, where international foods and entertainment were offered. On the top at floor 22, a costumed King Kong hammed it up with guests for the camera.

"There was a festive air about the whole event," said Bonnie Bing, the social scene columnist for the *Wichita Eagle-Beacon.* "It was just a big party."

On this night, 67-year-old Garvey, his family, and fellow employees were celebrating more than just the completion of another project. They were heralding a vision and a dream come true. Tonight, the entire city was celebrating with them. Everyone who laid eyes on the building was proud of the end result. The Epic Center is "as strong as it is spectacular," the newspaper proclaimed.

The celebration would not be long-lived. In its first two years, the building—which carried a $26 million, 11.25 percent loan from the Alaska Permanent Fund and the Boeing Retirement Fund—was about 40 percent vacant, double the vacancy rate for all of downtown. Some said the building "flooded an already overbuilt commercial real estate market." When the tenants never materialized, Builders, Inc. was left paying the bills, incurring a $100,000 monthly shortfall.

Parent company Garvey Industries tolerated the losses for two years. In 1989, the building was turned over to the lenders, in accordance with the "non-recourse loan" that protected Willard and his companies from further financial obligations. The Epic Center still stood tall, but Willard was out almost $5 million in the process.

"In hindsight, that was quite foolish," Willard said later. "We were trying to do something for downtown Wichita. ... I intended to put $3 million into it. But I made a $5 million mistake instead of a $3 million mistake."

Twenty-five years after the Epic's grand opening, those mistakes have long been erased. The building, with its mellowed copper roofline pointing heavenward, still defines the Wichita skyline. Embracing the Kansas state motto "Ad astra per aspera," meaning "To the stars, through difficulties," Willard Garvey turned an empty lot into a towering presence of business opportunity that rises above the municipal buildings at its feet. He built it—with or without profit—because he *had* to build it, as a symbol of individual, competitive action and private enterprise in a city he loved dearly.

2

DOWN ON THE FARM

"I have been most fortunate – particularly in the selection of my parents."–WWG

THERE WAS NO such thing as a skyline when eight-year-old Willard Garvey and his siblings first laid eyes on their new hometown of Wichita.

When the Garvey family pulled into the city of more than 100,000 in 1928, the Roaring Twenties were in full swing, Charles Lindbergh's *Spirit of St. Louis* had successfully landed in Paris the year before, and aviation was all the rage. In the air, there were Wichita-made biplanes from the E.M. Laird Co. and Travel Air, headed by Walter Beech. There were monoplanes from Cessna Aircraft Co. with instructors from the city's thirteen flying schools. On the ground there were streetcars, shiny new Model A Fords, flashing theater marquees, department stores, and a massive exhibition hall.

Even the rivers were full of activity. On the weekends, the banks of the Little Arkansas River near Murdock and Waco streets were full of spectators, some of whom lingered beneath the Corinthian-columned porches of the Riverside Boat Company, as canoeists navigated the shallow waterway beneath them. On the opposite side of the river, youngsters perched on a brick wall abutment to watch the boaters and even a few swimmers enjoying the water.

"It was a big deal coming from Colby to Wichita," Willard recalled years later. "You had a swimming pool and crafts and camps and all the good things. I was pretty excited about it."

Wichita was indeed a far cry from the farming community of Colby, whose population of about 1,500 lacked the excitement and activity of the largest city in Kansas. There, family entertainment was more about neighborly get-togethers, and the highlight of a child's early summer social life might be a dip in a farmer's swimming hole just north of town. For the Garvey children, even that fun was cut short one summer after Colby's warm, stagnant waters bred a nasty chigger infestation.

After more than a decade of living in Colby, where she watched her husband turn from lawyer to businessman, to farmer and land developer, to service station owner, Olive Garvey began "lobbying for a move" to a bigger city. Having grown up in Topeka, she longed to expose her children to the cultural and educational experiences of city life.

By 1928, Ray agreed, and the Garveys relocated from their two-story white clapboard house to an "old but commodious brick house" rented on North Clifton in Wichita's leafy and charming College Hill neighborhood. While the move was no doubt an exciting one, Ruth Garvey Fink, the eldest of the four children, remembered that the children didn't really have a say in the matter.

"Well, we went along," she recalled, laughing, eight decades later. "It wasn't anything you had an opinion about, you just did it!"

FOR 35-YEAR-OLD Ray Garvey, the move to Wichita took some getting used to. Born "a scrawny, peevish baby" in Phillips County, Kansas, the energetic and easy-going Ray was vastly comfortable in the big sky and dress-down world of the western Kansas High Plains farmer.

His paternal grandparents, Obadiah Garvey and Mary "Polly" Hale, moved to Kansas in 1879 from outside Bedford, Indiana. Like so many other immigrants of the late nineteenth century, they came in search of new life and the promise of rich soil.

At the time, Kansas had been a state for only 18 years. The scars of the Civil War, which began less than three months after statehood and ended four years later in 1865, still lingered. About 620,000 American lives were lost in the war, including 8,500 from Kansas, which had fought its own "Bleeding Kansas" battles over slavery prior to statehood. Across the region, Indian wars were still simmering as the nation's buffalo herd neared extinction, with more than 31 million animals killed in less than 15 years.

As the land opened up, the parade of homesteaders into Kansas continued. It was a parade that accelerated in 1862, when the federal government guaranteed title on up to 160-acre tracts to families who lived and worked the land for at least five years. Settlers could also buy their land for up to $1.25 per acre after six months.

Ray Garvey's grandparents came to Kansas in wagons with only each other, four of their twelve children, a few household goods, and $1,000 in cash. The other Garvey children were scattered: married with families of their own.

Farm life in Kansas and most anywhere in the country brought long days and grueling work. For the most part, Obadiah and Polly's children undertook the chores needed to help sustain their family. Only Seth, the youngest of the lot, ventured toward books instead of bales of hay.

Seth became a local schoolteacher, receiving a meager but steady pay of about $15 to $20 per month. Across Kansas, the first schools were often housed in abandoned sod houses, with students sitting on legged, half-log benches on dirt floors. Later, classes were held in stone or wood frame school buildings containing a few wooden desks and a blackboard.

Then considered an aging bachelor, the 20-something Seth Garvey was quickly distracted by the long black hair and blue eyes of 15-year-old "Nettie" Post. They were married a year later on October 4, 1881. Seth and Nettie began life together in a dirt-walled dugout on a farm owned by Nettie's father, Peter Post. The couple had three children: Della, Grace, and Ray Hugh, born in 1893.

A few years after Ray's birth, drought and depression yielded poor crops and little money. Seth decided to take his family on the road with the hopes of finding another teaching job. He ran a country store in Graham County before landing in Wyandotte County outside of Topeka. Eventually, the family returned to Phillips County and moved east of Phillipsburg along the south side of what is now Route 36 near Gretna. There, they built a six-room house on rolling land, with a barn and a building for storing grain.

As they watched their youngest child move through his teenage years, Seth and Nettie wanted Ray to stay on the farm. But like his father before him, Ray harbored a love of books and dreamed of going to college. He worked for a year as a schoolteacher, earning about $45 a month and saving what he could for college. In the fall of 1910, Ray Garvey traveled clear across Kansas to Topeka to start classes at Washburn University, a Congregational college on 160 acres then just southwest of town.

At school, the slim, blue-eyed competitive runner and Gamma Sigma fraternity pledge supported himself with three paper routes, delivering one and subleasing two others. Ray later became an accomplished debater and co-manager of the class yearbook. He met Olive White from Topeka, "the junior girl with the prettiest smile." The two became engaged during their junior year in January 1913.

OLIVE WAS BORN in Arkansas City, Kansas, on July 15, 1893, the fifth of six children born to Oliver and Caroline "Carrie" Hill White.

Her father, an entrepreneur who eventually became a "prosperous implement dealer," was born in North Carolina and moved to Indiana in 1858 when he was six. He met Carrie Hill—a very distant cousin, they learned later—at Earlham College, a Quaker school in Richmond, Indiana, and they married in 1880.

The couple first settled in North Carolina where Oliver worked in the lumber milling business. But when malaria—a common illness in the region's muggy, swampy heat—claimed their young son, the couple returned to Indiana, where they farmed and had two daughters: Mary Elizabeth in 1883 and Ione in 1886.

By then, the nation was changing at a rapid pace. Railroads were crossing Kansas lands, bringing passengers eager to settle in unclaimed territories. Oliver White felt the draw of prosperity in Kansas and followed his sister and her husband to Arkansas City in 1887.

Located on the south-central tip of the state bordering Oklahoma, Arkansas City was a destination for pioneers heading south to the new Indian Territories. Newcomers needing to restock their supplies for their journey were a boon to Oliver White's business. The couple had two more children: Florence in 1888 and Olive in 1893. Together, the family watched a young country spring up around them, as thousands of prairie hopefuls landed in Arkansas City for organized land runs that gave away claims to federal land once belonging to native people. When she was just three months old, Olive was part of the commotion of an Oklahoma land rush, when the government opened up more than two million acres of "unassigned land" in Oklahoma.

As the land rushes slowed, so too did the implement business. Oliver sold his company in 1899, and the family moved for a short time to a ranch near the Osage Indian Reservation in Kay County, Oklahoma. The two oldest White girls came of age and were sent to Topeka to attend Washburn University and Washburn Academy.

Olive and her parents followed in 1902, and the Whites welcomed their son Elliot that same year.

Olive learned all about Washburn from her sisters and enrolled there after three years in high school. She entered college in 1910 without a high school diploma by passing a few tests and receiving special admission. At the college's first social event, she met Ray Garvey. They were engaged by their junior year.

After graduating in 1914, Olive taught school in Augusta, Kansas, while Ray finished another year of law school. He graduated the following year, passed the Kansas Bar and then headed back to western Kansas for the harvest. Hearing of potential work opportunities, he went to Colby and met A.A. Kendall, a retired judge whose new profession was in real estate, farm loans, investments, and mortgages. Ray began working out of the office, and having lined up a steady career, in July 1916, he returned to Topeka to marry Olive. After the ceremony and a sit-down lunch at Olive's family home, the 23-year-old newlyweds took a train back to Colby, where they began to live out a classic entrepreneurial success story.

Law work with Judge Kendall earned him a living, but Ray could see from his clients that there were handsome profits in land sales. The growing country was demanding more wheat, and that meant more sales of farmland.

Sensing the opportunity, Ray took $500 saved from his Topeka paper routes and bought his first piece of land in Colby. By January 1918, he was concentrating exclusively on the land business, which earned him twice as much as his law practice. Meanwhile, the couple doted on their nine-month-old daughter, Ruth, and hoped for more children. For the Garveys, Colby was proving to be a fine place to live.

Ray Garvey often attributed his success to being in the right place at the right time. He joked that timing and conditions "forced" him to pursue new businesses such as service stations when farmers needed gas pumps near their fields, grain elevators when the nation was bursting with excess wheat, oil fields when he needed tax breaks and dust seemed to be the only crop the country's midsection produced.

But his timing was perhaps never better than in the waning days of World War I. Determined to help with the war effort even though he was granted a deferment for having a wife and child, Ray took out a $50,000 life insurance policy in Olive's name and enlisted in the Air Force. On November 11, 1918, he was in St. Louis working on his admission papers when the war ended and a cease-fire was declared. Ray Garvey was "forced" home to safety.

In the summer of 1920, Olive was expecting a second child and she was anxious about the delivery. The baby, it seemed, was in constant motion. There was no hospital in Colby, and after complications with Ruth's birth, Olive need more assurance. In July, the family traveled to the cool air and mountainous landscape of Colorado Springs to await the birth of Willard White Garvey on July 29.

Ray Garvey never forgot meeting his "red-headed lad" in the hospital more than a week after his arrival. Since fathers in delivery rooms would not become routine for another 50 years, Ray busied himself with work, while Ruth and her grandmother stayed "in a little cottage 'three blocks away'."

"Pappy" as Ray sometimes called himself, had just returned from selling "a half section of land at $85 an acre with $1,500 down" to a "Swede from Nebraska" named Ole Olson. With 640 acres to a section, it promised to be a $27,200 sale if the crops came in. Pleased with the outcome of his sale and with his son, Ray teased poor Olive by "saying the lad should be named Ole." But the name Willard White Garvey prevailed. At 27 years young, Ray and Olive had plenty to smile about.

Ole Olson wasn't smiling at the end of 1920, however. Corn prices that year dropped from $1.85 a bushel in June to 29 cents a bushel in December, leaving Olson's mortgage unpaid. Garvey resold the forfeited land the next spring for $70 an acre, and marked it down again and again for at least another decade, as western Kansas began a descent into two decades of agricultural depression.

In his first year, Willard Garvey's life was bracketed by the promise of profits and the realities of losses. He entered this world in the middle of a family business deal and was crawling as market forces began to shift. Family matters and business matters were often one and the same in the Garvey household. It would be that way for the rest of his life.

TRAINING GROUND

"Entrepreneurship is career education. . . cradle-to-the-grave on-the-job training." –WWG

THE DAWNING OF the 1920s brought a shift to modernity. The introduction of new types of automobiles and airplanes, along with household machinery that washed clothes, refrigerated food, and even shaved a man's face, spelled progress for America, fueling patriotic sentiment in a postwar world. Machines were also making farmers more efficient, with new gas-powered tractors replacing the mammoth, expensive steam-engine tractors of the past.

Ray Garvey and Judge Kendall happily participated in this progression. Over the course of about five years leading up to the 1920s, they had acquired and tilled approximately 25,000 acres of land in Thomas County, helping the region become one of the state's leading wheat producers. They succeeded in part by selling land that was already sowed with the new type of "winter wheat," planted in fall and harvested in early summer to avoid the baking Kansas sun and predictable onslaught of voracious pests. Farmers wanting to get in on the record wheat prices approaching $3 a bushel couldn't resist buying land from the Kendall Land Company. In a single day, the partners sold $50,000 worth of property.

But as the decade turned, so did wheat prices, deflated by the end of wartime government price guarantees. Like Ole Olson's corn prices, wheat dropped by more than half to below $1 a bushel in 1921, and the flood of optimistic novice farmers disappeared from sight. In the early 1920s, an aging Judge Kendall decided he had had enough and opted out of the land business, splitting the Kendall Land Company holdings with Garvey. Although the market had grown cold, for the next 20 years, Garvey hung on and added to his land inventory, leasing out whatever wheat production he could and using the proceeds to pay his taxes.

For the Garvey family, life in Colby was not negatively affected by the shifts in the 1920s economy. Two more children were born after Willard: James Sutherland in 1922 and Olivia Rae in 1926. Somewhere in the mix, the family also acquired a black and white dog named Beans.

At home the children were unaware of their father's burgeoning success. "All through my years until I got out of the Army, I wasn't aware that we had even more than an average income," Willard recalled later.

Time with "Pop" or "Daddy," as Ruth called her father, was usually reserved for fun. With his widening girth, broad smile, and gentle demeanor, Ray Garvey had a playful and hugely sentimental heart reserved for his children, whom he nicknamed "Toodles" (Ruth), "Willer" (Willard), "Skeeter" (James), and "Bunny" (Olivia). "Of all the projects a person has, perhaps his children are the most important, and ours are a particularly fine lot," he told them later.

Discipline generally fell to Olive, whom her children addressed as "Mother."

Vivid moments with his children were stored in Ray's head like a carefully preserved photo album. When Willard grew older, his father sentimentally recalled the day "when you cried yourself to sleep on my shoulder because your mother was giving birth to

James and you could scarcely be consoled because you could not sleep with her."

His father's mechanical ability to instantly recall places, names, and incidents in both family and business affairs led Willard to call Ray "the human Univac" after the name of the first commercial computer made in the United States. "He kept all of his business transactions in his mind," Willard recalled. "He could forecast income, estimate taxes, and allocate cash on his complex operations almost to the dollar without any help at all."

The Garvey youngsters gleefully visited with their father in between his car trips out buying, selling, and optioning land. There was always a car of some sort, sometimes one that had been acquired in lieu of land or lease payments. Occasional family outings involved a trip accompanying Ray in his seven-passenger touring car as he oversaw work on his various farms. During their days in Colby, the children witnessed the nation's transformation as prairie tall grass was churned into productive wheat fields.

Later, when years of drought and dormant sod produced giant clouds of dust-filled misery and forced migrations across the Great Plains, Ray Garvey's large-scale farming operations became a target of severe criticism. Locals said he was a threat to the family farm, and others cried that too many plows were stirring up the Dust Bowl conditions of the "Dirty Thirties."

Environmental and economic reasons for the Dust Bowl are still being debated today. "The idea that the Dust Bowl was caused by big farmers and irresponsible farming practices is way off," said the late Kansas historian and author Craig Miner of Wichita State University. "There had been Dust Bowls for hundreds of years. I guess it would have been a little bit less severe had they left all that country in grass. That would have been okay as long as you were willing to live like an Indian."

Garvey's operations used the "summer fallow" farming method, which left fields dormant every other year in an effort to let the soil rest, preserve ground moisture, and ultimately increase yield. "He was quite an environmentalist, actually," Miner said.

Still, the attacks grew with the dust, which rolled through more than one million acres at its peak, reaching from Texas to Nebraska and west into parts of New Mexico and Colorado. Garvey took on the critics, teaching his children a valuable lesson in the process. "My mother and father didn't think it was right to worry about what other people were thinking," Ruth Garvey Fink recalled later. Instead, they encouraged their children "to go ahead and do what was right."

And that's what Ray Garvey believed he was doing. It wasn't just one man's or one company's farming effort that brought on the dust catastrophe, he argued. Nature did its part, too. Cyclical weather patterns in a land that traditionally produced "electric winds" and unmanageable dust storms would show that the region was primed for accelerated problems in a prolonged drought. Anyone who managed wisely, operated efficiently, and held on until it rained again could come out the other side, Garvey believed.

Long before that time came, Ray Garvey discovered—or as he liked to put it "was forced into"—his next business opportunity. With all the new tractors out in the fields, farmers needed gas for their machinery, and they needed it close to home. As one of the nation's top petroleum producers with large refining capabilities, Kansas provided ample resources to serve Garvey's gasoline service business, founded in 1924. It kept him solvent through the Great Depression, as he worked his way to becoming the richest man in Kansas.

AS A CHILD, Willard displayed a hyperactive energy and natural curiosity that stayed with him through his life, according to his mother. Whether he was playing with his brothers and sisters or exploring the western Kansas fields during family picnics, he was in constant motion.

"He was always busy, always doing something," Olive told author Billy Mack Jones in August 1983. "Neighbors would call to tell me he was up on the roof and would be worried to death, but somehow I never worried about it because he always knew what he was doing … and Willard never did injure himself."

Photos from the summer of 1926 show him stopping long enough to pose with siblings Ruth, James, and baby Olivia and his mother while playing Indian scout games in the knee-high Kansas grass. The older children are dressed in costume, with the boys sporting lace-up shirts and feathered head dresses. Nine-year-old Ruth is dressed to be a part of the adventure but appears more concerned with looking after her baby sister than taking part in her brothers' mischief.

In a winter photo taken that same year, a six-year-old mitten-clad Willard is caught mid-motion fussing with the hood on his unbuttoned coat. This dislike for outerwear apparently carried over into his adulthood, as Willard was known to leave his office in bone-chilling winter conditions wearing only a tweed jacket, scarf, and gloves.

As the Garvey family grew in Colby, Olive was able to hire domestic help and later high school babysitters to free up time for her beloved community efforts. In Colby, Olive helped launch the town's first library and beautified the local cemetery. There were also afternoon card parties and occasional gatherings of the "Leisure Hour" club for some of the older ladies in town.

The children went to school during the week and attended Sunday school on the weekend. Olive, who had been raised a Quaker and was trained to recite daily Bible passages, now required Willard and the others to attend local Presbyterian Sunday school and occasionally the Methodist church services. Willard fondly recalled the "congenial" Sunday gatherings and Bible lessons from his youth. He once won a New Testament for regular attendance and good behavior.

But with that good behavior came a kinetic activity most likely inherited from his father's "nervous energy" and "constant motion." Willard also inherited his father's inquisitiveness, a trait which, when not well managed, could get him into trouble, even as a child.

In 1926, Willard received a toy taxicab as a souvenir from a trip his parents took to a Rotary national convention in Denver. "The clerk said it was indestructible," Olive explained to Ray as she gave her son the small iron car. Days later, Willard set out to prove the clerk wrong. He took a hammer and smashed the cab to bits. When she discovered what Willard had done, Olive was "outraged and reacted promptly," punishing him for the destruction.

Willard was also punished in kindergarten for biting a child who tried to steal his crayons. Despite a spanking from the teacher and some harsh words from his mother, Willard was not particularly remorseful over the incident because he believed he was only defending his property.

At the time, Olive Garvey failed to see the absolute veracity of her son's actions. What she would come to know and admire is that challenging accepted truths was an inherent part of her son's character. He would always stand up for what he believed was right, no matter the consequences.

Willard believed he was right about most things. One year, a Colby drugstore raffled off a child-size pedal-propelled automobile, and Willard announced to his mother that he intended to win it. Olive tried to gently explain to the boy that winning isn't always possible, but sure enough, Willard's name was called and the pedal car was his. "Mother, I was right," he told her. "I am almost always right."

❃

OLIVE, TOO, WAS right about Wichita, even though it took "a number of years" to persuade her husband to move there.

"I was always harping on it," but Ray "was not too interested in going to the city," she recalled later. "He said he didn't know how to make a living in a big town."

Her pleas "finally made an impression" and Ray agreed to move, handing over the management of his farms to a well-known and successful local farmer. Within months of his arrival in Wichita, he launched a company that packaged and sold farm mortgages to investors. Amortibanc Investment Company was his third major business venture, with at least three more still to come.

For the children, the Wichita move brought new schools and new friends. Willard enrolled in third grade at the Alcott School, with James behind him in first. Ruth, in seventh grade, went to Roosevelt Intermediate School, and Olivia stayed home with her mother.

Almost immediately, the older children began participating in local activities including swimming lessons at the YMCA. For Willard, "The Y was really hog heaven," he remembered. "It had an indoor pool and swimming was the love of my life." All the children enjoyed swimming, but for Willard, it became a passion and achievement. "He was a terrific competitor, and always had to be in the lead," his mother remembered.

In the water, Willard found a single purpose, a concentrated effort, a rhythm, and a meditation that brought clarity to his churning mind. Swimming would help Willard define his college career, enhance his army experience, think through business decisions, and come up with new ideas. In his senior years, lap swims kept his body trim and taut, often to the amazement of younger colleagues. In 1996 at age 76, Willard proudly wore his Army uniform to his 50th wedding anniversary celebration.

WITHIN A YEAR after arriving in Wichita, the Garveys moved out of the house they were renting and bought a white colonial-style home on the east side of town. The new house meant another school switch for the Garvey boys. A few blocks away, the brand new A.A. Hyde School—named for Albert Alexander Hyde, founder of Wichita's own Mentholatum Company, a well-known maker of ointments and heating rubs—was under construction.

It was the fall of 1929, and the nation was about to be rocked by plummeting stock markets, with Wall Street's financial panic drifting down Main Streets across America. By Black Tuesday, October 29, 1929, the Dow Jones Industrial Average had fallen 40 percent from its high the previous March. Always curious, nine-year-old Willard began "commiserating" with his father, asking if the stock market crash would affect the family.

"He laughed about it," Willard recalled, "and thought it was a lesson to be learned." Ray Garvey had "few if any" stock investments, but around that time, he did have a large and poorly timed investment in the cattle business, which cost him dearly. The lesson of the Depression, Ray Garvey believed, was about expecting too much from one investment. It was also about the ability to sustain risks and live within one's means. Later, it meant watching how government intervention impeded free markets. Willard Garvey learned these lessons on his father's knee. They would shape his outlook forever.

WHILE THE REAL-WORLD life lessons at home were coming fast and furiously, school lessons came a bit more slowly for young Willard. His mother thought at first he was an excellent reader, only to discover that he was memorizing various stories his sister Ruth had been reading to him. But when it was finally discovered that he was a "poor reader" who needed extra help, it was "painful to Willard because it required him to sit down."

Often easily bored, Willard was mostly a B student who excelled in math and spelling but was less skilled in writing and English. His mother knew school wasn't her son's favorite pastime but never doubted his ability. "Maybe it was because he was impatient with things that came easy for him, or because his teachers were always throwing Ruth's excellent scholastic achievements up to him—which of course didn't go over very big with him, given his competitive nature," Olive said later.

Relationships among the Garvey children were all close, Ruth recalled, but minor incidents of sibling rivalry were always present. Ruth admits she was "a bossy little brat," especially when her mother wasn't around. When he could find his chance, Willard would fight back, knocking his sister down. "I had it coming," Ruth admitted later. Roughhousing between Willard and James was also a regular event that began before the light of day. "I made their bed," Ruth recalled. "They had a wrestling match every morning, and their sheets were in knots."

Unlike his efforts with schoolwork, Willard seemed to enjoy his religious education experience. The Garveys joined the Plymouth Congregational Church on North Clifton Street, where Willard participated in Boy Scouts, hikes, picnics, and camping trips, even traveling to Colorado with some of the church's Sunday school teachers. For a while, he also attended services and activities at the Episcopal church, driven there by intellectual curiosity, the draw of attractive friends, or perhaps a combination of both.

"The concept of eternity and immortality in a universe created by God has been logical to me ever since my earliest inquiry on the subject," Willard wrote in 1994. But when it came to church doctrine, he had some difficulty as a teenager with certain beliefs. "I do not believe Christ to be more, at *most*, than a genius in formulating and applying moral principles, but scarcely divine," he explained in a school paper entitled "Why I Attend Church." Despite any youthful doubts, Willard remained a lifelong member of Plymouth

Congregational, maintaining his belief "that the mortal experience can and should be 'heaven on earth.'"

Between 1929 and 1933, more than 40 percent of banks failed, one in four workers were unemployed, and the hungry formed bread lines as they queued up for a free meal. In addition to the economic crisis of falling crop prices and farm foreclosures, the heartland experienced drought: record-breaking heat and dust-filled winds, called "black blizzards" or "black rollers." In 1931, temperatures in Colby hit 108 degrees the last week in July. Fourteen dust storms were reported around the country in 1932. The following year there were thirty-eight.

"It was horrid," remembered Sid Platt, who was a child in Topeka at the time. "It was so hot at night that we'd sleep out in the back yard with a sheet. Otherwise you'd just sweat to death." Even in Topeka, more than 300 miles east of Colby, a child had better be prepared for when the wind blew. "You had to wear a handkerchief or something over your face, so you wouldn't breathe the damn dust," Platt recalled. "It wasn't constant, but if you wanted to walk six blocks, you'd better be prepared."

The western Kansas region was hardest hit. Olive Garvey remembered driving through the region with her husband on a trip to California. "As we drove through western Kansas, the dead cattle were laying everywhere, and the prairie grass was clear down to the ground. It was dreadful."

John Kriss, the Colby manager of what became G-K [Garvey-Kriss] Farms in 1932, couldn't hide that dread when Ray Garvey came out to visit in the midst of the blight. "He met him with tears in his eyes," Olive recalled. The crops in 1933 and 1935 were a "total failure."

FOR THE MOST part, the Garvey children were insulated from the nation's difficulties. In 1932 the family moved again to a "large but not pretentious house" on Circle Drive in the leafy College Hill neighborhood about two miles east of downtown Wichita. Built in 1920, the two-story, ten-room house just south of Douglas Avenue had three full baths, and two half-baths, a finished basement, and down the driveway in the back, a bedroom for the boys over the garage. While it was certainly a comfortable home, in the record-breaking temperatures of the 1930s, "it was a bake oven," Olive remembered. "We wrung towels out of water and covered ourselves so that what breeze blew might be cooled."

By the 1932 presidential election, Americans were desperate and, seeking some kind of change, overwhelmingly voted former New York Governor Franklin Delano Roosevelt into the White House. FDR was inaugurated on March 4, 1933, and wasted no time launching his New Deal policies. On Monday, March 6, FDR declared a bank holiday, which closed the nation's banks, and he introduced the federal deposit insurance system. "The country was dying by inches," Roosevelt said of the days surrounding his election.

That same year, the newly created Agricultural Adjustment Administration began paying farmers to reduce their crop size, on the premise that cutting the nation's food supply would eventually drive up prices and get farmers back on their feet. In Kansas, more than 90 percent of the state's farmers agreed to cut their output by 15 percent, collecting instead from the government.

Ray Garvey was not among them at first. He took issue with the government's efforts, particularly calculations on existing crop sizes and the amounts each farmer was supposed to reduce in order to receive federal payments. As one of the largest landowners, he also qualified for the largest payments. But based on the federal standards, less than half of Garvey's 25,000 acres were eligible for the so-called allotment program. Garvey fought hard for a change and finally reached an agreement with the government for his 1935 crop, sustaining heavy criticism in the process.

The locals turned against him. Because he no longer lived in Colby, they labeled him a "suitcase farmer" who was taking advantage of the region's resources. The local press chimed in, and some residents even threatened to hang Garvey's effigy. "Just so they hang me in *effigy*," Ray told his family, laughing. Olive admired the self-control and good humor her husband continually displayed during such attacks.

FDR and his policies were rebuked in the Garvey household. Instead of helping Americans, Garvey believed the new federal aid packages only weaned them away from personal independence toward a dependence on government from which they would not recover.

A youthful Willard may not have completely understood his father's position in those years. But he would come to live, breathe, and profess it over time. "Roosevelt came in and made some really major changes which have adversely impacted us morally, socially, and economically," Willard would say later, pointing to examples of how New Deal programs often prolonged and amplified the Depression.

Despite bureaucratic aggravation, Ray Garvey prospered during the 1930s. Knowing that the only way to profit from farming was through the cost efficiency of a large operation, he bought foreclosed land from the New Deal agency set up to provide financial assistance to farmers. His Wichita-based Amortibanc Investment Company also bought the assets of more than a hundred banks around the country.

When asked about why he criticized the government and still did business with it, Garvey would simply reply, "We operate under the program, we don't set it." The phrase would become a familiar refrain in the family business.

THE BRICK HOUSE on Circle Drive held 16 years of happy memories for the Garvey family. Olive reconfigured and renovated the house in 1941, as it became the gathering place for the young people and their dates, for college students home on holidays, for family and guests at the marriage of Ruth to Richard Lloyd Cochener in 1942, and for parents and a younger sister anxiously awaiting mail from two boys at war.

It was also the place from which Willard departed on his first ride as a 14-year-old licensed driver in a "topless, battered relic" of a jalopy, purchased with his own money. In those days, it was legal for 14-year-olds to drive and for 13-year-olds to drive in the company of an adult. Driving would never be one of Willard's strengths. And some would even rue the day that Willard Garvey got his license. His brother James was the first on that list.

At the start of the summer of 1934, Willard, who had just finished ninth grade, left Circle Drive in his "new" car and drove about a mile west to Roosevelt Intermediate School at 2201 East Douglas, where James, finishing up seventh grade, was stranded with his bicycle and an abundance of books.

"I put his bicycle on the front end of the car," Willard recalled. James, a wiry jokester with a penchant for mechanics, playfully climbed on the outside of the car and held on to his bike as his brother made his way back down Douglas.

Willard's lack of experience—or perhaps his reckless demeanor—brought the trip to a sudden halt. Willard somehow hit a truck, and James was tossed across the pavement, cutting his thigh. A local grocer rushed to help, and James was taken to the hospital and later home to nurse his scar. The traumatic incident left Willard grounded for two years. It is unclear which he found more frightening, the accident or his punishment.

Even without a car, Willard was a popular student at Wichita East High School, a sprawling, ivy-covered brick building not far from downtown. Activities trumped academics as Cs won out over As on his report cards, and victories trumped losses on the swim team. Unlike his father, who had mastered debate as captain of the team at Washburn, Willard landed a C in debate class but still rustled up a confident grin for the debate team's photo in the 1936 East High yearbook.

Later interests in journalism may have been sparked by his work as a reporter for the school newspaper. An interview with Norman Thomas, a six-time socialist candidate for president, stayed with him for years. "What exactly is the socialist platform?" Willard asked his subject. "We don't have one," Thomas replied. "The New Deal has taken it all." At the conclusion of the interview, Willard knew his parents' views on Roosevelt were absolutely right.

In high school, Willard's outgoing personality, athletic physique, deep hazel eyes, and full lips attracted plenty of female attention. His love of music and aptitude for dancing made him a much sought-after date. Girlfriends were plentiful, and a substantial amount of correspondence with female friends collected over the years.

"I can match your story of eight different dates in eight evenings," a female acquaintance wrote him in June 1939. "At the present time, your list must have mounted to 12, and by June 24, even giving you the leeway of a toothache, one evening I will be Number 19."

In the summers, Willard temporarily left the girls and joined his brother James for more manly work, helping with the wheat harvest and earning between 15 and 20 cents an hour. After his graduation in 1937 at the age of 16, Willard took $20 from his wheat harvest pay and hit the road on a solitary hitchhiking and freight train-jumping adventure. The journey took him from dance halls in Salt Lake City, where he listened to the early swing band sounds of Glen Gray's Casa Loma Orchestra, to the casinos of a Nevada mining town, where he lost the rest of his money.

His companions were often professional roamers— Depression-era hobos and families running from the arid dirt and dust of the heartland. It was an era captured by John Steinbeck in a series of articles in the *San Francisco News* and later in *The Grapes of Wrath,* a time when human suffering pitted man against man as the promise of work remained elusive.

"All walks of life were on that train," his sister Ruth recalled, remembering her brother's trip that summer. At the time, Ruth was living in Topeka with her grandmother and wasn't privy to how her parents were taking news of Willard's absence. "We knew that he was gone, but then we didn't take it very seriously," she said, laughing. "We didn't worry like mother did. Olive Garvey tried hard to hide her concern about Willard's well-being but later admitted to spending a few "sleepless nights" contemplating his whereabouts. "Could you imagine having a child in that kind of company all the time?" Ruth recalled of the situation.

Flat broke and not yet tired of his sojourn, Willard eventually landed in Sacramento, California, where he hawked his electric razor for $5. Hoping to find work, he headed 40 miles north to Yuba City and Marysville, site of the first federal camp for hungry migrant workers from Oklahoma and Arkansas.

Unlike the more dismal "Hooverville" shantytowns of homeless people that were popping up across the nation, the Marysville camp had toilets and running water for about 200 tent-dwelling families, many of whom, like Willard, were working for 20 cents an hour picking peaches at local farms.

By the time he turned 17 in July, Willard felt the grip of the Great Depression with every fruit he plucked from the trees. He heard it in the profanity-laden voices of the unsavory and downright dangerous characters who boasted about doing time in the McAlester, Oklahoma, prison and knowing the notorious gangster Charles Arthur "Pretty Boy" Floyd. He saw it in the caravan of "beat up old cars" carrying mattresses, rusty pots, and a pack of weary children as they moved across the country.

Willard Garvey, son of the soon-to-be richest man in Kansas, was picking fruit, sleeping in freight cars, and barely earning enough cash to survive. But he was not uncomfortable. Like his father, who could be mistaken for the janitor in his own office building, Willard had the warm ability to relate to people of all social and economic status, most of the time. Once, when he made a "smart remark" among the migrants, one of the workers "took me aside and said I was running a risk of being knifed," Willard later recalled. He may have been witnessing the Depression firsthand, but at 17, he was also a bit naive.

After two months on the road, Willard took his earnings and went to find a friend in southern California. By then, his mother had had enough of his travels, sending him money to get a bus ticket home. Instead, he began to hitchhike, but when he got stranded in Bakersfield, California, the bus option came in handy. Olive Garvey remembered the "unkempt, dirty smelly object" that returned to her in the late summer of 1937. She didn't dwell on her son's departure or scold him for his activities. "Mother let it go, because she felt you should let people do what they wanted to do," Ruth said.

Throughout his life, Willard often told the tale of his stint as a migrant worker, romanticizing it as a wide-eyed adventure. "It was a wonderful experience, and I think it aged me quite a bit," he said.

RECIPE FOR WAR

"It is better for a person to know why he is doing something, than for him to merely be following someone else's rule blindly." –WWG

WITH SOME LIFE lessons behind him, Willard returned home to Wichita to pursue a more formal education. At the urging of his father, in the fall of 1937 Willard enrolled at the nearby Municipal University of Wichita, now Wichita State University. Not certain of what he wanted to study, he instantly found a spot on the swim team and kicked up his heels at Alpha Gamma fraternity, where future university president Clark Ahlberg was a fraternity brother.

Financially, the Garveys were doing quite well, despite a tough time in the farming business. The wheat crop lost out on a projected $150,000 profit; however, income from the service stations and Amortibanc, which was busy buying loans from hundreds of failed banks, propelled the Garvey income.

By 1937, the country's unemployment fell to 14.3 percent from 25 percent four years earlier, but Americans were still worried. Across the oceans, the world was churning with conflict. In Japan, Hideki Tojo ordered the invasion of eastern China. In Germany, Adolph

Hitler began to segregate Jews from the general population, stripping them of citizenship and imposing restrictions on marriage and work. In Italy, Benito Mussolini annexed Ethiopia and withdrew from the League of Nations, joining Japan and Germany in establishing the Axis alliance. The ingredients for another war were being carefully laid out on the counter. In four years, they would be fully mixed and baked.

Willard, his family, and his schoolmates continued to cram in as much fun and travel as possible during those late teenage years. There were family vacations to Mexico, California, and Wyoming's Yellowstone Park, where Ray Garvey later wrote of watching Willard's "lithe young body flashing through the water to release the anchor in Yellowstone River." In the summer of 1939, Willard's wanderlust took him to work as a seaman on freighters out of Houston, Texas. He wrote friends about hoping for a chance to see Cuba or travel to South America. He began dating Kathleen, an intense, dark-haired honor student one year his junior.

It was, in many ways for all of them, a last gasp of normalcy. Deep down, everyone seemed to know what the future held. Another war was coming and they were headed straight for it.

EVER RESTLESS, WILLARD sought to graduate from a bigger, out-of-state university. He considered going west to Stanford University in California, where high school chum David Jackman, Jr., was studying. He also thought about going south to the University of Texas, or back east to Harvard, Yale, or the Wharton School at the University of Pennsylvania. In the Midwest, the University of Chicago and the University of Michigan both interested him.

Ultimately, it was a national championship swim team that locked in his decision. Michigan swim coach Matt Mann was beginning his thirteenth of twenty-nine seasons with the Wolverines that year and was well on his way to winning a seventh consecutive national collegiate championship. To learn from the best and be a part of that dynasty was an opportunity Willard didn't want to miss.

In September 1939, Willard headed to Ann Arbor and moved into the Allen-Rumsey House, a two-year-old gothic brick residence hall built for about a hundred male students. Named for Ann Arbor settlers John Allen and Elisha Rumsey, the dorm was the first of what would be several connected buildings in what is now the campus's West Quadrangle.

For Ray and Olive, their son's departure was bittersweet. Ray, who always delighted in the company of his children and who, Olive later wrote, "thoroughly enjoyed being victimized by them," knew that it was natural for a youngster to go away to school, as Ruth had to Topeka years before.

But Willard and James were becoming more than his companions. They were his business associates. Letting go of the two young boys—who left him "helpless with laughter" when they turned him upside down in search of loose change—would not be easy.

By the time Willard arrived in Michigan, German troops had invaded Poland. On September 3, 1939, FDR took to the radio airwaves to broadcast one of his fireside chats. His message: Britain and France had declared war on Germany. The world was at war again, and America was standing by. Exactly how long peace might last and what would happen if it didn't was on the minds and lips of every American in the years that followed. On campus, the subject was perhaps more consuming than the disciplines of higher education.

Willard joined the Reserve Officers' Training Corps (ROTC) and pledged its fraternal organization, Scabbard and Blade. He made the freshman swim team, with the intention of getting to the varsity team as soon as possible. He audited classes and scouted out a Greek fraternity to pledge.

In between his thoughts of war, Willard, as usual, went into his junior year at full tilt. He boasted to friends about his heavy course load in economics, English, philosophy, zoology, and other classes. Like most 19-year-olds of the day, he had never been away from home for such an extended time. Perhaps in a period of homesickness or simple teenage disquietude, Willard typed out a contemplative essay examining life and the choices he was about to make.

"Keeping busy is one of the most stimulating and invigorating things he has done yet," he wrote, referring to himself in the third person. "He hoped these full schedules will continue, he doesn't want his life to become narrow. Because, sometimes he thinks, with a little wistfulness, that there is only one life to live and one should get everything out of it every minute."

Friends in Wichita took note of Willard's jam-packed days on campus. "You sound like you might be quite a busy young man," high school pal Betty Ann Bassett wrote after receiving an update on his activities. "Please don't try to do too much. Remember when we were talking before you left and you agreed that you had tried to do too much here?"

If anything, Willard thought he was not doing enough. In his first semester, he squeezed out four Cs and three Bs, including one in zoology and another in ROTC. He admitted to being restless and bored again. In one angst-filled moment of darkness, he sat down at a typewriter and let the strokes on the keyboard bang out a stinging, single-spaced self-evaluation of his progress. "You, sir, have been passing through a particularly listless period within the last few weeks," he wrote to himself on the newsprint-quality thesis paper reserved for English assignments. "School work is slipshod, if at all. Horseplay, insipidness and generally haphazard pursuits do nothing beyond 'killing time.'"

The self-assessment is most jarring, coming from a young man of seemingly limitless drive who bragged of having eight dates in as many days. In this note to himself, Willard goes on to act as his own disciplinarian. "I am willing to consider any excuses you might offer, but there seem to be none," the typewriter keys bark back at him, asking if it is the "fear of work" that is so befuddling. He concludes that he is suffering from "lack of initiative and self-confidence." Of that thinking, no one could or would ever agree.

The subject of war also found its way into Willard's college essays and personal correspondence. He even penned a poem on the topic, entitled "Europe's War." His viewpoints, like those of his father and many Kansans, were largely noninterventionist. The proper course of action was clear, he thought. "Defend our own land, if attacked, but not until," he wrote in an English paper that September, a full two years before Pearl Harbor.

"If the United States goes to war, I shall be rationalized into going too, although now I am very much against such action," another paper said. "It is difficult to justify getting killed to alleviate a temporary condition in Europe. ... My sense of values requires that I derive some years of further benefit from the mind and body which I have already spent 19 years developing.

"Multiple elements might help direct us toward war," he continued. "Business interests, honor of the country, gullibility of our officials, newspapers, sympathies for the underdog (in case England is losing, or causes us to believe so), fear of invasion, all might tend toward declarations. Moral principles, such as aiding to suppress the aggressor, or other as yet undeveloped or (new) propaganda" would move the country toward joining the war, he opined.

Willard's free-thinking, contrarian philosophy had made its debut. College was a forum in which he could experiment with the voice that would unabashedly challenge governmental and educational authority into the next century.

By the end of his first school year at Michigan things turned more bleak. On May 9, 1940, the Nazis invaded Holland, Luxembourg, Belgium, and France. In a sense of both optimism and dread, the staff of the 1940 *Michiganesian* dedicated its yearbook "To Peace."

That summer, Willard spent six weeks at Camp Custer in Augusta, Michigan, as part of his ROTC training program. The camp, built originally as a military training ground in World War I, was later that year renamed Fort Custer and became a permanent military training base. As an incoming senior classman, Willard was officially a lieutenant, having completed ROTC classes in weaponry, military history, and warfare tactics. During the school year, he had also worked out in twice-weekly, hour-long drills that often included a two and a half-mile march. At Camp Custer, he was assigned to Company C, an eighty-man unit made up of students from Michigan, Illinois, Tennessee, Wisconsin, and Pennsylvania.

In these pre-war days, Willard viewed ROTC as part of a long-range survival tactic. Higher-ranking officers, he surmised, had a better chance of staying off the battlefield should the nation go to war. As it was, his current rank as lieutenant machine gunner was risky, since it was well known that those boys had a short life span in battle. "It might be well to attain as high a rank as possible as a safety precaution," he wrote in an English paper about ROTC. "The higher the officer, the safer the epidermis."

Years later, Willard reflected on the nation's temperament at this point in his life. "Roosevelt had been unable to solve the Depression," he said. "Things had gotten worse and government spending had gone up. He hadn't been able to solve employment problems and the Germans were making economic inroads in Argentina and Brazil and were hurting our economy because we had a socialist economy and they had another aggressive capitalist economy. ... (FDR) tried one thing after another. Being unable to solve the economy, he decided to create a foreign enemy."

CAMPUSES ACROSS THE country were brimming with talk of war. Willard turned some of his thoughts to poetry.

Europe's War

Hitler causes us consternation
He's beating up the British nation.
He promises his people approbation,
For present substitutes deprivation,
Wooden clothes and tea for rations.
By bombing and in placing liaisons,
He carries on national vivisections.
To "limbo," add soul relegations
And his own, for lies at delegations.
He above God, himself stations,
Causing some Christian alienations. And America's same clamor
"participation,"
Reviving old dupe, "democratization."
Make our armies an English annexation
Add to this much subsidization,
Revive England from intimidation,
Defeat forever this bounder Hessian.
America issues treaties through dictation
On Brotherly love and Golden Rule Relations
And fondly hopes for reciprocation
Disillusion follows cries of "patronization"
Can find no system of complete satisfaction.
Another offers himself as militarization,
Efficiency, glamour and acquisition,
More for all through utilization
World supremacy for direction
inferiority complex compensation.
And the cycle completes another revolution.
A dictator issues on this rotation.
America again wastes its reformation.

As Willard returned to Michigan for his senior year, prospects for peace grew dimmer still. On September 7, 1940, the *New York Times* reported that 1,500 German planes had bombarded London with incendiary bombs, marking one of its largest offensives on record. The massive Saturday evening attack, which left the city in an "unbroken sea of licking flames," marked the beginning of a 57-day "blitz" of bombings that crippled Britain's capital and at its conclusion left more than 12,000 dead. As news of the bombings made the daily headlines, cries for American support grew louder and louder. Legislation to create a peacetime draft began to make its way through Congress, as Wendell Willkie, a Republican convert and former utility executive, was challenging President Roosevelt's effort at a third term. America was not adequately prepared for war, Willkie argued, and the New Deal programs were hurting American business.

Again with an unparalleled energy, Willard began the new school year at full speed. He pledged the Delta Upsilon fraternity, was named to Michigan's varsity swim team, continued with ROTC, went after his pilot's license, and began another full course load.

His sister Ruth, active in Greek sorority life in Topeka, wrote to approve of his fraternity selection. As his closest sibling, Ruth often looked to her younger brother for personal guidance and to hear her out on her own political views. "You are surely one of the finest boys I've ever known, and I know you're going to have the grandest year you have ever had," Ruth wrote.

In Wichita, James began attending the local university, often accompanying Willard's girlfriend Kathleen to various local events. Younger sister Olivia, a "gay, sensible, vivacious birdie," according to her father, was active in high school and anxiously awaited any and all news from her big brother.

Despite his father's warning—"better get Bs or better at school"—Willard remained a fair student at best. His daily routine got him up at 7 a.m., to classes until 3:30 or 4 p.m., to swim workouts, to dinner at the frat house, and to the library until midnight, with bed shortly after. His grades suffered in part because he was unable to clearly set down on paper the rapid-fire thoughts that were racing through his mind.

"Rewrite. Too vague," was the order from his journalism professor on one assignment. "You must discipline yourself to write exactly what you mean," scribbled an English professor, giving his scintillating December report on "mistletoe" a D grade. "As it is," the professor wrote, "you sacrifice clarity to verbal gymnastics. Why?" With days left until Christmas break and a visit with his hometown sweetheart pending, Willard might just have been saving his clarity for actions under the mistletoe itself.

Ray and Olive Garvey each wrote regular weekly missives to their son while he was away at college. It was a pattern they would continue through the war, reporting on ongoing changes in Wichita and politics in general. Ray often wrote of the farming conditions, including specific references about pieces of land that they gave to their son that year. "The wheat is up fine this fall, including the wheat on your half section," Ray wrote. "They also planted a section to milo in June on summer-tilled land where the wheat did not come up and it looked like a 20 or 30 bushel yield." John Kriss, manager of the Colby farming operations at the time, had 6,000 lambs pasturing on wheat and other forage.

On the political front, family members were quick to provoke discussion of the nation's future. Ray Garvey's dislike for Roosevelt prevailed in most of them.

"Mr. R. is so full of chicanery that one never knows whether he wants to get into the war in Asia or Europe or is just using and stressing the emergencies for purposes of his campaign," he wrote his son. Ray felt that FDR was leading America "to war far faster than into preparation for war," and while he was supporting Willkie, he saw that FDR was destined for a political victory.

On the other hand, he knew there would be no victors in the coming war.

"While I favor Britain in a mild way, I think they are all going to dislike us regardless of who or [if] nobody wins, and that it will be tough for foreign trade as well as domestic trade for us when the war is over," the elder Garvey wrote.

Ray was proud of his son's activities at college and wrote to tell him so. His only disappointment was that his son was a less-than-dutiful correspondent. "Judge Alexander and I were at Wolf's cafeteria today and Mrs. Hinkle started waving me over to shake my hand as the father of the boy of whom she was proud because he made the varsity on swimming," his father wrote. "We are also, and would like to know more about your meets. Can't you send us some headlines or at least some clippings, or describe them to us?"

Occasionally, Willard would receive a bit of parental advice about how to manage his full schedule. "You have done a lot of things this last semester, what with swimming, flying, ROTC, school work, auditing classes, etc.," Ray wrote. "[You] may have learned that such a course is fine for a few months, but is suicidal in the long run. ... Doing some things well, while knowing a smattering of many is a fine combination."

While Ray Garvey typed out letters to his son after hours from his office in Wichita's Bitting Building, Olive more than likely wrote from home. Her handwritten letters, on blue woven stationery imprinted with her name and address, contained a mix of community and household news as well as political observations.

In the city, preparations for the war were already beginning, and Wichita's aircraft industry was gearing up to play a major role. Local industry executives had been to Washington to learn of Roosevelt's plans to quickly build 50,000 planes, or more than double the number of planes in existence. "The airplane industry is filling up the town and there are lots of new houses being built," Olive wrote Willard in November 1940. "All the plants are expanding tremendously and the traffic downtown is so heavy one can scarcely drive." To accommodate the aircraft workers, "hundreds" of new homes were sprouting up around Wichita. "Even Daddy is building a couple of *very* small ones, west of the university," Olive reported. "I'm thinking of building one too!"

Ray Garvey became part of the city's next building boom. It was yet another example of him being "forced into" a business as he laid the groundwork for what would become Willard's favorite company, Builders, Inc.

BY NOVEMBER 1940, the weather in Kansas turned cloudy and damp, as winter was about to unleash its piercing furor. That month, a ferocious 1,000-mile wide Armistice Day storm raged from Kansas to Michigan, killing 150 people while in some places dropping about 27 inches of snow in a 24-hour period.

Olive Garvey probably could have used some snow days that year. Her numerous activities, including the annual Community Chest drive, which allocated money to local charities, could sometimes be draining. "I've been Community Chesting all week and hope to finish tomorrow," she wrote her son. "I should like to retire to a desert island where they have no organizations for a while." Generations of Garvey women, who have remained involved in their own communities, no doubt understand their grandmother's statement today.

Having witnessed her husband's battles against the government in the New Deal administration, Olive too, shared a repugnance for Roosevelt, who won the November election, carrying thirty-eight of the forty-eight states. "I'm having trouble keeping out of hearing of the radio these days," Olive told Willard. When FDR was making a speech to the nation one evening, "I stuck my fingers in my ears and read."

Despite the family small talk, Olive's letters held a deep and seemingly angry concern for her son's future safety. Willard's long-range survival plan to move up the ranks and get assigned a non-combat job might be thwarted by his decision to get a pilot's license from the Civil Aeronautics Administration (CAA). That move did not sit well with his mother.

"Quite frankly, I don't care if you don't pass your CAA tests," she scolded. "However, don't flunk them while in the air. With our election over, the next thing in order is no doubt a program of 'defense' which will try to encircle the globe and put Hitler and the Jap [*sic*] emperor in their places all to the glory of FDR. We may not 'declare war.' Who does these days? And the air-pilots are going to be the first sent into service. So I think it's smarter not to be an air-pilot," she told him.

Olive repeated her plea a few months later. "I hope you are not taking the advanced flying course. First, because you have enough to do without it, and second because I think it is very foolish to take any more flying at this time. The first thing that is going to be required is pilots to transport [troops] across the ocean. You have your commission in the army with a chance to work up to a better place before actual action develops—we hope! And I can't see why you want to put yourself in a position to be sent into actual combat first."

Again the contrarian, Willard ignored his mother's notes, choosing to take more advanced air tests. "What in _____ did you take some more air tests for?" she scolded after learning of his air adventures, her tone a bit more desperate. "Don't you know everybody with training and qualifications will be put in that service when they're needed whether they want it or not?" The risk of Willard flying just didn't sit well with Olive. The papers that week reported news of a young man's suicide in a plane at the airport, which killed an onlooker who was trying to stop him.

"War on the ground is bad enough," Olive wrote. "Why try to hasten it in the air?"

WILLARD SUCCEEDED MOST that year in his best element, water. In the fall, the Michigan swim team was getting ready for what would be an undefeated swimming season and still more championships. That Christmas, Willard's parents and his two sisters traveled to Fort Lauderdale, Florida, for the annual East-West swimming gala at the Fort Lauderdale Pool, a 55-yard saltwater pool with a Spanish-style façade enclosure. This same meet, now called the College Swim Forum at the International Swimming Hall of Fame, attracts more than a thousand student athletes every year.

The trip gave family members an occasion to be together over the holiday. "Ruth is giving up several attractive functions to come along, so I hope you'll try to see she meets some of your friends and has a good time there," Willard's mother wrote beforehand. Ruth was not disappointed. The Michigan team's early season performance was a show-stopper. Coach Matt Mann's "Blitzkrieg Battalion of Chlorine Crawlers" represented the West, taking the meet's honors with a performance that was "nothing short of amazing," the Michigan yearbook proclaimed.

While his parents were headed back home to Kansas, Willard continued his break with friends, traveling to New York and Pittsburgh. He learned later that on their way home, the Garveys got into a car accident. "A woman from Chicago ran into us sideways," Olive reported. No one was hurt, but the crash, which happened in Lake Wales, about 185 miles northwest of Fort Lauderdale, left a serious dent in the door and front fender of their new Ford Coupe.

Afterward, the family continued on to Tampa, where Ray traded the dented Ford for a Mercury sedan, giving everyone "considerable" room for the remainder of the trip home. When they got to New Orleans, the family stopped to see the French Quarter, had lunch at Antoine's, and Ray "indulged" in buying more cameos for Olive's growing collection and other trinkets for his family. They headed home Friday, January 3, driving all night, arriving back home at Wichita at 5 a.m. Saturday, January 4.

Whether driving or riding in them, cars and the Garveys never made for the greatest companions.

"THE FUTURE LOOKS awfully unsettled doesn't it?" Willard's friend David Jackman asked as the calendar page turned to 1941. Jackman, like so many of Willard's friends, would soon be awaiting news on his permanent commission to the U.S. Army. By the time of FDR's inauguration on January 20, the United States was debating the merits and means of sending Britain substantial military aid—without sending Americans to war.

"Give us the tools and we will finish the job," British Prime Minister Winston Churchill pleaded in a worldwide broadcast that helped persuade Congress to pass the Lend-Lease Act allowing the United States to send aid to Britain (or any other country by the president's orders) while demanding no specific terms for repayment.

Americans were heavily divided on the issue. Proponents of the act viewed the support as necessary to keep the advancing Germans at bay. Opponents, including aviator Colonel Lindbergh, a spokesman for the antiwar America First Committee, believed involvement was "another step away from democracy" and would break America's promised neutrality policy. The country had no right to "police the world," he told a Senate committee in February.

Ray Garvey and his family sided with Lindbergh and the noninterventionists. "Did you see Lindbergh's testimony before house and senate? That lad is good," he wrote his son in March, months before the former flying ace was thrown into controversy for his remarks against a relentless push for war.

Nonetheless, America was getting ready for battle. In May 1941, the last truck for civilian use rolled off the assembly plant floor of a Michigan factory, as all the state's auto plants were being converted for production of war materials.

With just months to go before graduation, Willard, who had moved to the grand, ivy-covered Tudor Delta Upsilon house on Hill Street, savored the last of his college days at the height of the Big Band era. He wouldn't have missed a chance to be among the more than 2,500 "rug-cutting swingeroos" who danced to jazz greats Gene Krupa, Raymond Scott, and "King of Swing" Benny Goodman at the annual "J-Hop" put on by the Class of '42 or swayed on an open-air dance floor at the Senior Ball to popular tunes like "Green Eyes" and "Blue Champagne."

Willard's sister Ruth and brother James were on hand to celebrate with their brother during his final week in Michigan. The pair started out for Ann Arbor on Sunday, June 15 and arrived by train from Chicago on Monday afternoon. Ruth, an active Delta Gamma member, stayed at the sorority house for the week.

"Congratulations and best wishes for the future," Olive Garvey wrote to her son that final week before graduation. "I suppose James and Ruth are already in Ann Arbor and you'll have lots of fun the rest of the week and on the way home. … Don't try to drive too fast, nor too far in one day on the way home," she added. "The family seems very small and we'll be looking for all of you home." Olive's fear of cars remained a healthy one, especially if Willard was at the wheel.

On Saturday, June 21, Willard and his fellow graduates of the Class of '41 joined together in the processional march for the school's 97th commencement exercise. Before he and 643 other graduates of the College of Literature, Science and the Arts received their Bachelor of Arts degrees, university president Alexander Grant Ruthven tried his best to offer them hope in remarks entitled "Our Moral Heritage." "Although technological achievements have intensified and extended 'man's inhumanity to man' to an extent never before known," he said, "it remains as clear as ever that the bodies of men can be destroyed but not their consciences, hopes, and aspirations."

The next day, Germany invaded Russia. Hitler was getting closer to taking over the world.

5

"WE'RE IN IT. LET'S WIN IT."

"The war and the military gave me a global view, a world outlook." –WWG

BACK IN KANSAS, Willard and James spent part of the summer covered with salty sweat and wheat dust working the harvest with John Kriss at G-K Farms, the Colby wheat and lambing partnership he ran with their father.

It was a good year for farming, thanks to the end of the drought and a war-fueled increase in demand for farm products. Ray Garvey thought it was also a good time for his sons to be exposed to a taste of Kriss's "fatherly discipline." At 36, Kriss was a skilled veteran farmer with a no-nonsense and meticulous approach to his work. His pairing with Garvey had created one of the nation's most successful farming operations.

Willard's time away from home and his break from the teenage years apparently gave him a new maturity in Kriss's eyes. "I enjoyed the day spent with Willard last week very much," he wrote to Ray that summer. "He has certainly grown up since he was here two years ago." There would be more growing up to come. By the end of July, Willard had his military commission and was ordered to active duty with the Air Corps in November with a Christmas deferral. For the rest of the year, he also spent time with his father at Builders, Inc., putting up brick duplexes all across Wichita.

About 1:30 p.m. on Sunday, December 7, 1941, Willard was trying to sell a small brick home on North Chautauqua Street near the university when he heard the news about the Japanese attack on Pearl Harbor in Oahu, Hawaii. Nineteen U.S. ships, including eight battleships, were sunk or heavily damaged. About 150 airplanes were lost. There were 2,400 Americans killed. The United States was at war, as officially proclaimed by President Roosevelt the next day.

The start of World War II in America would mark the largest single unifying effort the country had ever seen. Willard, his brother, and all their friends, parents, and siblings would somehow participate at home and abroad.

"Wichita won't like this—and neither do I," a friend from Three Rivers, Michigan, wrote to her pal "Will" the day after Pearl Harbor. "The world is really aflame now, consuming itself with its own stupidity. I have been so excited inside and mad, perhaps mostly I feel gypped to think that with only one life to live, we must live it this way. ... I spent last night thinking up patriotic speeches about America where the individual is emphasized as much as he can be in this world. The tools and fools of Japan (and most other countries) certainly hold human life as little and the individual as nothing. We'll never get out of the Middle Ages."

Willard was opposed to Roosevelt's policies, but now the nation had been attacked and he had a job to do. "We're in it. Let's win it," he told his parents, who used the phrase and a picture of their helmeted, Army-outfitted son in their 1942 Christmas card. His brother James would follow him into the war, reporting to Fort Knox for training soon after.

"We hadn't raised our boys with the idea that they would be soldiers," Willard's mother wrote. "Although we had serious reservations about the way we had become embroiled in the war, once declared, both as a family and individually, we had no thought but to do what was required of us."

In January 1942, Willard reported to Wright-Patterson Air Force Base in Dayton, Ohio, where he became assistant depot supply officer for the Air Transport Command, moving people, aircraft, and mail outside the United States. When he saw the outfit was in desperate need of organization, Willard began setting down a few administrative procedures that improved its efficiency. Years later, Willard credited the army for exposing him to organizational systems that dominated his business operations for decades. "More money has been spent on running armies over generations and centuries than anything else," he observed. "They have developed technique and administrative capability that I think is worth copying."

Although her sons were still stateside, Olive Garvey tried to remain stoic about the future by keeping busy with motherly chores in their absence. "What shall I do with all your clothes?" she wrote Willard in a letter whose envelope carried a postal plea to "Buy Defense Savings Bonds and Stamps." "Do you suppose they'll still be in style when you need them again?"

Willard had been gone only a few weeks, but she still longed to see her son in civilian clothes again. Losing him—in any number of ways—seemed a real possibility. "I hope you are over your cold," she told him. "And remember, if you should get really sick, telegraph us. More people died of pneumonia in the last war than on the battlefield."

Years later, she would write: "There are no words to express the feeling one experiences at the prospect of sending two boys whom one has nurtured all their lives, into such an uncertain holocaust."

With such unpredictable futures ahead of them, many of Willard's friends, including Stanford graduate David Jackman, decided to get married. Not so for Willard and his hometown girlfriend Kathleen.

Although their time together was full of admiration, it was also peppered with provocation and debate.

Willard still enjoyed having a variety of female companions, and at this stage in his life was ambivalent about marriage. Kathleen, an honor student at the University of Wichita, toyed with the idea of marrying Willard but wanted to first pursue a teaching career. Time and distance eventually forced a decision on their three-year romance, which sometimes left their parents guessing about its outcome.

"I wish you would find out if you can, just what position Kathleen holds in the scheme of things," Olive wrote her husband during one of his visits to see Willard. "Is she just a friend, an ex-friend, or a potential member of the family? There might be times when one would really want to know." Later, Olive said she was "deeply grateful" that both her sons got off to war "without leaving a daughter-in-law on my hands."

Despite their sons' inactivity in the marriage department, the Garveys did their part for the national wedding boom. While he was stationed in Dayton, Willard's sister Ruth became engaged to Richard Lloyd Cochener, an engineering student she met at the University of Kansas while she was helping to establish a Delta Gamma sorority house there. Willard, who was always close to his sister, made a surprise visit home for the February 1942 wedding on Circle Drive. "This makes it perfect," Ruth said when she saw her brother walk in the door in his Army uniform.

It was perfect for Ray Garvey, too. A house full of children, grown though they were, was the way things should be in his eyes. Soon, he would be reduced to communicating with his children through carbon-copied letters addressed, "Dear Children in Absentia."

JUST AS HE DID in college, Willard took full advantage of the educational experience the army had to offer. In March, he went to Baltimore to attend Motor Transport School, and he returned to Columbus, Ohio, as commanding officer of a troop of black men assigned to a truck company at the Air Force Storage Depot on the Ohio State Fairgrounds. Like so many other businesses that were transformed for war production, one of the nation's oldest fairs went on hiatus, instead housing airplane engines, gliders, and other Air Force equipment.

Racial segregation was a fact of life in America at the start of World War II, and enlisted blacks were often assigned to service and manual labor jobs supervised by white officers. When he arrived, Willard learned that the men in his unit had not been paid for three months. He got them their checks but warned them not to follow others who had gone AWOL: absent without official leave. "This is the army; democracy is dead," the lieutenant told his soldiers. Members of the troop respected his command, and some even befriended him, inviting him to their weddings.

By August 1942, Willard was promoted to first lieutenant and that fall headed to adjutant general's school in Maryland. "You will go thru [*sic*] those ranks just like Eagle Scouts, I imagine," his father wrote, congratulating him on the promotion. "I think you have the temperament, ability and ambition to be and will be a fine officer and soldier."

They were not easy words for Ray Garvey to write, even though he knew them to be true. It was easier, perhaps, for Ray to write about business; about the "21 duplexes and 56 houses" he was building that fall, or the 20 fourplexes just completed south of Wichita's Kellogg Avenue and east of Hydraulic Street. With so much effort and materials being diverted to the war, Ray could feel the pinch on his own businesses. "The labor problem is getting quite critical," he wrote. "We have plenty of carpenters, but only three or four laborers. Materials and utilities, particularly water lines, are hard to get." The story on the farms was similar. "It is getting a little more difficult all the time to get competent help," he wrote. Since the war was taking all the strong men, those left behind were either too old or too young.

As Willard's departure overseas drew nearer with the fading autumn light, Ray swallowed hard before writing his son. "You mentioned once that perhaps you ought to make a will," he wrote. "I am sending a couple of forms in case you wish to do it now. If you wish to send it home, we can put it in the safety deposit box." He signed off like he did so many letters, "With best wishes, Sincerely, Pop."

Westover Air Force Base in Chicopee Falls, Massachusetts, was the next stop for the young soldier, as he awaited orders to ship out. While there, Allied troops, including 70,000 Americans in 600 ships, moved into French North Africa in an offensive move designed to stop the Germans from occupying the region. Newspaper and radio reports were grim reminders of a soldier's potential fate. "300,000 Allied Soldiers Thunder into Tunisia," one Massachusetts newspaper proclaimed.

Assuming that Willard was headed straight into the war zone, Ray Garvey went east to say goodbye to his son. Olive stayed in Kansas, thinking she "would behave better" from afar. Ray went first to New York City and stayed at the Hotel Taft. He made arrangements to meet Willard at the Springfield train station, about 11 miles south of the Westover Air Force Base.

Every step and action the pair made that last week of November played over and over in Ray's mind for the next three years. He would remember the sound of Willard's voice on a phone at the Hotel Taft or the sight of his "good-looking new car" and his "good-looking new uniform." The two spent four or five days together at Westover, until in the last full week in November, Ray Garvey bade his son one final goodnight as news of fighting in North Africa still loomed large.

"I was shocked and scared, and perhaps you were too," he wrote his son later. They said farewells as men, but Ray "only wanted to throw my arms around you and kiss you as when you were a smaller boy." Willard left his father, like so many boys that year, not knowing if they would ever meet again.

NEW YORK CITY commemorated the one-year anniversary of the Pearl Harbor attacks like dozens of other cities in the country in 1942. Schoolchildren observed a moment of silence. The American Women's Voluntary Services held a rally in the Bronx. Students at Manhattan College donated blood to the American Red Cross, and Brooklyn dock workers hollered vows to build more ships faster in honor of the dead.

For Willard and about 10,000 GIs, the day was marked at New York Harbor, boarding the HMS Queen Mary as it prepared to sail for England. A handsome 81,000-ton, three-stacked British luxury liner with a 3,000-passenger capacity, the Queen Mary was turned over to the United States and transformed into a no-frills transport ship that could hold as many as 15,000 troops at a time. Her sleek black, white, and red exterior was sacrificed for a wartime grey, earning the ship the nickname "Grey Ghost," because it would disappear in and out of sight on its top-secret, zigzag course across the Atlantic horizon.

Carrying about a hundred pounds of gear, including his rifle, duffle bag, field pack, and personal supplies, Willard headed to a stateroom and claimed the highest spot in a row of five-level canvas bunk beds. The ship pushed out of New York Harbor the next day, as soldiers hunkered motionless in their bunks to keep the heavily loaded ship on an even keel so as not to break through the Holland Tunnel beneath them.

Once outside the harbor and into the wide-open seas of the Atlantic, the Queen Mary and other transport ships became vulnerable to attacks from German U-boat submarines trolling for prey. Early that month, Willard's parents heard reports of a troop ship hitting a mine and waited "an eternity" to hear of Willard's safe arrival in Gourock, Scotland, on December 14.

The Queen Mary may have eluded enemy U-boats, but it did not escape the fury of the seas. With the gyroscopes turned off so the ship could keep changing course, the ship's natural tendency to roll with the waves made for a bumpy ride in North Atlantic winter weather. "The Queen Mary tossed like a cork," Willard remembered later. "We broke dishes at every meal."

Willard and his family never knew how close he and his fellow soldiers came to tragedy during that weeklong Atlantic crossing. One day before they were scheduled to arrive in Scotland, a 75-foot rogue wave suddenly leapt up and pummeled the ship's port side, pushing it into a near fatal roll. The force of the impact smashed windows that were 95 feet above water level. It tossed GIs out of bed and landed others with broken arms and concussions. The Queen Mary listed 52 degrees to starboard, remained suspended amid a rush of frigid water, and then slowly began to right itself. Another three degrees of list, experts say, and the transport would have capsized, tossing Willard and others near his main deck stateroom to an unknown grave on the icy open sea.

Years later, Willard described the incident in a far more detached manner. "One night a wave broke a porthole on the main deck," he recalled. When he woke up in an empty room, he saw a mattress propped up against the void on the main deck. "Everyone had abandoned their staterooms," he said. Knowing he and others were virtually helpless to do anything more in the situation, Willard did something he could always do best: He rolled over and went back to sleep.

FROM THE MOMENT he stepped off the Queen Mary and onto foreign soil, Willard viewed his Army experience not only as a duty but as an adventure. "I had about the most interesting wartime job of anyone I've ever run into," he would say later.

For almost a year, the war for U.S. soldiers in England was an administrative one, as more than 1.5 million men, tens of thousands of planes and vehicles, and tons of equipment were amassed and readied for the invasion of France. While America was fighting a bloody and relentless war against the Japanese in places like the Solomon Islands in the South Pacific and the Komandorski Islands in the north near the Bering Sea, Willard's footsteps echoed across the marble floors of the Hotel Berystede in Sunninghill, Ascot, a turreted Tudor mansion known locally as a "country home" transformed to accommodate members of the Eighth Air Support Command.

During the day, Willard worked for Colonel Lloyd R. Garrison in the Adjutant General's office at Sunninghill Park, where he was responsible for supervising personnel issues, including orientation programs for incoming troops. The job, as he described it to his mother, was "to account for every individual unit and individual of the entire command at any given time."

At night, he was a young man immersed in a very active social life that evolved around 35-mile trips to London for evening theater, dinners at the private Royal Automobile Club, and swims beneath the barrel-vaulted roof of the Marshall Street Baths.

When the bombs of 500 Allied planes were gouging Naples on a push to defeat Italy's fascist dictator, Benito Mussolini, Willard and the U.S. Army swim team were making headlines in *Stars and Stripes,* the daily newspaper for America's military. Led by Detroit Olympian swimmer Taylor Drysdale, the team swept six events to capture the Chelsea Trophy Meet cup, its ninth victory in ten meets. Willard brought home the meet's 100-yard freestyle trophy, finishing the distance in 59.8 seconds. A month later, just before his promotion to captain, Lieutenant Garvey took four medals in the European Theatre of Operations swimming and diving championships. By May 1944, he had shaved nearly three seconds off his time in the 100-meter swim.

Willard's brush with British royalty came when Colonel Garrison took him to a party at a country estate. Willard met Queen Victoria's septuagenarian granddaughters, Princess Marie Louise and Princess Helena Victoria. He charmed them with news that he owned a 20,000-acre ranch—a gift from his father—and instantly propelled his social standing into what the British dubbed "landed gentry." The party invitations started pouring forth. Evenings at the home of Sir Archie and Lady Weigall for "port and roulette" helped make Willard's war a memorable one.

There was much to see and do during those years in England. Often in the company of a 20-year-old Austrian expatriate named Elizabeth Letner, Willard bicycled past ancient stone walls of the British countryside and feasted on roast turkey, lamb chops, ice cream, and hot dogs—food choices that perhaps were more abundant than what his parents were getting through food rations back in the States.

The daughter of wealthy Jewish parents who fled Austria and then Czechoslovakia for England in 1938, Elizabeth lived at the Berystede and worked at the Women's Voluntary Service (WVS), taking care of children whose parents sent them out of London to the country during the Blitz. After the war, she married Edmund de Rothschild of the international de Rothschild banking fortune, one of the wealthiest families in the world. She and her husband remained friends with Willard and his family for the rest of their lives.

Willard grew so fond of his English environs that he considered staying there after the war. "I have become rather settled in the [headquarters] here and returning to the wide, terrifying vastnesses of the USA don't [*sic*] hold too much appeal," he wrote his parents. "Amazing how wet weather, plugging along, jumbled roads, nothing to do, in or out of London and general inadequacy of vitamins can make one content."

True to his nature, he was not content for long. He wrote to his parents about his discouragement with the Army bureaucracy and his continued restlessness over his job. It was here in the war that Willard developed his animosity for wanton government spending. "I want to see someone in the government who will cut out 90 percent of the bureaus and departments," he told his parents. "Those parasites are self-generating and vicious."

Despite his distaste for bureaucratic waste, the promotions came quickly, as his family predicted. Willard was named captain in the summer of 1943, earned his glider wings in 1944, and in early 1945 became one of the Army's youngest majors at the age of 24.

And yet, during his three years overseas, Willard would swing from moments of complete immersion to intense boredom with his work. "Nothing could be farther from our minds than the war," he wrote his parents. "When you are this near it and not in it, there is a certain yearning to be. Those ditches and long days in mud don't seem too attractive however. It would be nice to be spectacular and lead a swashbuckling life as an aviator in fighters or captaining the infantry."

Willard wrote home anywhere from once a week to a couple of times a month, which never seemed enough for his father. "We had a letter from you last week and hope to get another one this week and every week," came the directive from home. "If you do not have time to write a letter, why not dash off a postal card, one or two of them a week."

Later, communications came through "V-mail," a government system designed to reduce the bulk of mail being delivered to and from the troops. Senders would write or type their letters on a single page of specially designed stationery and then send it to a central repository where it would be reduced to microfilm and shipped overseas. The film was then developed and the letters were printed out in 4 x 5-inch miniatures and sent to the recipient. For security reasons, every soldier's letter was read and initialed by a censor who blacked out any sensitive information. Willard censored his own letters, which frequently displayed the churning mind of a young man contemplating career moves after the war. Despite the ample opportunities his father was willing to provide, Willard sometimes talked of a career in the newspaper business—an idea he would never let go of. Unlike his father, Willard did not make profit the main reason for taking on a project.

Willard's V-mail to his parents, September 10, 1943

This letter is intending to be poetic extemporaneous in short bursts, but not words. Satisfies Pop, not Mom (contemporaneous) (A la [Gertrude] Stein O.[gden] Nash).

There's a hell of a lot of noise in this office, with clerks babbling and ranting about,

Making my bliss more than somewhat odiferous, this postworking lout deserves a clout.

Took a semi-weekly trip to London, for the purpose of taking a plunge,

Got beat by the other team's Bundin, drowned sorrow with dancing and orange.

Saw "Elliott" R. on the dancing floor thar—looks surprisingly well among the myriad.

But his friend and a frail caused me to "Har!" when she said, "He likes to talk period".

Got a cab in the rain, and soft in the brain, not remembering the prior Sunday's chaos.

Resulting from Pimms, no sleep & no swims, the orgy, work, left me in a daoz,

But twelve hours sleep, without a peep, much benefit reaps, and relaxes heaps.

Not so last night, our girls bright, went home to bed, after they'd been fed.

So returning to the flat, we chewed the fat, up before dawn, on the train & gone.

On the way to the train, to vary the refrain, took bus, less fuss than Tube.

Which wheezes under Westminster & Misses, Misty Parliament, Abbey and Thames Danube.

Quite light for the walk over the bridge down the street into the passages of Waterloo.

Seeking a paper, watching them sweep through the gate, onto the ramp off on the choochoo.

In the compartment home, there quite alone, daydreaming serene with the passing scene,

of fighting at Rome, a slaphappy crone with the buses' careen, and a self-centered bean.

Wondered what's good, to study for skill, with music, paint or quill

Or to build an abode, satisfying your mode, or to organize a nation, within one's ration,

Or to pause with a query, what is your theory?

Isn't to live, to live fully within each moment, enhancing each instant, and what of looking forward, back, to others, for a divine-soliloquy.

Ray Garvey did his best to offer encouragement to his son's postwar plans, long before Allied troops ever hit the European continent. "A lot of things will appear as hooey to you Willard, as doing big or little things is largely a matter of getting in position to do them and learning the trick of the thing. ... So, if you want to succeed, shoot high, learn the trick of whatever business it is you want to get into, and then go to it. I would have liked newspaper work but did not know how to get into it in a profitable way and just grabbed what seemed easiest and quickest, most interesting and most profitable from time to time as the opportunities presented themselves."

A hardy man who could eat four slices of Vienna bread, two slices of bacon, and three eggs in the morning, Ray Garvey became increasingly lonely for his children during the war years. "We have very little wise cracking and spontaneous wit around our dinner table in volume anymore," he told his faraway children, in one of his weekly carbon-copied letters to each of them. With both boys in the service, Ruth married, and Olivia away at college, a lonely Ray Garvey used his letters to give a brief overview of the goings on in the farming business, which by then had reached more than 100,000 acres.

Ray grew melancholy when he recalled the time James and Willard literally picked him up and then dropped him in a hunt for their father's pocket change. "You boys can come home anytime you can, and are welcome to all the loose change you can shake me down for," he wrote, pleading for their safe return.

To assuage the pain of separation, Ray Garvey turned to his dog for comfort. He began writing letters to his children in the "voice" of Muggs McGillicuddy, the family's beloved wire-haired terrier (see page 76). Muggs's never-ending efforts to engage "Pop" in a game of stick or ball throwing, his pleas to his "former playmates," and observations of the family's activities no doubt brought smiles to Willard and all who read them.

THE AMORTIBANC INVESTMENT COMPANY

BITTING BUILDING

WICHITA, KANSAS

Muggsyville,Wichita,Aug. 13,1943

Ruth,Willard,James

Dear Former Playmates:

Doubtless you recall that I wrote you and Willard,
James, a couple of weeks ago giving you some advice on how I have made
what is generally acknowledged to be asuccess of the two principal
businesses in which I indulge,namely ball and sticks,by keeping my eye
on the ball. I thought it might have some military valueto a couple of
young rookies in the tank and air corps. Well,that was two weeks ago.
One lives and one learns. But I supppse you have heard. Anyhow,as you know
I like to play ball and I like to play sticks,and I not only am eager but
am good at them. But a special delivery postman pulled a fast one on me.
As I nipped for his pants leg,he swang a mean bat. I was the ball and I did
not like it. When I woke up a few minutes later,I am told,he had run away.
Mrs. Jenkins,Mrs. Lyons,Mrs. Garvey,(your mother) and Olivia were moaning
over me. I was all right,but they took me to the dog hospital for a half
days observation. It was hot there and nothing cool to drink,and was I glad to
get in the Mercury when Pop stopped for me that evening. Two dollars,said
Dr. Bogue's secretary. Give me a blank check,says Pop. Was I hot'. We drove
down on S. Hydraulic and looked over the project and finally I found some
water in which to wade,but I was glad to get home to my tub. Since that time
I have stuck to the milder pleasures,just a faint growl even for the garbage man.
It reminds me of the time,James,when you and Keith and some of the rest of us
were in your Model A. car and I jumped overboard. Well,I am feeling fine
again and I noticed when I was let out this morning,my muzzle was on. The
muzzle is for protection of other people. I guess they still do not trust
me too much. Nothing much else exciting around here,and you lads will
need to work out your own systems of defense,I guess,as I was a little slow
on the trigger. Maybe a person should learn tomswing a mean bat. Certainly
I would rather be at the other end of the bat. Pop and I have been heaving
a retrieving sticks in the back yard nearly every evening. I get hot and
make for the tub for a few seconds two or three times usually. Last night
we had a slight rain,and it was a little cooler,so I did not need to tub
until it was over. The game usually ends when Pop throws a swish instead
of the stick and puts the stick up on the window ldge. He says I lose
too many good sticks and what would we use the next evening. He loses about as many
in the trees,however. When he throws a swish and walks off with the stick,
I obligingly play the game by running to where tho swish should land and
look for it awhile. It makes Pop feel as though he had pulled something,so
I humour him. If either or all of you figure out a plan to nip the postman's
leg safely,drop me a line. Drop me a line anyhow. I understand you have
just two weeks more,James and then perhaps you too will be a shavetail.
How is the water in England,Willer? I have heard it is cold. Do you boys
get to keep up on Orphan Annie,Dick Tracy Skeezix and Lil Abner. Annie has
had her share of submarines. There is some infantile paralysis in town.
Olivia does not have many at the swimming pool now,15 or 20,where is was
running 200 to 300. Mom has a slight leaf posioning on her feet,from trimming
shrubs,we think. Pop isn't any thinner. We had a letter from Kathleen Setzer
a couple of days ago,thanking for a dish,saying they soon are going to Fla.
from Seattle,she thinks,enjoys Seattle and asks to be remembered to you scattered
members,Willard and James,and hopes all can be together for a chat soon. My
paper is out and so are my thots,so long,good luck,with love. Muggs. His X Mark.

Letter from Muggs

Ray may have been lonely, but not his son. Willard's opinion-ated wit and unbounded athleticism made him particularly popular with women wherever he went. His mail call brought dozens of letters addressed to "Will" or "Bill" Garvey from some obviously charmed female acquaintances met while he was stationed in Ohio. These fawning communications replaced the evaporated letters from Kathleen, who married a university classmate and Navy ensign and moved to Seattle six months after Willard sailed for Europe.

"I shall write this kind of a letter tonight and enclose a couple of clippings," wrote Olive Garvey, who attended Kathleen's ceremony at Plymouth Congregational Church, where Willard himself would be married three years later. "The church was very pretty, although roasting hot and [the groom's] whites and the other costumes very striking. I am glad you displayed such a sensible and generous spirit toward the affair, and we have been trying to meet comment in the same spirit," she wrote. "I think a number of people have been somewhat critical of Kathleen for her apparently hasty action, and a number who have so expressed themselves were not at the wedding but there may have been other reasons."

DESPITE THE EFFORTS of Willard's family and friends, day-to-day news of his hometown became like the images of a fading photograph. The setting was familiar, but the details were hard to decipher. Wichita, like so many communities across America, was changing, all for the sake of the war. The town was virtually emptied of young men. Gas and food rations reduced consumption to an as-needed basis. Local aircraft plants like Boeing went to 10-hour shifts in an effort to churn out aircraft parts and planes at full speed. Support for the war even wafted into local theaters. "You should see the people applaud in the picture show when soldiers are shown," Ray wrote his son.

Parents with boys serving overseas often stuck together and supported each other in times of grief. "They are having a service at the Commons for Stan Diamond Thursday afternoon at three," Ray wrote Willard. "He was married a little over a year when his plane collided on its first mission over Germany with another of our planes over the North Sea. The tail gunner was the only one of the two crews that lived. ... As you say, we are losing many of our best boys."

Ray and Olive Garvey could only pray their sons wouldn't be among them.

IN ENGLAND, PLANS for Operation Overlord, the code name for the Allied invasion of France, were coming together. As D-Day grew closer, so too did the danger. The Germans continued to shell Britain. "Our bombings have been heavy around here lately," Willard wrote his parents in February. "The war is now personal. They bombed my swimming pool and favorite club."

With his top-secret clearance at what had become the Advanced Headquarters of the Ninth Air Force Command, Willard was privy to details of the invasion, which would bring "150,000 men, 1,500 tanks, 5,000 ships and 9,000 planes" across the English Channel to the coast of France beginning June 6, 1944.

Days before the Normandy invasion, Willard longed for a faster-paced world of rapid-fire orders, high commands, and last-minute changes. "Confidentially, while this is supposed to be a fairly exciting time, I am a little bored," he wrote his parents.

He was not bored for long. In the days and weeks that followed the invasion, Willard flew between England and France with the sad task of finding the identification tags of missing men. In the horrific aftermath of battle, Willard walked along the sandy beaches of the Cherbourg Peninsula and the bomb-pitted streets of Sainte-Mère

Eglise, where paratroopers from the 82nd Airborne were shot out of the sky while dropping behind enemy lines. He went to the countryside, where the smell of death and spent ammunition overpowered the beauty of the dense French hedgerows, which had been transformed into a maze of armed enemy obstacles for the foot-weary liberators.

Willard remembered a smothering silence as he watched detached fellow soldiers collect the dead. "It was a tragically impressive day," Willard said, recalling the sight of so many "magnificent physical specimens" in their final sleep far from home. Leaning down to check the identification of one fallen soldier, Willard's mind raced back to Wichita. He thought he recognized the face of a neighbor boy on Circle Drive.

What he saw in France kept Willard away from any kind of veterans pilgrimage to Normandy in his later years. The cemeteries would open too great a hurt.

Like so many other parents back in the United States, Ray and Olive Garvey followed the progress of the Allied troops through news reports. While the British and Canadian troops attacked Utah Beach, pushing through to the French countryside, the Americans landing on Omaha Beach did not fare as well. More than a thousand were killed and another thousand were missing by midnight that first day at Omaha.

Because Willard worked with Air Force Headquarters, his parents could never be sure where he might be at any time. After the invasion, they waited three weeks to receive word he was safe. They waited another year—on top of the two that had already passed—to hear their son's voice again.

"I notice the casualties are mounting toward 400,000 for this war," Ray wrote Willard in August. "We hope you are successful in dodging the robot bombs which the paper reports knocks out or damages 17,000 houses per day as they move through France."

As the summer of 1944 progressed, so did the Allied march to liberate Paris. In June, Willard moved to France and worked first in the Advanced Headquarters of the Ninth Air Force along the beach at Normandy. He wrote home about contracting a painful ear infection while swimming off Omaha Beach, and of his disappointment in missing his first shot at promotion to major. He noticed the "certain air of mild apprehension & reminiscence" in his parents' letters, and perhaps fueled their fears in his response.

"I am afraid that if I get knocked off it will be all the more ironical because it will be some fluke, stumbling over a mine, having some flack drop through the tent, etc.," he wrote from France in July.

By the time Allied troops were preparing to move into Paris in August, Willard was comfortably back in England working for the newly formed First Allied Airborne Army, which was designed to plan airborne attacks coordinated with ground forces. He spent nights on the terrace of a local country club watching "hundreds of searchlights practice following planes across the sky." They would be followed by rockets, or "shooting stars," as he called them, which were "nothing compared to the superior fireworks kicked up at any provocation over our tents in France."

But London wasn't exactly safe either. A week after Normandy, the city was once again terrorized by German bombings. Hitler's secret jet-propelled robot bombs, also called "V-1" or "buzz bombs," were falling silently from the sky at an alarming rate. In mid-June, one of the bombs killed 200 officers and men worshiping inside Guards Chapel, including a colonel on General George S. Patton's staff.

With the move to the European continent, General Dwight D. Eisenhower, Supreme Commander of the Allied Expeditionary Force, decided to combine all Allied airborne forces into a single unit. Willard was transferred to the group, now called the First Allied Airborne Army, a combination of the British 1st and US 82nd and 101st airborne divisions.

Working for Lieutenant General Lewis Brereton and his chief of staff, Brigadier General Floyd L. Parks, Willard again got a ringside seat to machinations of war. Plans for Operation Market-Garden an ill-fated mission in which the Allies hoped to move across the Rhine at Arnhem in the Netherlands, were revealed at the Sunninghill Park headquarters. The September 1944 attack, well chronicled in the book *A Bridge Too Far*, was called "one of the most daring and imaginative operations of the war," but when supplies and reinforcements were delayed in reaching cornered British troops, the British First Airborne was decimated. More than 17,000 men were killed, wounded, or missing.

Years later, historians would attribute the loss at Arnhem to a number of missteps and misfortunes including bad weather and infighting between the British and American commanders who led the operation, Field Marshall Bernard L. Montgomery and Eisenhower. "If we fought as much against the Germans as we did among ourselves in headquarters, we would have been in Berlin in 1942," Willard said later. Despite the failure of Market-Garden, the First Allied Airborne Army forged on. Willard regularly visited the continent, helping to open an advance headquarters for the group at Hotel Royal at Maisons-Laffitte, just outside of Paris. Much as he did in England, Willard managed to find a few prominent local women to accompany him to the theater and shows. Among his French companions: Anne Marie Perochia, the daughter of a baroness.

As 1944 came to a close, an ailing Roosevelt was re-elected for a historic fourth and final term, dying in office five months later. Willard spent his third Christmas in Ascot, looking out 12-foot windows of the Sunninghill Park country home onto frost-covered grounds and the lake beyond and wondering how life would resume after the war.

Two things interested him now, business and travel. The army taught him administrative organization and systems. He knew how to "select and train men, systematize procedures, streamline functions, and operate with minimum personnel." Still, by his own admission, he was easily distracted and had much to learn about "sticking to one subject and following it through," he told his parents. There were plenty of opportunities in the world at large, if only "We might let our 'entrepreneurs' spread out a little to develop some of the world's resources."

It was a big world out there, and Willard wanted to be a part of it all, well beyond the Kansas Plains. Before he could do so, there would be some final tasks to complete in Germany.

"FDR WAS SHORT of War in '40, Short of Alert in '41, Short of Planes in '42, Short of Rubber in '43, Short of Shells in '44 and seems destined to be Short of Food in '45," Ray Garvey wrote his children the first week of the new year, when he would launch a major farming expansion in eastern Colorado. "We are thankful that all of us are well and in one piece and hope that continues just that way."

While the U.S. casualty count topped 80,000 in the final days of the Battle of the Bulge in Belgium's Ardennes forest, Willard was ordered back to the First Allied Airborne Army headquarters at Maisons-Laffitte, where he would stay until May. "France is quite pleasant," he wrote to a friend in February, as Russian troops crept closer to Berlin. "We have a lovely old town all to ourselves built on an estate belonging to a chateau near Paris." The setting was almost surreal, given the extent of death and destruction just a few hundred miles away.

As a line of 6.7 million Russians moved westward toward Berlin, the world began to see the true horror of Hitler's reign. In January, the Soviets came upon more than 7,000 prisoners at the abandoned Auschwitz killing camp, part of Hitler's sinister plan to eradicate world Jewry. More than 1.1 million Jews and tens of thousands of other prisoners died at the camps outside of Krakow, Poland, under Hitler's direction. Days before the Russians came upon the grisly scene, 60,000 weak and starving Auschwitz prisoners were forced to make a 35-mile relocation death march. To the world at large the war had grown almost incomprehensible.

ON APRIL 13, 1945, Ray Garvey was in Wallace County, Colorado, inspecting work on a newly acquired 19,000 acres of farmland when he heard the radio news of President Roosevelt's death the previous day. The president was eulogized as the man who presided over the end of the Great Depression. Willard's father was among many Americans who believed otherwise. He found the whole scene "disgusting." Ray saw FDR's programs as economically destructive to the country because they created a government dependence that replaced individual responsibility.

"It appeared ... they were trying to impress everyone with the idea that he was a very great man," Ray told his son. "I thought it was somewhat unbecoming in view of 80,000 young casualties per month to spend so much time on an old worn-out lad like Roosevelt. ... No president before was ever such a poor administrator or was so lacking in integrity, veracity, judgment and common sense." Vice President Harry S Truman, the former senator from Missouri, would be a fine replacement, Garvey thought. "The country will be far better off in his hands."

Now a major, Willard could only hope so. The war was growing old. Days after FDR's death, Berlin was on the brink of collapse. Hitler was ensconced in a concrete bunker under his Chancellery, on the verge of suicide. When Germany surrendered in early May, Willard was in Paris, celebrating with a female British officer outside the seventeenth-century buildings of the Place Vendome. Hundreds of thousands of exuberant people filled the streets all around the city. The Champs d'Elysees was a sea of humanity. France was its own once more.

Newspaper pictures of the European victory celebrations flashed across the world. From Britain to New York City to Toronto, horns honked, ticker tape flew, and people took to the streets. In London that evening, landmark buildings were floodlit, hundreds of bonfires burned victoriously in the parks, and singing and dancing crowds filled the streets. In Kansas, which was still losing boys in the Pacific, there was simply a collective sigh of relief. There would be no festivities for the Garveys until Willard and James were back on Circle Drive.

"Surprisingly, only in New York City was there wild celebration of V-E Day in the U.S.," Ray Garvey reported to Willard. "Here and in most places, most people worked as usual, and felt only the German phase was closed with Jap phase still on and the hope that there would be no more phases. Not that all of us were not happy about the German surrender, but we felt a celebration was premature."

After V-E Day, Willard and his headquarters staff moved to Bielefeld, Germany, and then to Halle, Germany, on the Elbe. The most exciting and perhaps the most impactful days of the war were still ahead of him. Arriving by car in Halle at noon one day in mid-June, Willard was told, "Be prepared to take three of your enlisted men with General [Stuart] Cutler to Berlin in one hour."

Willard picked up his three sergeants, outfitted them with updated uniforms, and flew in a DC3-C47 with Brigadier General Stuart Cutler into Soviet-occupied Gatow Airfield in Berlin. There, they were picked up by a group of Russians who drove them to meet Major General Floyd L. Parks, overseer of the local American forces.

Berlin was still smoldering from the relentless Soviet assault in April. The entire city, it seemed, had been blasted into a pile of pulverized masonry. Bricks and glass littered the streets lined with collapsed building façades. A bullet-riddled Volkswagen, its door ajar, was among the abandoned cars forever stalled near the shelled Reich Chancellery, where Hitler and Eva Braun, his wife of one day, killed themselves April 30. The charred marks outside Hitler's infamous bunker, presumed to be from the gasoline used to cremate their bodies, were still in plain view.

Willard said that he, Parks, and Cutler were the first three U.S. officers to witness the devastation after the city's fall. The Americans' Second Armored Division wouldn't arrive until July. From Berlin, the group traveled south through the suburban cities, which sustained far less ruin.

The real damage appeared on the faces of downtrodden refugees walking along the road, Willard recalled. More than a million Berliners were now homeless, including scores of starving women and children left vulnerable to the vicious brutality of their Russian conquerors. Many of the refugees were older couples, weighed down with whatever personal belongings they could carry. Occasionally, a single person would pass, pushing a baby carriage filled with household possessions. Willard wondered if some of these people were coming from where he was headed.

The U.S. officers traveled 10 miles southwest to the suburb of Potsdam, an unscathed country town on the shores of Lake Griebnitz. There, Willard would help establish an advance headquarters for the upcoming Potsdam Conference, where the victorious Allied leaders from Britain, Russia, and the United States would divide up Germany, determine the future of Poland, and enlist Russia to defeat Japan. For two weeks, the world spotlight would be focused on Potsdam for what one newspaper called "the most important international conference of our time."

At the site, American soldiers set up in a two-story wooden building about 50 yards away from the sprawling Cecilienhof

Palace, a 176-room mansion built in 1917 for Kaiser Wilhelm II's son, the Crown Prince, and his wife, Cecilie. In about a month, President Truman, Soviet Premier Joseph Stalin, and British Prime Minister Winston Churchill, along with his elected replacement Clement Atlee, would meet at the Cecilienhof to chart out a new world order and, some historians say, initiate the tensions that led to the Cold War. During the meetings, Truman would also receive news of the successful test of a powerful new U.S. weapon: the atom bomb.

Three miles from the Cecilienhof, more than twenty-five "abandoned" private homes in the lake village of Babelsberg would serve as private residences for the visiting dignitaries. In reality, the Russians cleared the area ahead of time, telling many of the homeowners to take what they could and leave in an hour.

Willard witnessed the aftermath of the Russian efforts, remembering, "Their idea of cleaning up the houses was to move everything possible into a pile into the street, and then trucks came along and carried it away." "Everything" included rare books, china, and objets d'art, or as one former resident said, "the wealth of a cultivated house was destroyed within hours."

Preparations for the conference got under way immediately. "We came in and used about three times as many people as necessary to polish up the old place and fixed it up pretty flashy," Willard wrote his parents. The Russians put their stamp on the outside of the building, planting hundreds of red geraniums forming a 24-foot five-pointed red star, the symbol of the Russian army, at the center of the building's circular courtyard. Inside the palace, a vaulted reception hall on the first floor was turned into the main conference room, sporting three separate entrances for the triumvirate of world power. The room's focal point became a 12-foot round conference table with a centerpiece of three miniature country flags. Twelve hardback chairs, along with three wider armchairs crowned with gold-colored cherubs, were reserved for the participants. The conference was veiled in secrecy. A news blackout limited virtually any release of information about the goings-on behind the ivy-laden walls of the Cecilienhof, prompting loud squawks from the Berlin-based media, who objected to the "insulting" tidbits of news they did receive, such as what officials were eating and what they wore to dinner.

Willard's role as adjutant general, the chief administrative officer for the event, gave him a front-row seat to the historic conference and cast a light on his view of politics that would last a lifetime. He saw how government spent excessively on personnel and how the rules were bent for presidential supporters from Missouri who came to visit. "When I'd see a colonel or a general officer that was a new face at my office, I'd say, 'Are you from Missouri too?' More often than not they would admit to that."

Although his lifelong disenchantment with government was in its infancy, Willard nonetheless thrived amid "all the high brass" at Potsdam, where meetings and dinners stretched into the mornings' wee hours. Years later he recalled sitting two rows behind the president during Sunday church services, being "practically walked over" by Churchill, and having a rather close and potentially fateful encounter with Stalin.

"I happened to walk out of my headquarters one day unexpectedly and started to cross the street. Not 50 feet away, Stalin emerged from a house right at the end of this lake and strolled over to his limousine. ... I had my .45 sidearm ... and it occurred to me that I could have shot him," he recalled later, adding with a quip: "It would have been my last shot, and I would prefer to be here." In the retelling of this story, Willard sometimes said the incident was "a vivid reminder that opportunities with alternative options occur."

The Potsdam Conference ended on August 2, 1945, with agreements on how to divide Germany, provide Soviet war reparations, and re-establish Poland. Another called for "unconditional surrender" from Japan, threatening "prompt and utter destruction" otherwise. The Japanese government refused. Four days later, while Truman and his entourage sailed back to the United States, the atom bomb was unleashed on the Japanese city of Hiroshima. Three days after that, on August 9, 1945, another was dropped on Nagasaki. By August 15, the Japanese agreed to unconditional surrender.

"The atom bomb was a total surprise," Willard said later. "I thought I was really wired into everything, but that thing was a total surprise."

After Potsdam, Willard celebrated the victory over Japan by flying to the Riviera with friends, taking a two-hour swim, then traveling to Nice, Cannes, and Frankfurt, and returning the next morning to Berlin, where he planned to attend an afternoon ballet. His "interest ing" war was coming to a close.

In Berlin, now governed in the East by the Soviets and in the West by France, Britain, and the United States, Willard worked for the Allied Kommandatura, the governing body charged with polic-ing the area. His credentials allowed him to move easily between the heavily guarded checkpoints separating the two sectors, marked by the mammoth columns of the Brandenburg Gate.

World War II exposed Willard to a global perspective that few in Wichita had seen or would see for many years to come. He saw the gentility of the British, the hospitality of the French, and the gregariousness of the Germans as they returned to bombed-out Berlin to rebuild their city.

"They were accumulating together in one spot with nothing but their own labor. ... They rebuilt a city and an economy by serving one another." He saw how his young, U.S. compatriots defeated the enemy in a foreign land and began to think of how he could bring his experience back home. "Willard says he is getting ready to be a civilian," his father wrote the family. "Finally. We will be glad to see you at your early convenience." With a promise of the return of his elder son, Ray Garvey was resting a little easier.

After the anticipation in England, the danger in France, and the victories in Germany, it probably wasn't easy for the young, independent Willard to think about returning to a much simpler life in Wichita, Kansas. "Don't be discouraged about your future, Willard," his sister Ruth told him. "There will be plenty for you to do when you return. Daddy has a job and then some for you; I don't know how he has managed all these years."

A LIFETIME DEVOTION

"My wife is my most fortunate association." —WWG

AFTER JAPAN'S SURRENDER on September 2, Willard put off an immediate return to Kansas, choosing instead to stay in Europe for a few more weeks and take in the sights in Austria, Switzerland, and Italy. Before he left, he shipped home a trunk of correspondence, the first U.S. flag that was flown over Berlin, and a massive sixteenth-century Martin Luther Bible discovered after the postwar looting ruckus of German homes.

The delay disappointed his parents, who tried their best to remain enthused about their son's overseas adventures. "I can just see you shimming up the mountains ahead of the others," Ray wrote, hoping his son would leave the army behind and Berlin to the Berliners. "Leave it to the peacetime police, Mr. Willard, and try your hand and presence at home. ... There are lots of opportunities for those who can do."

At the end of October 1945, home had beckoned loud enough. Twenty-five-year-old Major Garvey bid adieu to the European theater and headed back to Circle Drive as a well-traveled man full of confidence and hope. Willard's confidence came from more than three years of a charmed army life at a time when the world was near historic implosion. His hope came from a father's reassurance that there was a place for him in the growing Garvey empire. "It was a happy day when Ray and I drove to Fort Leavenworth (Kansas) to meet him," his mother later recalled. "He was rosy-cheeked from the English climate, and fit and eager to conquer the world."

A lot had changed in Wichita since Willard left for war, and the city, like the rest of the country, was on the verge of another new chapter. The 60,000 aircraft jobs that once sent the population surging by 36 percent began to evaporate. Men who were paid $1 an hour making airplane parts didn't want to revert to farm work, earning $4 a day on a tractor crew. Gasoline rations were lifted, and the streets once again grew congested with cars. But as more people started driving longer distances, they found their "reclaimed rubber" tires—the result of wartime conservation—weren't up to the task. "I heard 300 cars were stalled between here and Colorado with tire trouble," Olive Garvey wrote her son.

With throngs of GIs returning from war and ready to settle down, marriage and family life became burgeoning industries all their own. Willard was now ready to be a part of the newlywed class. Drawing from his experience in the service, he decided to treat matrimony as he would any assigned project. A list of objectives and criteria was needed, a list he shared with his brother after James began contemplating a marriage of his own earlier that year.

"Is the girl physically attractive, both face and figure, and will she remain so?" Willard wrote, counseling his brother. "A good idea is to look at her parents and consider whether a woman like her mother would appeal to you in 20 or 30 years. It may appear a little like buying a good horse, but is the physical and mental health of her family good and free from hereditary diseases? Is she mentally alert, intelligent, and stimulating? Does she keep you interested; have new ideas which appeal to you? Is she generally quite pleasant? Do you both want the same things—family, vacations, friends, etc.?"

It was a formidable list. And yet, knowing that perhaps any eligible woman might have her own horse-buying specifications in the search for a suitable mate, Willard knew he would have to settle on a career before any husbandly aspirations could come to pass.

Ray Garvey's businesses offered plenty of options. Operating with a handful of employees, including his secretary and a construction superintendent named Clarence Drake, Garvey's Builders, Inc. had begun to construct communities of five-room brick houses throughout Wichita. Some of the homes had doubled in value during the war. On the northwest side of town, new homes with basements that sold for between $6,000 and $7,000 in 1941 were now worth $15,000. Several smaller brick houses sold for $3,300 in the fall of 1941 and "between $3,700 to $4,500" four years later. "Wichita may have lost some population, but there is still a good demand for housing, and ours fill up rapidly as people move out," Ray told his son.

Willard was interested in construction, but he was also curious about business opportunities in the oil, newspaper, and manufacturing businesses. He began his career search, spending "the most boring six weeks of my life" talking to executives in those industries. Eventually, his father steered him toward a decision. "Why don't you take Mr. Drake and go build some houses?" he remembered his father suggesting. "I did that and everything took off from there."

Across town, 23-year-old Jean Kindel's life was about to take an abrupt turn. Born in February 1922 to electrical contractor George Kindel and his wife Leota, a dedicated Christian Scientist, Jean and her brother Jim enjoyed an idyllic childhood in their two-story white frame house in Wichita's Riverside neighborhood. The children were never without things to do, whether it was playing alongside the nearby Little Arkansas River, roller-skating down Riverside Avenue, watching silent films in the neighboring park, or listening for the nocturnal roar of a lion wailing from a cage at the Riverside zoo. Jean grew up loving music and theater and was devoted to her parents and her church.

After graduating from Wichita's North High School in 1940, Jean worked in a downtown clothing store while attending the University of Wichita, where she was studying to be a Latin American diplomat. With her saucer-shaped brown eyes, hypnotic smile, sense of humor, and shapely figure, Jean was a striking beauty. In 1940, her good looks caught the attention of a popular bandleader, who chose the Wichita freshman to be the year's "Parnassus Queen," an honor named after the university's yearbook and one usually reserved for a graduating senior.

When the war came, Jean left school and went to work for Swallow Aircraft (which later became Boeing) and later as a file clerk in Boeing's cost accounting department. "I couldn't imagine staying in school and not doing something for the war effort," she recalled later. The end of the war sent Jean 160 miles northeast to Lawrence to finish college at the University of Kansas in the School of Business. "I wanted to find out what I'd been doing (at Boeing) all those years," she recalled. For fun, she socialized with a number of sorority girls, including sophomore Olivia Garvey, a member of the Delta Gamma sorority.

Jean Kindel was exactly the kind of woman that the KU sorority wanted in its ranks. Hoping to persuade her to join, Olivia asked her handsome older brother Willard if he would accompany the young woman to Wichita's Christmas "Triad" dance, which was put on every year by three of KU's popular sororities.

Thrilled at the prospect of an escort for a party she wanted to attend, Jean primped to perfection that night after Christmas. "I got out my long dress, and got all fixed up," she recalled. As it happened, Jean had met Willard Garvey once before, when he was dating Kathleen, the president of Jean's sorority back in Wichita.

Willard apparently did not remember the pre-war meeting with his former girlfriend's young sorority sister and left Circle Drive feeling "extremely suspicious" of his sister's set-up. Within moments of meeting Jean, the suspicion turned to gratitude. Willard would always have his sister to thank for the blind date, which began what he called his "most fortunate association."

As she watched Major Garvey approach her in his formal winter uniform with the belted tunic jacket, Jean's heart skipped a beat. Willard was dashing, and he instantly captivated her with stories of Europe and his take on world affairs. "I knew within the first few minutes that this was the most interesting man I'd ever met in my life … and he was just about the best dancer I had ever seen," she recalled more than 60 years later. And Jean Kindel—kind and attentive, intelligent and engaging, with a distinguished radiant charm—certainly fit all of Willard's criteria for a wife. Olive Garvey remembered how her son "came home in a daze and remained disoriented" for some time after that sorority dance.

Still, there was an air of practicality on both sides of the budding romance. "Willard came back from the war and he was looking for me and he found me," Jean remembered. "We both realized before we met each other that we were at a time of our life when we were supposed to settle down. … On our second date, he started to talk about getting married."

Getting Jean to buy in to his partnership plan took a little convincing. Willard kept at it on January 6, 1946—two weeks and four dates into their relationship. He was staying at the O'Pelt Hotel in Colby, Kansas, while helping his father ship "several thousand" head of sheep and cattle just before a stockyard strike. "It seems to boil down to the cold, simple conclusive summary that we are a couple of equally wholesome, intelligent, healthy individuals with sufficient past experience and thought to make the most of an intelligently planned and mutually executed future," he wrote in a twenty-page treatise while sitting out one of his father's bridge games in the next room.

In the letter, he wrote of a "little fantasy I was dreaming up under the heading of 'the 50-year plan' or 'a long-time married.'" Always one to practice visualization, Willard was downright prophetic on that point. He admitted he was "charging forward like a bull in a china shop" but was of no mind to stop. Somehow, Jean understood Willard and his impatience, perhaps better than he did himself. That spring, she quit her job at a local business and accepted his proposal. "I left school because he might not ask me again," she joked to friends.

AT 11 A.M. ON April 18, 1946, Jean and Willard were married at the Plymouth Congregational Church, a gothic stone landmark in Wichita. The wedding was billed by the local newspaper to have "outstanding interest in society circles" but was in fact quite modest. Jean, touted in the local newspaper as "an attractive member of the debutante set," wore a Larry Aldrich suit with a cocoa-brown pleated skirt and a beige waist-length, double-breasted jacket with turned-back cuffs and a Peter Pan collar. A small straw brown hat decorated with buttons and trimmed with beige ribbon bows adorned her head. During the ceremony, the couple was surrounded by arrangements of white snapdragons, carnations, and Easter lilies while the organist played Schubert's "Serenade," Liszt's "Lieberstraum," Dubois's "Can-tilene Nuptiale," and Bizet's "Dreams."

Family friend Lois Senter of Tulsa, Oklahoma, daughter of well-known art-deco architect Leon B. Senter, who played match-maker to Jean's parents, was the couple's maid of honor. Willard's high school friend David Jackman was the best man. Willard, dressed in a dark brown suit and tie, sported a mile-wide smile that matched his crisp white shirt as he celebrated another goal met in record time. Two months after his discharge from the Army, he was a husband.

After the wedding ceremony, the guests went to a local banquet room for breakfast, where Willard and Jean took the ceremonial cut of a ring-shaped cake encircled with Easter lilies, lilies of the valley, and yellow jonquils. Their honeymoon, according to the newspaper, was "an extended motor trip through the East."

In making their travel plans, Willard asked his bride where she had been and where she would like to go. When she replied that she had been as far east as Cincinnati to visit her grandparents, west to Green Mountain Falls, Colorado, south to Tulsa, and north to Kansas City, Willard set out to change things in a hurry.

"We went about 2,000 to 3,000 miles on our honeymoon," Jean recalled. "We went across the country, along the East Coast, up to Canada, and back here." The couple visited Willard's friends and relatives, including an aunt, uncle, and cousins in Baltimore, an Army colonel in Washington, D.C., another in Amherst, Massachusetts, and a third at East Leavenworth, Kansas.

The first leg of their trip was a 200-mile drive to Kansas City and a night at the Muehlebach Hotel, where they might have crossed paths with President Harry Truman, who often used the penthouse at the grand hotel as his in-town headquarters. It was early evening, and Jean by that time was ready for "dinner and relaxation." Willard, however, had other ideas. "We're going to go swimming," he told her. The couple ventured over to the nearby Phillips Hotel, and Willard launched himself into the water. Having taken the plunge of a very different sort earlier in the day, Jean braved the water as her husband observed her swimming style. "Willard and I started off our marriage in a swimming pool, and that's the way it's been the whole time," Jean recalled.

Swimming became part of the daily routine in what would soon become a very busy Garvey household. Whether in the throes of an ice-gripped winter or an oppressively hot summer, the faint smell of chlorine or a pile of heavy wet towels was as recognizable as the family dog. "We were all waterlogged," she said.

JEAN AND WILLARD GARVEY are remembered for being a glamorous Wichita couple, but they began their life together in a simple brick fourplex on South Hillside, in one of the tiny new homes built by Ray Garvey's Builders, Inc., then on its way to becoming the city's largest homebuilder of the postwar boom. Every day, Willard drove their Chevrolet into downtown Wichita to work with his father at Builders, Inc., while Jean, trying once again to finish college, took the bus back and forth to classes at the university and rehearsed for a lead in a community play.

Within months, the diploma was put on hold once more when Jean learned she was pregnant with John, the couple's first son, born in 1947. Over the next 10 years, there would be five more children: another son, Jim, and four girls, Ann, Emily, Julie, and Mary. All grown up, those children and even a few grandchildren would be on hand when Jean Garvey eventually did finish college. In 1988 at the age of 66, she received her Bachelor of Science degree in human resource management from Wichita's Friends University. Willard beamed at his wife when she walked to get her diploma that day, telling friends later, "I was the Class of '41 at Michigan and my wife is the Class of '88 … She's a nice young wife!"

In Jean, Willard found the perfect partner. Friends and family say she was the one who softened so many of Willard's rough edges. She was charm to his belligerence and patience to his furor. She attended family business meetings and came to understand the inner workings of the successful Garvey companies. She got involved in a host of community projects and reflected her husband's energy and enthusiasm at every step of the way. It was Jean, observers say, who often made Willard more tolerable.

"He did have a temper," said Cheryl Gillenwater, Willard's administrative assistant at parent company Garvey Industries for almost two decades. "If it hadn't been for Jean, I don't think I would have stayed as long." Gillenwater, who occasionally overheard the couple's spats from the speakerphone in his office, recalled that "he adored Jean. You would hear him bark at her. She would say, 'Willard, calm down.' She hung up on him a few times, but she never got upset. They were very, very close."

In Willard, Jean found a worldly, driven, good-looking, and athletic man who idolized his parents, valued his siblings, and believed in American production and liberty. He was also reliable. After a day of roughing up people in the office, floating out dozens of new ideas, barking out challenges over the cost of building materials or the nonadherence to his ever-changing but mandatory organizational procedures, Willard would call Jean every evening at 5:30, ask if she needed him to pick up anything on the way home, and be home for dinner promptly at 6 p.m. "He'd come in and give her a big smooch and we'd have dinner together every night," said daughter Mary Theroux.

For more than 50 years, Jean could usually be found at her husband's side, traveling with him to six continents, attending countless trade meetings and gatherings of first the Young Presidents Organization and later the YPO alumni group, the Chief Executives Organization, with hundreds of their lifelong friends.

Her days were often filled with children, travel, community projects, or a combination of all three. At night, the couple could be spotted at numerous business, cultural, or charitable events, dancing and smiling the night away. Together, their love of theater brought about repeated trips to New York City and Broadway, where they collected mementos from shows such as the 1948 performance of

"A Streetcar Named Desire" starring a young Marlon Brando, Karl Malden, and Jessica Tandy, or one of Willard's favorites, "Man of La Mancha" staring Richard Kiley in 1965.

At local social events, Willard was hard to miss. "He was an *arresting* person," Jean said. "If he was around, you'd know he was there. If you stayed a few more minutes, you'd find out what his opinion was."

Guests at a formal party one night in Wichita executive Stanley "Bud" Beren's home found out much more than that. As an orchestra serenaded guests alongside Beren's indoor swimming pool, a tuxedo-clad and fancy-footed Willard twirled a dance partner out over the open water. He successfully returned her to dry land but sacrificed himself in the process, falling into the pool full-throttle. "Unabashed, Willard climbed out of the pool, slightly embarrassed, drove home, and returned in a dry tuxedo," Beren recalled. "We surmised that Willard was the only man in Wichita with two tuxedos."

Tuxedoed or not, some people cringed when they saw Willard Garvey at a cocktail party for the simple fact that he preferred a spirited debate over the woes of public education to the velvety taste of a rich red wine. As one partygoer put it: "He was always all business. Jean was a diffuser in the situation."

With Jean on his arm, the gruff, demanding boss often surprised his employees with a gentle side. "When Willard was with Jean, he was a different person," said Alex Dean, the president of Builders, Inc., in the late 1980s. "He was kind and generous and gracious. ... It was just in his weekday work thing that he got worked up about things."

The Latin American diplomat's job may have eluded her, but Jean's role as Willard's wife and mother to their children made her all that and then some.

FATHER AND SON

"He was a dreamer who made most of his dreams come true." —WWG on Ray Garvey

THE EARLY 1950S were prosperous years for America and the Garvey family. Returning World War II veterans were buying houses, building businesses, and tending to their growing families. The nation was in the midst of a "baby boom," with about four million babies born each year. That boom also created an economic crest as consumers filled their homes with big-ticket items such as washing machines, refrigerators, and stoves. Production of goods and services hit record levels, and money spent on business equipment and new facilities was continually on the rise.

By 1951, Willard's father was overseeing a very successful and diversified enterprise that owned more than 100,000 acres in Kansas and Colorado; a thirty-station service oil company; a wheat and farming business with sixty tractors, sixty plows, and forty trucks; an oil drilling company that produced oil runs of about $100,000 per month; a fledgling grain elevator that could store much of the nation's wheat surplus; a mortgage company; an insurance agency; and the Wichita-based Builders, Inc., which owned about 1,400 rental units and had just finished building another 500 postwar homes.

With profits that year estimated at about $2.2 million, Ray Garvey poured a lot of it back into the businesses, particularly tax-advantaged operations like oil exploration. As it was, profits over $400,000 were taxed at 92 percent. "We have a family income of considerable amount, all of which, nearly, we would have to pay out in tax and might not have the money to do it," Ray told his children, now in their 20s and 30s and heavily involved in company operations.

Willard was managing Builders, Inc.; James was in the farming business along with Olivia's husband, George Lincoln; and Ruth's husband, Dick Cochener, who would die three years later from lung cancer, worked in the grain storage business. Even with their involvement, Ray always remained firmly in charge, organizing meetings and prodding each family member along the way. "To be acquainted with the high-strung, always-pressing businessman was to respect him," Olive Garvey wrote of her husband. "He was restless and fidgety in all his waking hours, but had a rare ability to relax totally in almost instant sleep."

Perhaps it was his clear conscience that brought him such deep sleep. Or maybe it was his resolute commitment to "demonstrate that free enterprise is the foremost laboratory for all the American virtues," Olive thought. Ray Garvey's hope for all his children was that they would find as much satisfaction in business as he did. "In all of this work, the chief thing is that all of us keep occupied at interesting work, at constructive and productive labor," he told them. "That adds to the happiness and importance of each of us, I think, and keeps us out of mischief."

Working with his methodical, confident, and demanding father in the real estate business wasn't always easy for Willard, who could spit out ideas with the intensity of a horizontal hailstorm. While the family was fully engaged in building a one million-bushel grain elevator in Topeka and more than 400 housing units at the Fort Riley military base in northeastern Kansas, Willard lobbied to begin construction of a 14-story Wichita apartment building dubbed "The Jayhawk," commemorating the free-staters who opposed slavery in the days leading up to the Civil War.

The speculative project did not sit well with Ray, who convinced his son that The Jayhawk should wait and be reviewed by the entire family once the two larger projects were completed. By November, The Jayhawk was officially tabled due to high construction costs and labor shortages brought on by the Korean War, then in its seventeenth month. The cancellation was likely a disappointment to Willard, who longed to break out of his father's constraints and find success of his own.

"Willard thinks I interfere with him, and I guess I do," Ray wrote in April 1951. Throughout the decade, Willard and his father would clash like two dissonant cymbals in a prolonged symphony. Ray often criticized his son's affinity for creating systems and organizations designed to help manage a growing operation, preferring instead to handle business matters personally and act like a "ramrod in there ramming." Willard was forced to defend his techniques to his father, explaining how his method of holding weekly meetings with staff members taught them to understand the complexities of projects and track progress against various items each week.

In the mid-1950s, Ray chided Willard on his plan for the Bonnie Brae subdivision, a development of custom homes in an up-and-coming eastern Wichita neighborhood. It would be one of the first of twenty subdivisions Willard was credited with developing. In Bonnie Brae, Ray wanted a quick turnaround on the lots out of fear that another depression would leave the Garvey enterprise in trouble. As it was, interest rates were rising to postwar highs and federally supported mortgage money was growing scarce. Willard, ever confident, was willing to wait it out, even though construction costs were rising. Working with local architect Sid Platt, Willard stood firm, telling his father the development was a good one. It took time and patience for the sales to be made and the homes to be built, he argued.

Words of disagreement between the two men fell just short of hostile in 1956, when Ray grew anxious over the inventory status at Builders, Inc., fearing that taxes could devour the company if business slowed. Willard, in response, felt his father was "needling" him and wrongly "harped on" his business decisions. "I know you have been having a bout the past two years with Management by Generalities or Management through Secret Enigma, Willard, but you should be snapping out of that," Ray wrote. "You cannot appoint a business and make it succeed."

That kind of comment "shows how little you know about administration," Willard shot back. "I have tried to do what I think you have never tried to do—namely systematize my work so that I run it rather than it runs me. ... Naturally, I am groping, having had absolutely no example by my seniors here in administrative systems so that I will not be harassed day and night but will have each problem bucketed with an individual whom we hope by training will develop into a competent manager."

Willard was trying something new with Bonnie Brae and wanted to show his father that success was possible even if he wasn't working like all the other developers in town. "If I want to copy all of the peanuts in town, why, we can continue to be a peanut. Maybe it would be smart to be a peanut, but on the other hand, by showing a little imagination, innovation and individuality, it might be that we can come up with our own program rather than copying the current flash in the pan," he told him.

Weeks later, the hurt that Willard felt from his father's criticism was still evident in angry correspondence. "I don't care to have any implication on your part that I give orders or will screw up these companies by giving orders as I have not done it and don't care to hear any more remarks to that effect. ... Obviously, I am interested in carrying out the family's interest, but I think I am not as effective as I would be without your constant reminders."

He gave his father a simple proposal aimed at halting the familial discord. "I wish a small emancipation proclamation to be brought up at the family meeting wherein I would like to have you volunteer to drop off my back and participate only in a regularly held monthly board of directors meetings of Builders, Inc., wherein I would be glad to entertain all of your suggestions and would care to hear nothing from you between the board of directors meeting as far as Builders operations are concerned."

The proclamation apparently went nowhere. In the months and years that followed, Ray would still critique his son's business methods in lengthy memos that addressed up to a dozen subjects. When some of Willard's real estate ventures were losing money, Ray blamed Willard for "constantly upsetting the organization by trying experiments."

He attacked Willard's sales organization, saying the "deflated morale" of the sales force was hurting business. "A sales force that does not have an exuberant morale cannot do much selling," he wrote. On another occasion, Ray warned Willard about being in too many businesses at the same time, something Wichita critics would echo years later. "Of course you should have the privilege of expanding your business by going into related lines, although you are in so many businesses now that you will find it easy to acquire a reputation for making losses in a number of businesses and of being a 'Jack of all trades and a master of none.'"

"Dad was right. I was unduly complex," Willard reflected later. Despite his father's reproach, Willard publicly remembered Ray as "gently leading by the hand."

That guidance eventually helped Builders, Inc., become a formidable force in Wichita's development. The company that began in 1946 with two or three employees went on to train more than 600 returning World War II GIs to become bricklayers and carpenters. Many of them went on to launch firms of their own. Builders, Inc., was behind the construction of more than 5,000 homes, the management of more than 3,000 apartments, and the development of Parklane Shopping Center, one of the first strip malls in the state. "Willard's involvement in homebuilding in this community as well as worldwide is probably unparalleled," said Elton Parsons, former vice president of development for Builders, Inc. "There's not too much in this town that Willard Garvey didn't touch."

Still, the lingering reverberations of parental discord were ever present in Willard's head. They would also be heard among Willard's own children, many of whom, like their father, wanted a symphony of their own.

AS ENJOYABLE AS it was, the prosperity of the 1950s was wrapped in a bundle of fear. Creeping communism, atomic destruction, and domestic espionage emerged as new U.S. enemies. By 1950, the Russians had their own atomic bomb after Soviet spy Klaus Fuchs passed along its secrets while working on the Manhattan Project in Los Alamos, New Mexico. FBI Director J. Edgar Hoover warned President Truman about suspected communists working for the U.S. government, but it was the crusade of Wisconsin Republican Senator Joseph McCarthy that served up the issue to the national press.

Having witnessed the early days of U.S.-Soviet discord back at Potsdam, when Stalin reneged on its agreements and set down firmer stakes in Eastern Europe instead, Willard believed communism was a verifiable threat. President Truman left Potsdam thinking Stalin was "a son of a bitch" whose global communistic push must be stopped. When Soviet-occupied North Korea invaded U.S.-led South Korea in violation of the agreements at Potsdam, a showdown between the burgeoning superpowers was inevitable.

The U.S. Congress never officially declared war on the North Koreans; however, more than 36,000 American lives were lost in a conflict that lasted from June 1950 to July 1953. Dissatisfaction with Truman's handling of the situation overturned a 20-year stay of Democrats in the White House.

In 1952, Kansas-reared Republican Dwight D. Eisenhower became the thirty-fourth U.S. president, riding on his popularity as military leader of the European invasion in World War II. His vice president was California Senator Richard Nixon, a politically ambitious conservative selected in part for his stance against communism. Nixon's perseverance as a congressman against alleged spy and former State Department official Alger Hiss in 1950 propelled him into the political spotlight.

The election outcome was welcome news in the Garvey clan. Willard and his father may have disagreed at times in their business approach, but politically they were identical. Ray Garvey, ever the epitome of the independent, free-thinking Kansan, abhorred entrenched New Deal policies and the liberal press that supported them. When McCarthyism and the hunt for communists took the national stage in 1952, Willard's father rose to his defense, believing that "McCarthy had something important and real under exposure."

He tweaked McCarthy opponents in the media with tongue-in-cheek letters inviting recipients to get active in "The Committee to Protect Subversives by Smearing McCarthy." Publishers such as Henry Luce of Time-Life and Palmer Hoyt of *The Denver Post* were puzzled at the correspondence, which only pleased Ray Garvey more.

Willard would also become known for his own brand of letter writing, firing off commentary to newspapers and politicians with the volume and regularity of an all-day e-mailer. "He wasn't out to build goodwill," recalled Gillenwater, Willard's assistant, who typed out hundreds of the dispatches, including some of his last protesting a downtown Wichita economic development district. "He was out to say what he thought was wrong and how it could be corrected."

Fortunately for many, the technology of the time limited Willard's communications to letters, memos, telephone calls, or facsimiles, all of which he used to capacity. Family, friends, and co-workers smile with relief when trying to imagine Willard equipped with a cell phone, text messaging, or e-mail, jamming their inboxes with the questions and ideas that filtered through his head 24 hours a day.

Willard also believed in McCarthy, a year before the senator dominated television networks in congressional hearings that took on the U.S. Army. Willard embraced McCarthy with the same fervor as his father, writing Kansas City banker Arthur Eisenhower, after the president's older brother called McCarthy "the most dangerous menace to America."

"I hope that your statement that McCarthy 'has done the party no good' is a misquote," Willard wrote. "McCarthy's rabble-rousing approach awakened the public to what a stinking mess existed in Washington. Your brother's remarkable public appeal made the needed change possible. We need Ike ... we also need McCarthy."

During the 1950s, Willard decided to fight communism with capitalism, launching an international residential construction program that built affordable homes in developing countries. When the United States agreed to sell excess wheat to foreign countries, Willard pushed to have local governments set aside a portion of their payments for local mortgage programs for working people. His "World Homes" effort was a way to whet the working-class appetite for private property rights in communist-leaning countries. "Every man a homeowner, and every man a capitalist," was Garvey's battle cry during the Cold War.

Jean Garvey heard plenty of cries during the 1950s. Mostly it was the cries of her six children, born within about two years of one another. Meanwhile, other cries from her husband encompassed creeping communism abroad and domestically against union membership as a condition of employment, also known as the "right to work" movement. He also protested the bidding practices of Wichita construction projects and minimum wage requirements for builders of low-income housing projects.

Willard's viewpoints on everything from McCarthyism to right to work laws were passionate and unshakeable at a time when young people were being criticized for their indifference to the world at large. "Youth today is waiting for the hand of fate to fall on its shoulders," *Time* magazine wrote in 1951, introducing readers to the spoils of "The Silent Generation." With all his cries and causes, Willard Garvey was anything but silent. By the end of the decade, however, his civic cries would turn to tears of grief.

OVER THE YEARS, Ray Garvey had been troubled with health problems. At six feet and 190 pounds, he had an insatiable appetite and a penchant for pie a la mode, peach cobbler, sausage, and other fattening foods. By 1953, at the age of 60, he was diagnosed with diabetes. Five years later in January 1958, he suffered a heart attack in California, but he recuperated enough to return to work at year's end.

Always one to love his work, Ray Garvey began 1959 equipped with a big to-do list. His oil company, Petroleum, Inc., was expanding into Canada. Nine huge Garvey Grain elevators were already in operation, including two in Nebraska, one in Fort Worth, Texas, and two more under construction in North Dakota.

Nationally, the Garvey name was becoming quite well known. Big-city bankers from the East Coast were more than happy to finance Ray Garvey's massive grain elevator expansion, even though they had no concept of its function, preferring instead to think of it as some kind of moving staircase and not the tubular storage facility of the Great Plains harvests. The family's reputation was so good in financial circles, it had little problem receiving a $50 million business loan tied to personal guarantees from Ray and Willard. Such hefty borrowing was risky, but Ray Garvey knew his limits.

Elsewhere in the country, people who imagined Kansas as nothing more than a farmer's flatland read a profile of Ray Garvey in the June 8, 1959, issue of *Time* magazine. Entitled "Garvey's Gravy," the article not only highlighted the acumen that led to Ray Garvey's fortune, but condemned him for receiving millions of dollars in government loans and subsidy programs for growing and storing wheat. According to the article, the U.S. Department of Agriculture paid Garvey $14.7 million a year to store the country's excess grain.

"Of all the harvesters of the U.S.'s scandalous farm subsidy program, none have harvested more profitably than a bulky, hearty Kansan named Ray Hugh Garvey," the story began. The article hit a painful nerve, eliciting Garvey's familiar response: "We operate under the program. We don't set it."

A week and a half after the *Time* article hit the newsstands, Willard, Jean, and sons John, age 12, and Jim, 9, left Wichita for a month-long trip to Asia and the Middle East. Giving his children a worldwide perspective was a priority for Willard, who started first with his two boys.

John Garvey left Kansas thinking about his grandfather. "He was starting to become very interesting to me. ... I made a specific conscious goal to get to know him better." John liked to play catch with his grandfather, an activity that eluded Willard, who was more likely to jump in a pool with him instead. John also remembered admiring his grandfather's "Socratic approach" to dinner table discussions, where he would pose a series of questions encouraging the grandchildren to think through their answers and statements.

For the Garvey boys, the 1959 trip was the first of several memorable family trips they would take with their parents. They traveled first to San Francisco on their way to Japan, Hong Kong, Thailand, and then Pakistan, where Willard's world changed forever.

On June 30, Ray Garvey woke up ahead of his wife and went to the kitchen of his handsome yet modest two-story wood-frame home on a tree-lined street in Eastborough, a tony Wichita suburb. He fumbled around to make himself breakfast, an act practically unheard of in his 40-plus years of marriage.

Alone at the kitchen table, he considered how the day's business would bring another milestone—the final mortgage payment on a grain elevator in Salina, Kansas. He and two associates were taking a 90-mile drive out to the property to conduct the transaction and celebrate it with a smile. By the time Ray was ready to leave, Olive stood at the sink in the kitchen. As he always did, Ray gave her a kiss goodbye and walked out the door to the attached garage. Minutes later, he returned and inexplicably kissed her again.

That afternoon, his business complete, Garvey was napping in the passenger seat of the Ford sedan headed back to Wichita, traveling the U.S. Highway 81 bypass just west of McPherson. A truck pulled out from a roadside service station directly into the car's path. The impact sent the right-hand side of the Ford directly under the truck's bed. Ray Garvey was dead within hours. He was 66 years old.

THE SUDDEN LOSS of their patriarch was a blow to the close-knit Garvey family. Willard's brother and two sisters had rushed to their father's side from Colby and Topeka and were with their mother when Ray died. Willard's exact whereabouts were not known, but Olive enlisted the help of an international grain company, which found him in Pakistan. The boys were told their grandfather had been in an auto accident but had no idea how dire the situation. At dinner that night, Jim Garvey broke the meal's leftover wishbone and hoped that his grandfather would be okay. On a plane out of Karachi, Pakistan, that evening, Jean Garvey sat next to her sons and told them their grandfather was dead.

Trying to get back to the United States in 24 hours was no easy feat, said John, who remembers his father's serious tone while negotiating a complicated and lengthy itinerary to get them home quickly. "We were on a whole series of planes from Karachi back to Wichita," said John. Willard's emotions over his father's death were not evident to his children, muted perhaps by the planes' deafening propellers, unsteady trajectory, and unyielding seats. There was little rest on this long, unexpected return trip. It took more than a day to get back to Wichita—just in time to get to the funeral.

Two hours before the Friday, July 3, funeral services at Plymouth Congregational Church, Willard, Jean, and their sons landed in Wichita and were reunited with the younger Garvey children ages 8, 6, 4, and 2. They joined Olive, Willard's siblings, and a throng of mourners to pay tribute to a man with "restless energy and a sense of fun."

Kansas had lost one of its most prominent citizens. Once vilified for his business choices, Garvey was praised in local newspapers for his leadership and down-home compassion. "Garvey was Millionaire Who Didn't Act Like Tycoon," wrote the *Topeka Daily Capital,* the newspaper Garvey delivered while a college student at Washburn University. "He "valued health above wealth" and "outside of his family, business was his only passion."

More tributes came posthumously. Garvey's pioneering farming techniques and his entrepreneurial spirit gained him a place in Kansas history. In 1993, he was inducted into the Kansas Business Hall of Fame, and in downtown Wichita, the ten-story R.H. Garvey Building and its companion Olive W. Garvey Building have been a mainstay for local businesses, home to Garvey executives, and landmarks on the city's horizon since 1966. In the lobby of the R.H. Garvey Building, a bronze relief of his image bears an inscription testifying to the attributes he held dear: "Imagination, Courage and Integrity."

Ray Garvey's shoes left a deep impression on Kansas's fertile soil. After his death, "everybody realized that the genius was gone," his daughter Ruth said. And so it was up to Olive, who considered herself "a half-person with no balancing prop," to carry on his legacy. At 65, she began what she called her "third life" as chief executive of a multimillion-dollar family enterprise. Willard, who was as restless, fidgety, and high-minded as his father, would work hard to see the Garvey legacy reach well beyond his Kansas grain.

"You always wonder what would happen if he were still around," Willard once said. "I wish I were half the entrepreneur he was."

OUR FELLOW
OF PERPETUAL MOTION

"I am happier in the pursuit." –WWG

A FATHER'S DEATH tends to mark time. "Before and after Dad died were totally different eras," Willard once said. Few could disagree.

With Ray as patriarch, the Garvey business was regional in scope, investing in wheat, oil, and residential construction. But with his death, the company was thrust into trouble across the country. First, it had to assure dozens of lenders that the business was financially sound, and second, it had to fend off estate taxes, which threatened to wipe out everything Ray Garvey had built.

Ever stoic, Olive Garvey stepped into the role of corporate decision-maker immediately after her husband's death. She presided over the family meetings and coordinated visits to the East Coast, assuring bankers their loans, including the $50 million personal note co-signed by Willard, would not default.

In addition, Willard and his siblings began to take responsibility for different aspects of the business, although each was pursuing his or her own interests. "Mother decided we should all have our separate responsibilities so we didn't second-guess each other and have family trouble," Ruth said.

James and his wife, Shirley, worked first for Garvey Farms in Colby and later moved to Fort Worth, Texas, to oversee a grain facility there. Ruth, widowed since 1954, remained in Topeka with her new husband, Bernerd "Bun" Fink, and ran C-G-F (short for Cochener-Garvey-Fink) Grain Co.. Olivia and her husband, George Lincoln, whom she married in 1949, lived first in Colby, then moved to Lincoln, Nebraska, to head up the grain business there. Willard remained in Wichita, overseeing the building division and Ray Garvey's long-lasting legacy, the half-mile, 246-silo grain elevator just southwest of town. Although they were operating different companies, Ray Garvey's children remained in business together until they were financially untangled in 1973.

Overseeing day-to-day operations and administration of the $10 million estate was a young accountant named Bob Page. A no-nonsense, brilliant tax expert with a hard-charging personality, Page worked at a local accounting firm, and Ray Garvey was his client. Garvey came to trust and respect Page so much he was a pallbearer at his funeral. That endorsement was enough for Olive, who convinced Page to come work for her in 1960.

The youngest of eighteen children, Bob Page was inherently confident, with an unflinching practicality. When he was orphaned at age 16, he asked the courts to declare him an adult so that he could enter into contracts without a guardian. He earned a degree in accounting and another in law from Kansas University, sporting a powerful one-two punch in business precision and legal finesse. He admired Olive Garvey and became her loyal adviser.

"Mother and Page had a perfect relationship right from the start," Willard said later. "He worships her and she totally relies on him." For more than 30 years, Page worked tirelessly as the company controller, guiding first the Garvey businesses, until they were split up among the children in the early 1970s, and then Olive's personal affairs until her death in 1993 when she was 99 years old.

As Page worked in those early days to finalize Ray's estate and fight Internal Revenue Service disputes dating back to 1951, Willard's business curiosity shifted into overdrive. He started a new newspaper and an international homebuilding program. He also turned down at least one memorable opportunity, questioning Frank and Dan Carney when the local entrepreneurs asked him for $20,000 to build their first building in exchange for a 20 percent interest in their new upstart pizza company. "Who eats pizza?" he quipped to the founders of Pizza Hut, which grew to be the world's largest pizza franchise.

Page did his best to prudently steer Willard and the rest of the Garveys in a beneficial direction, especially in moments of intense family disagreement. During business meetings, it was not unusual for him to witness a caustic interaction between Willard and James, Ruth, or Olivia, as mother Olive officiated. Back then, the family fights included decisions about Willard's international housing project known as World Homes. While his siblings never challenged Willard's motives for wanting to increase home ownership worldwide, they did press him on when the project would make a profit. After all, it wasn't just his money at stake.

A year before her death, Ruth Fink remembered the family meetings in a gentle light, saying her brother was "not too realistic sometimes," often jockeying for control of more Garvey companies. It wasn't greed, but the honest belief he could run businesses better, Ruth said. In the meetings, "nobody held anything back," she recalled. "If we disagreed with (Willard), we told him."

JAMES "HARVEY" CHILDERS was a 32-year-old accountant at a Tulsa, Oklahoma, broadcasting company in 1962. Tall and thin, with a sense of calmness and consistency one would expect in a numbers man, Childers was examining his career path when he heard about an auditing job working with Page at the Garvey organization in Wichita.

By then, Willard's World Homes project was in full swing, with construction in Lima, Peru, and Bogota, Colombia, well under way. On the domestic front, he continued his personal quest against high taxes and big government and launched *Washington World*, a weekly newspaper designed to promote private enterprise and embrace Jeffersonian individualism.

Between the travel involved with these projects and his much-loved gatherings of the Young Presidents Organization, there were periods when Willard and Jean spent more time in airports than in their own living room. "Willard would get a thought in his head and suddenly we were on a plane," was how one associate described his on-the-go personality. It was not unusual for Garvey, who opted to get the most from every minute of the day, to ask Childers to meet him at the Tulsa airport, where he and Jean had a 45-minute layover en route to Wichita from Memphis. What was unusual, at least in Childers's mind, was the race that interview entailed.

Shortly after deplaning, Jean and Willard got separated in the terminal. As soon as Childers greeted Willard, he was recruited to help locate Jean. The men walked from one end of the terminal to the other and did not spot her. After two passes through the building, departure time drew near and Willard grew anxious. "Let's double-time," Willard barked at Childers, who soon found himself running through the airport and getting plenty of odd looks from strangers. Garvey, 10 years his senior yet fit as a 25-year-old, sprinted ahead with little effort. He looked back at the lagging Childers and said, "What's the matter, can't you keep up?"

❧

KEEPING UP WITH Willard Garvey was a challenge for anyone. "He lived life like a cavalry charge," said Wichita businessman Martin Eby, whose construction firm worked on several Garvey projects. "It was full speed —always."

For more than 35 years, Childers did his best to keep up with the charge, working first as chief financial officer for the Garvey organization and then for two decades as an executive vice president for Willard's companies. He worked with managers of Willard's building company, his ranch properties, grain businesses, and countless entrepreneurial investments, among them a flour mill in Trinidad, a new television network, and an ethanol plant.

Childers estimates he spent about 11,000 days with Willard and talked with him every day, save for a period in the summer of 1965, when Willard, Jean, Jean's mother, and the six children took a 10-week trip around the world. "Every day, he'd say, 'What's new? What's new?' And if there wasn't something new, he'd say, 'Let's create something new,'" Childers said. "His passion was his entrepreneurial spirit. Willard felt like he could motivate anybody, that if you had the energy and the right attitude, anybody could do anything. ... He would take on anything, anywhere, anytime." Childers is among dozens of former Garvey executives— many now successful business owners in their own right—who credit Willard for giving them a chance, and the responsibilities that went with it, to prove their worth. "Willard opened an awful lot of doors for me," Childers recalled. "In fact, he pushed me through a lot of them."

The longer he was in business, the more Willard believed in giving others a chance. "I am personally committed to helping build independent self-starting individuals, and providing places and prospects—golden opportunities—for them to work out their individual destinies," he said.

The opportunities came to those who could keep up with him. If Willard wasn't at an airport at 5:30 in the morning, he was in his office by 7 a.m., ready to chair a breakfast meeting. Mondays brought weekly lunch meetings of the Wichita Rotary Club, and other days, he spent his lunch with area executives at the members-only Wichita Petroleum Club. By about 3 p.m., when the day's decisions reached a crescendo, Willard religiously left for a swim at the downtown Wichita YMCA. It didn't matter what documents needed signing, what calls needed to be returned, or who might have been sitting outside his office. Swim time was re-energize time and his routine never varied. "If I have an addiction, it is swimming," Willard said. "Swimming is my drug."

To get his daily fix, Willard would leave his office on the tenth floor of the R.H. Garvey Building and drive six blocks over to the Y, where he would change, shower, swim twenty laps (never counting them), shower, dress, drive back to the office and return, still damp, but with a dry toupee on his head and a wet bathing suit in his briefcase. The whole process took about 30 minutes. "No matter where in the world I go, if there's a swimming pool nearby, I'm just 30 minutes away from feeling good," he once told Childers, who shot back, "Willard, no matter where in the world *I* go, if there's a Diet Coke machine, I'm 30 *seconds* from feeling good." Willard didn't get the joke.

In the evenings when he was in town, Willard was home for dinner by 6, after which he would head out with Jean to a social or civic event, perhaps a presentation from the Council on Foreign Relations, a church fundraiser, or a dinner at the Wichita Country Club to meet a foreign dignitary. To any outsider, Wichita might seem like a nondescript midsize city smack dab in the middle of the country, but to Willard and Jean, it was a pretty exciting place.

At just about any social event, they might run into prominent Wichitans such as Olive Ann Beech, who like Willard's mother took over the helm of her husband's company, Beech Aircraft, after his death in 1950. Or they might have stopped to talk with Fred Koch, who gave his name to the industrial conglomerate Koch Industries, to recap the events of a recent John Birch Society meeting at his home. Fiery talk of education issues might have come up in chats with Robert Love of Love Box Company, with whom the Garveys helped launch Wichita's Collegiate School before Jean started her own Independent School in 1980. Bill and Moya Lear of Learjet fame might chat with them about luxurious private planes, and visits with hometown entrepreneur Sheldon Coleman might bring news of the latest in camping gadgets.

Last, there was an equal chance they would meet up with Olive Garvey, an active philanthropist dedicated to the arts, education, and holistic health. Willard liked to joke that if his wife was ever too tired to go out (and she never was), his mother was always a willing standby—even well into her 90s.

"He was curious—totally curious," said Mary Knecht, the former general manager of WTQW TV-49 in Wichita, Willard's low-power community television station, whose initials mirror a home-grown privatization project known as Total Quality Wichita. "He and Jean would have invitations for four or five things a night. It wasn't just to be seen, it would be to find out what was going on!"

Willard's business week didn't end on Fridays either. On Saturday mornings, he would join a small group of men for coffee and rail against government excess at meetings of the Home Owners Trust Foundation, a citizens' anti-tax group he launched under a slightly different name in 1959. He might also pop over to the office, where Childers, Page, and others were putting in Saturday hours as expected. Holidays like New Year's Day might also find Willard in the office, making plans for the upcoming week or catching up on his reading, using his signature red ballpoint pen to check off what he had read or add comments on memos.

"Willard reminded me of the Energizer Bunny," said Gary Bengochea, who has managed the Garvey ranching operation in Nevada for nearly three decades. "He was always on the go and never slowing down." And he expected the same of his employees. "When he hired me, he told me I only had to work half a day, and I thought that was absolutely fantastic!" Bengochea recalled. "He didn't care if it was the first 12 hours or the last 12 hours."

THE DICTIONARY DEFINES an entrepreneur as someone who organizes, operates, and assumes the risk for a business venture. Academics might add to that, saying entrepreneurs often have trouble running mature businesses, choosing instead to seek out new ones.

Willard may have wanted to be "half the entrepreneur" his father was, but instead became one with a style all his own. "He was always trying to start something new," said Craig Miner, the late historian who worked as a writer and project manager at Garvey Industries from 1985 to 1995. "When you were around Willard, everything you saw was seen as a business opportunity."

When Miner mentioned he was taking his dog to a dog trainer, Willard immediately envisioned new large-scale business opportunities. Garvey TV stations could put the trainer on television; sell pre-recorded videos packaged with dog collars and leashes. The merchandising opportunities, well before Cesar Millan and "The Dog Whisperer," seemed endless. Miner was charged with pursuing the venture. However, once the dog trainer got a whiff of the true potential of the plan, he decided to go it alone and took the Garvey plan with him. Willard was out some money on the deal, but it was the lost opportunity that bothered him most. As a reminder of every half million-dollar investment he lost or passed up, Willard placed a symbol on the top shelf of his office library. When the number got to five or six, including losses in India, Germany, Bolivia, and Nevada, he got rid of them, deciding instead to remind himself of successes of $1 million or more. Eventually, there were just as many successes, earning him twice as much as he had lost.

New ideas came to Willard with the cadence of his Evelyn Wood speed reading class. On the civic front, why not halt big government by privatizing everything from the local water company to city trash collection to public housing and the county jail? Or help poor and underserved citizens solve persistent problems by matching them with up with a neighbor who has the solution? Why not create vouchers for public education? Impose term limits on career politicians? Give public land back to the Western states to manage for the benefit of local citizens?

On the business front, he proposed using vacant space at the grain elevator for a fish farm or an ice rink. The fish farm idea got off the ground, but then all the fish died when the water temperature went awry. Forty years before a publicly funded arena was built in downtown Wichita, Willard proposed building one of his own, a private venture with seating for 50,000. In Nevada, he bested the opposition and built a quarter-mile long dam in the desert, improving irrigation and creating a premium spot for boating and fishing. He forever pondered a law school for business executives and a television home shopping network to boost local business.

"Willard probably had 10,000 more ideas than the time he had to put them into action," one long-time colleague proclaimed. Those ideas kept people like Bob Page hopping. Page, who was charged with protecting the family's financial interests, often lost patience with Willard over his penchant for prophecy and seeming disregard for profit. "My job each month is to pick the thirty or thirty-one ideas that come out of Willard's head and get rid of twenty-nine or thirty of them," Page once said.

But Willard wouldn't stop. Creating *more* ventures and *more* competition in business was the whole point. "My attitude is to create a bigger pie," he said. "Don't worry about the competition; create competition. Business makes business!"

At Garvey headquarters, figuring out exactly how to bring his ideas to fruition—and on a shoestring budget—was usually someone else's job. Any employees willing to take on a new project could have at it; Willard was happy to push them through the door. Those who hesitated were likely met with one of his favorite mottos: "Ideas are cheap; implementing them is what counts."

In Willard's mind, all good ideas could be implemented only through a good set of methods and processes, and his GO System would do the trick. Based on the "five-paragraph field order" from his army days, the GO, or "Goal-Oriented," project management system was essentially a way to synthesize ideas or actions into actionable results.

In the 1960s, Willard used the GO System to help him keep track of his multitude of businesses and the goals he had for each. For example, on Monday, he would meet with executives from the company's life insurance, ranching, and grain operations; Tuesday was reserved for Builders, Inc., and his international homebuilding projects; Wednesday would be for mortgage and equipment leasing businesses; Thursday, communications companies; and Friday for management businesses, oil operations, and farming business.

By the 1980s, GO itself was synthesized into a four-point system for all Garvey employees requiring them to (1) set goals, (2) prepare a plan for each major goal using what he called a "Form-1" to define the specifics of the project and how it was to be funded, (3) write a progress report for managers, and (4) achieve profitable results.

Willard was quite married to GO, which he also dubbed a "Golden Opportunity," or a "Get Organized" system with a "Goal Overall" to create better managers, starting with him. If you worked for Garvey, you might be a "GO-Getter" who read the company's GO Newsletter. Some employees rolled their eyes over the moniker, and yet others came to respect its fundamental organizational principles, as muddled as its creator may have made it sound. "The Go System is tailor-made to overcome my shortcomings," he once said.

Mentioning the GO System to any of Willard's children usually evokes a reminiscent smile about their father's drive to organize. "The idea of the GO System can be helpful in communicating effectively within any business or organization," admits daughter Julie Sheppard. "It can also come in handy by helping to identify projects that should be avoided, and the weekly reports can act as a good record-keeping system." Daughter Mary Theroux believes GO was Willard's never-ending attempt to devise the unified system that would solve all problems, worldwide. "One entire summer, all I did was redraw the Form-1 over and over again because he had this obsession that he could create this perfect form that would fit on one piece of paper."

Emily Bonavia remembers how her father's love for his system even found its way into his efforts to meditate during the height of the Transcendental Meditation craze in the 1970s. "One day, he conspiratorially drew me aside and said, 'Hey, Em. I'm going to give you your own mantra.' I thought he was going to whisper it, giving it to me for my ears only. Then he said, 'Your mantra ... is ... GO, Em!'"

"What Willard had was the ideas," said Bob White, who joined the Garvey organization in 1969 as a part-time accountant during his college years at Wichita State University. "He was an entrepreneur, not an operator." Good operators like White could go far in a Garvey organization. Growing up in Arkansas City, about 60 miles southeast of Wichita on the Oklahoma border, White saved money for school by working at the New Era Flour Mill, one of the oldest businesses in the community. His experience there helped him land the job at the wheat-laden Garvey organization. White went full-time with the Garveys after he graduated from Wichita State, disregarding the advice of a former boss planning an exit strategy of his own at the time. "Don't come to work here," the executive told White. "Willard is a nut. He's crazy and he'll ruin your career."

"It was the worst advice I ever got in my life," said White, who became controller of international operations. At age 21, the small-town Kansas boy was spending half his time traveling outside the country while Willard was building a thousand homes in Mexico City and hundreds more in Costa Rica. "We had a bus-manufacturing plant in Costa Rica and a flour mill in Trinidad," White recalled. "One of the great things about Willard was that no matter how old you were, if he thought you could do a job, he would throw you in."

White hit the Garvey waters with aplomb, becoming president and later owner of Garvey International, an Illinois-based grain, long-haul railroad, and marine shipping business. He sold the renamed White International and retired a wealthy, successful man, at the ripe old age of 56.

THOSE WHO GOT close enough to soak up Willard's energy and entrepreneurial enthusiasm paid a price for their proximity, however. Along with his swirling ideas and it-can-be-done attitude, he brandished a sharp tongue that could level unprepared or uncertain executives in mid-sentence.

"Willard would fire off a hundred questions in about 30 seconds," White recalled. "You couldn't answer the first one before the second question came out." Bad news like cost overruns or bureaucratic red tape was not received graciously. "He would blow sky high," White said.

"Everybody was scared to death of him, because he did a lot of yelling," remembered Charlotte Weidman, a former Petroleum, Inc., executive. A salty, quick-witted championship bridge player who could go one-on-one with any tough-talking, hard-drinking oil man, Weidman was recruited by Ray Garvey to work in the office in 1950. When Ray Garvey invited her to the office to meet "some of the boys," Willard was among the group. "He talked a mile a minute," Weidman said. "I thought he was the craziest man I'd ever met." Three years later, Weidman went to Denver as Petroleum, Inc., expanded. She became corporate secretary overseeing expansions in Dallas and Shreveport, Louisiana. She retired as president of Petroleum, Inc. in the early 1990s.

Those with the gall to challenge Willard's tirades often ended up on good terms with him. Like a well-placed strike in a canine fight for dominance, an intelligent argument or a fact-based confrontation seemed to ignite Willard's respect for his challenger. After one particular upbraiding from Willard, Weidman struck a memorable blow. "I'm not deaf," she told him. "You're yelling in my face and I don't like it." Although somewhat taken aback by the comment, "The next thing I knew he and I became pretty good friends," she said.

Sometimes, the insults would get personal, sending some employees right out the door. "People would quit because they didn't want to take that kind of abuse," recalled Builders, Inc.'s Alex Dean, who experienced the ire firsthand.

One executive, hired to run a resurrected business unit in November 1981, locked horns with Willard over the plans to move and upgrade his group's allocated office space. Willard, known to be tightfisted when it came to corporate expenses, required any additional expenses be outlined and approved by him via the Form-1 before the work could move forward. The executive tried to skirt the process but was pulled up short.

"With reference to your slow move to the first floor, please take the office as is and make no structural or physical changes," Willard wrote in a January 1982 memo. "Any step in any office change is to get your plans so that we can all see and review them. Since you weren't able to get your plans prior to my absence, please do not make any changes until I've approved them and the purchase order. Meanwhile, I would like to have you make your move to the office on the first floor prior to the end of January. My original intention was that you would have completed this move prior to the end of December."

The executive would not back down. "After I was given authority and responsibility to move into and modify the new space, apparently I have no authority to make any small decisions without checking with you," he responded.

This time, Willard mustered no newfound respect for the man's argumentative efforts. He fired off a retort: "Form-1 with attachments is THE policy for projects! ... [Purchase orders] approved in advance is THE policy for project or ANY expenditures ... Hope you can quickly become comfortable with and accelerate this essential basic discipline as [senior vice president] for you and everyone else, including me." By July, they reached an impasse. "For the last several weeks you have dropped a continuing stream of critical innuendos about my people, placements fee ... management, etc.," the executive wrote to Willard. "These are undermining, damaging and totally without substance. ... It is obvious from the events of the last few days that you really don't care if I or my people are happy, or motivated, or have any real control over our responsibilities. I cannot continue to contribute to or manage an organization if I am being undermined at every turn. Therefore this letter serves as my resignation."

"There is little herein with which I can disagree," Willard responded in a handwritten note at the end of the resignation letter. "My regret is that we did not work this out together." Despite all his fire and brimstone, Willard accepted responsibility for his role in their parting of the ways.

"As much as I admired Willard, I could *not* have worked for him," his sister Ruth said. "I think he was a wonderful idea man, and a wonderful leader, but I think that in developing a strategy I could work with, it wasn't there."

If employment with Willard was better suited to the thick-skinned, Cheryl Gillenwater knew she better toughen up fast. A divorced mother with two young children in 1984, Gillenwater had relocated to Wichita and was relieved to find a much-needed job as Willard's new secretary. On her first day, the other secretaries took her aside and gave her a warning. "Don't ever let him see you cry," they told her. "If he gets to you, go to the restroom or something, because that's a sign of weakness." She heeded their advice, and her skin grew thick enough to last for two decades. "People who worked for Willard either worked for him a week or two or stayed forever," Gillenwater said. "There didn't seem to be anything in between."

In the office, Willard may have resembled a hummingbird that moves up, down, forward, backward, sideways or stops in mid-flight. He could call out a question to a colleague while talking on the phone and writing a memo at the same time. "People thought that was rude, but that was just him," one employee said. "He just couldn't do one thing at a time. If you thought he wasn't paying attention, you could be very, very wrong."

Business problems or issues were usually addressed on the spot. If a tenant called Willard about a problem at one of his apartment buildings, he would put that person on hold, call the building manager, and conference them both in until the situation was resolved.

That desire for immediate answers sometimes spelled trouble for the unsuspecting employee who happened to walk by his open door. As a young woman in her 20s, daughter Julie Sheppard remembers trying to sneak by her father's office without him seeing her. "If he did, he would drag me into his office and try to get me to take on whatever project someone in his office was trying to sell him."

The real risk in being with Willard, though, came when he was behind the wheel. Obeying speed limits and traffic signals, staying a safe distance behind other cars, keeping your eyes on the road or wheels on the pavement are rules that never factored into Willard's signature driving style. If he had someplace to be, he was going to get there any way he could, pulling out in front of drivers while turning his head to continue a conversation. Anyone who ever rode with Willard—southern executives, terrified family members, Nevada cowboys, and even grown-up Boy Scouts, who remember hitting their heads on the ceiling after an ambitious crossing of a railroad track—have a story about Willard's audacious driving habits.

"He drove with the exuberance and energy that he did everything," said Marge Page, who traveled with her husband to various off-site Garvey meetings. She remembered a particular southern trip in a car with the Garveys when Willard gave a classic exhibition of his speeding and tailgating habits. "I could have *shot* Bob for putting me in that car," she said. "I swore that I would never ride with him again."

In her recollections, Jean never mentioned Willard's terrifying driving habits. Others remember that she usually said nothing, aside from an occasional guttural exclamation when it appeared her husband was careening out of control, and taking their family with him.

"Will-ard!" Jean would warn after a particularly treacherous move.

"Jean!" he replied, warning her to back off. Car rides peppered with the escalating refrain of "Willard! Jean! Willard! Jean!" are a familiar memory to all the Garvey children. "Jean had the patience of Job," said Willard's sister Ruth. "She didn't really like driving with him."

The story wasn't much different when he was piloting an airplane, according to the late Bud Beren, president of MISCO Industries, a Wichita oil field supply company. Beren had two harrowing flights with Willard at the controls after agreeing to fly with him from

Wichita to St. Louis and then to Kansas City for two meetings of the Young Presidents Organization.

Piloting the rented silver and red Cessna 180 to St. Louis, Willard hit some thick cloud cover about 15 miles outside the airport. Instead of slowing down and dropping through them gradually, Willard went full throttle into them. The clouds grew thicker as they neared the airport, leaving Willard—an unrated instrument pilot—flying blind.

Beren looked over and saw his companion gripping the plane's control wheel and staring at its instrumentation. Willard began to repeat a three-word phrase he had learned in the military. "Needle. Ball. Airspeed," he chanted. "Needle. Ball. Airspeed." The recitation kept Willard focused on the needle for his turns, the ball for the plane's bank, and the airspeed to make sure the plane was going fast enough to stay in the air.

"Before we came out of the clouds, I knew we were in a spin. But Willard was able to pull the wheel back and pull that airplane out of that drop." The pair made it safely to the event in St. Louis and another the next day in Kansas City. But on the final leg back to Wichita, Beren got another fright. Once again, clouds socked in their airport, but Willard took off anyway, maintaining a low altitude so that he could navigate by sight.

"We were flying 50 feet off the ground," Beren recalled. "At 50 feet, you can run into bridges, flagpoles —buildings!" Just outside of Topeka, Beren's nerves were shot. "Willard, I can't take any more of this," he told him. "You are going to have to take me back to Kansas City."

Willard obliged, returning home to Wichita alone. In retelling the story, the aging Beren, who passed away six months later, understood how years can play tricks with a man's memory, but he was most certain he escaped great danger on that particular trip. "It may have been 50 feet of visibility, it may have been 100, it may have been 1,000," he said. "But to me it was 50 feet!" Despite being nearly killed by Willard twice, Beren laughed as he thought of how he and his friend both approached life. "I consider myself a middle-of-the-roader, but Willard was driving on the other side of the road and he was going fast!"

Ruth Garvey Fink also knew that accompanying her brother in any kind of motorized vehicle was always a challenge. "It wasn't a smooth ride," she said. "Someone once joked that Willard had quick reactions—and he needed them!"

Olive White college graduation portrait, 1914

Ray Garvey college graduation portrait, 1914

Olive with Ruth and baby Willard, 1920

Olivia, James and Willard

Willard in his Boy Scout uniform. He went on to make Eagle.

UNIVERSITY OF MICHIGAN, WINNER OF THE N.C.A.A. CHAMPIONSHIP AND WESTERN CONFERENCE TITLE

Front row, left to right: Wilkinson, Burton. *Row 2:* Barker, Wolin, Heydt, Beebe (C), Welsh, Thaxter, Garvey. *Row 3:* Matt Mann, coach, West, Williams, Skinner, Riedl, H. Muller, assistant coach. *Back row:* Houlenko, Allen, J. Sharemet, G. Sharemet, Patten, Morse.

Matt Mann's championship University of Michigan Swim Team.

Ray and Olive's Christmas card for 1942 featured this photo of Willard.

Paris, 1944

Willard being decorated for serving as Adjutant General of the Potsdam Conference by Brig. General Floyd Parks, Berlin, August, 1945

Maj. Willard Garvey, son of Mr. and Mrs. R. H. Garvey, is now serving as an adjutant at the Big Three conference in Berlin. He writes that he is meeting many notables and having interesting experiences.

Hometown newspaper coverage of Willard's service in postwar Berlin

Jean and Willard's second date, New Year's Eve, 1945

Most people were no happier flying with Willard than driving with him, but despite some near misses, Jean smiled through it all

Garvey Family Annual Stockholders' Meeting: (left to right) James and Shirley Garvey, Bernerd "Bun" and Ruth Garvey Fink, Ray Hugh and Olive White Garvey, George and Olivia Garvey Lincoln, and Willard and Jean Garvey

Bun, Ray, George, James and Willard at a Garvey Drilling rig

As a Young President

Pictured in *Forbes* magazine as President of Builders, Inc., April, 1952: "The building boom is breaking all the rules and records."

Photo credit Dan Weiner: Copyright John Broderick

Swimming with John, left, and Jim

Devoting full time to the start-up of the *Washington World*, Willard relocated the family to a former tobacco plantation outside of Washington, D.C. for the summer of 1961

Garvey's World Homes venture provided opportunities for residents of poor countries to move from substandard housing (above) to owning newly built homes (below). World Homes developments were built in countries including Mexico, Taiwan, Morocco, Ecuador, Colombia, India, Thailand, and Peru (pictured, with local manager Rod Salinas in foreground).

Photos courtesy of Special Collections and University Archives, Wichita State University Libraries

After Willard's death in 2002, Jean made a return visit to their Lima, Peru, World Homes development, where the homeowners association honored her with a reception and a plaque commemorating World Homes and Jean and Willard. Former World Homes manager Rod Salinas joined her in the plaque's unveiling.

Combining his lifetime practice of involving his children, no matter how young, in his businesses, and dealing with the top leadership of countries in which he operated, Willard took the entire family on a tour of his global operations in a 10-week around-the-world trip in 1965. Pictured here, an audience with India's Prime Minister Shastri: left-to-right, Willard, Jean, Julie, John, Shastri, Mary, Jim, Emily, Ann, and World Homes Indian partner Tony Ray.

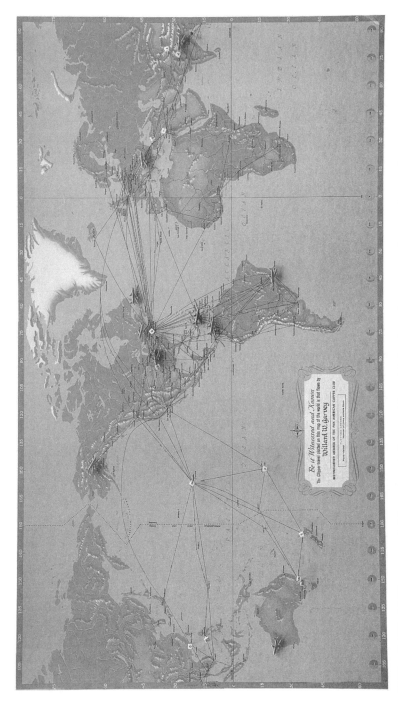

Willard's World Homes took him around the world multiple times in an era when such travel was rare, warranting the presentation to him of this map from Pan Am Airways.

The Garvey Center was Willard's bulwark in revitalizing downtown Wichita, which had been ravaged by disastrous urban renewal policies.

Family Christmas card portrait, 1971. Front: Emily, Jean, Julie.
Standing: Jim, Mary, Willard, Ann, and John

The only place he really relaxed, Willard relished trips to the Nevada
ranch with family, friends, and associates.

Willard and his hunting buddies at Stonehouse Ranch, Nevada. From left: Bob Redfearn, Burt Lance, Charles West, Bo Calloway, Ray Riddle, Willard Garvey, J. B. Fuqua, Ed Noble.

Willard and Jean's 50th anniversary portrait, 1996 (left). Always fit, Willard proudly donned his Army uniform for his 50th wedding anniversary (right).

Willard and Jean never lost their fascination with each other

Three generations
enjoyed an Alaskan
cruise in celebration
of Willard's 80th
birthday.

Among their successful collaborations, the Independent School combined Jean's passion for education with Willard's passion for building

The Independent School
20th Anniversary
1999-2000

The Epic Center stands as a testament to Willard's relentless quest to make dreams possible.

9

GROWING UP GARVEYS

"My mother thought her greatest achievement was that her children were productive and constructive people. I feel the same about our children, our grandchildren, and our posterity."
—WWG

WHEN THE PERPETUAL motion machine that was Willard Garvey collided with the kinetic activities of his six young children, the results could be chaotic. To combat that potential, Willard was a disciplinarian who insisted his children be orderly, respectful, engaged, and responsible—for themselves and one another.

"Willard liked to bring up the children in military fashion," Jean Garvey recalled. Dad-as-drill-sergeant is a lasting memory for the Garvey children. On any given evening, Willard's deep, affected bellow might suddenly summon them upstairs from single, dormitory-like bedrooms in the basement of their Douglas Avenue home.

"Re-PORT!" would come the holler from just off the kitchen, its reverberation bouncing down the stairs and into two common living areas dubbed the "girls' side" and "boys' side." Any dawdling would bring the unwelcomed "Second Request!" command, along with some serious scorn for the tardy. After scrambling upstairs, the children lined up and shouted out not their name, but the number of their birth order. John, the oldest, was number one, finishing with Mary at number six. To add to the theatrics, Jim, the second oldest, suggested they end each count-off with a formal military pronouncement. And so it would go, "Number One reporting for instructions, sir!"

The system may have been at times efficient or even amusing, but it wasn't a foolproof way to keep track of the brood. On a 1960s road trip in the family's converted camper bus, everyone assumed that the silence from "number four" meant that 13-year-old Emily had fallen asleep in the back. Instead, Emily was left behind at a Nevada gas station, where she was treated to candy bars and milkshakes until her family returned.

Willard and Jean's frequent travel during the late 1950s and early 1960s meant the children were left with live-in nanny/housekeeper Dorris Easley, a widowed mother who lived at the Garvey home with her teenage daughter, Karen. A religious woman whose husband, Fred, died in July 1957—just six weeks after they had moved in with the Garveys—Easley wrote a rosy memoir of her time with the family, as busy and as chaotic as it must have been. "I wish the general public knew the Willard W. Garvey that I know with his family around him," she wrote. "[He] loved his wife and children very tenderly and was constantly planning how to add to their pleasure and comfort."

Traveling with Willard must not have always been so comfortable for Jean, who usually acquiesced to her husband's insistence that she accompany him. To this day, she rarely complains but admits there were times it was hard being away from the children when they were young. A four-week excursion through postwar Europe in 1952 was one such time.

"Willard was dying to take me to see where he had lived," Jean recalled. But leaving three children—including one-year-old Ann, who was getting ready to take her first steps—tugged at Jean's heartstrings. On the trip, Jean also learned she was pregnant with Emily, which made for more than a few "woozy" moments in the passenger seat as Willard peeled around the British and French countryside en route to whirlwind visits with old friends. When the couple finally returned home, Ann was walking and for a few moments didn't recognize her parents.

Some of the children relished the freedom and fun that came with their parents' travels. "We liked it when Mom and Dad were gone," daughter Julie Sheppard said. "It was so much more relaxed. We got to eat hamburgers and fish sticks." Younger sister Mary was too young to appreciate that freedom, saying she felt "miserable and abandoned" when her parents left.

Souvenirs from foreign countries sometimes helped smooth over any hard feelings. "We purchased a couple of guitars in Mexico for the children," Willard wrote his mother during one trip in 1964. "They are taking care of things at home, while their parents, I'm afraid, are neglecting them."

Child rearing, at least in Willard's mind, was a practical task that could benefit from a business approach: identify the problem, map out a plan, and then solve it. In the Garveys' case, a household with lots of children and pets needed a plan all its own. Assigning chores such as feeding the fish, the dog, and the ducks in the pond was one part of the plan. Another was to teach each child to look after his or her younger sibling, a lesson that helped create a strong bond between the four Garvey sisters, all of whom remain extremely close today.

Once the "big family" problem had been identified and the plan was mapped out, Willard could only hope a solution would follow. "Establishing principles and moral fiber for the children was a big part of the discussion at our Mexico City conference," he wrote his mother after one trip. "Jean and I are devoting ourselves to a program to compensate for our frequent absences."

In their younger years, the children had little choice but to endure Willard's volatile side, withstanding his explosions over typical meal-time shenanigans that might see their table's oversized lazy Susan spin out of control, or food "accidentally" land in a sibling's drink. If too much dinnertime horseplay led to a careening glass of milk, Willard's belted reprimand was soon to follow: "Get my belt!" Daughter Mary Theroux remembers her experience in such a scenario. "I admit, I'd probably been leading up to it by being obnoxious, but I didn't appreciate being belted," she said. While sagas like this one unfolded, Jean yielded to her husband's discipline. "She wasn't crazy about it, but she wouldn't stop him," Mary recalled.

Despite his frequent eruptions, Willard's children prefer to remember their father's fun-loving and compassionate traits. In one minute, he could jump in the car to take one young daughter shoe shopping and in the next assuage another's fear of skiing with positive visualization techniques. They loved when he told a corny joke, showed them how to symphonically tap spoons against water-filled glasses in fancy restaurants, took them to foreign films or hit musicals, or simply worried about their whereabouts.

When it came to delicate matters like dating, Willard plied his trademark brand of interrogation to the parade of boys finding their way to the Garveys' front hall as they waited to take out one of his popular daughters. Standard queries focused on the boys' background, their parents, their church, or anything else he could think of in order to know exactly who his girls were dating. When his oldest daughter Ann stayed out with a boy well into the morning hours, Willard took his four girls into the den and gave them a private talk about what type of woman men respect and what kind they don't. "It was a very unemotional, conversational thing, and very sweet," daughter Mary Theroux remembers. "It was explaining the world as he saw it—as a man."

As adults, Willard and Jean's children made their own choices about marriage, and each would later deal with the pain of divorce. Some of the breakups were hard for the parents to accept, especially in light of their dedication to each other. However, Willard remained true to his beliefs about the power of individual choices and personal responsibility and ultimately abided by his children's decisions.

"We are very sad that you (have) parted," he wrote one former son-in-law, "but recognized decades ago that free individuals will and must be responsible for themselves and their 'free' associations and actions." As the years went on, various remarriages brought new sons- and daughters-in-law, all of whom were welcomed graciously into the Garvey family.

WILLARD DIDN'T WANT to teach his children about life beyond the grain of the Kansas wheat field; he wanted them to experience it for themselves. The world was teeming with potential, and Willard wanted his children to see it with their own eyes. "By taking the boys (and often the girls) on my business calls with me, I feel they will be years ahead in professional operations," he told his mother.

"I want [my children] to live as fully as my dad did and I have," Willard told a group at the University of Michigan in November 1987. "I want them to be free to take their risks and make their mistakes and collect their dues while finding the way their God-given talents and tendencies can best contribute to the building and the managing of a better world. I want them to be operators, awash in the give-and-take of reality and intensely aware, moment to moment, of the stakes of living well."

One way to heighten that awareness, Willard thought, was through travel. Family trips across country, and later around the world, became important lessons in the Garvey children's upbringing. In the late '50s, the trips were more adventurous than luxurious, as the family traveled in an old Trailways bus that had been converted into a rustic family camper with eight vinyl seats that folded into beds. One summer before Mary was born, the family piled into the bus to visit Willard's parents at their summer cabin in Colorado, which Ray and Olive nicknamed "Garvilla." The trip took them through Rocky Mountain National Park, where Jean remembers making dinner in a skillet over a wood fire. Later, there were family holiday trips to visit Willard's brother James and his family in Fort Worth, as well as more comfortable ski trips to Vail, Colorado, where the family had been early investors. In 1962, the three oldest children accompanied their parents to South America.

Sightseeing with Willard was almost as unique an experience as driving with him. His itinerary made it possible to see *all* of Paris *and* the Louvre in one day. On one 1964 trip, Willard and son John arrived in Paris at 11 a.m. and proceeded to whip through the city like contestants in a treasure hunt, catching glimpses of the Sorbonne, the Petit Palais, Champs d'Elysees, Place de la Concorde, and the Tuileries, finishing up the day with a two-hour jaunt through the Louvre. In the evening, they visited the Eiffel Tower, the Trocadero, and several other sites before grabbing a taxi, subway, and bus to the airport in time for an 8:30 departure to Madrid.

Whirlwind tours were standard fare—even with grandchildren. "I saw the Grand Canyon with my grandfather ... through a car window ... going 60 miles an hour," Nick Bonavia dryly recalled. "He asked me and my brother, 'Did you see it?' 'Yes,' we said. 'Okay, good,' he replied, and that was that. That was characteristic of the way he did things. He would show you where the canyon was, but it was up to you to discover it for yourself."

Not every trip went smoothly, however. In the fall of 1964, John Garvey accompanied his father on a trip to Berlin with forty members of Willard's beloved Young Presidents Organization, many of whom were anxious to visit the country they had fought against in World War II. When the group began its two-hour tour of Communist-controlled East Berlin with a mandatory stop at "Checkpoint

Charlie," the Cold War demarcation point, Willard realized he was in trouble.

In his pockets were brochures describing the World Homes housing projects and Willard's personal crusade to "stop the onslaught of communism" by making every man a homeowner. The pamphlets were intended for the other YPO members on the trip, but East Berlin authorities would not tolerate such anti-communist propaganda. In front of his son, Willard was taken off the bus and detained for two hours, while the others completed their tour of East Berlin.

"It was the most nervous I'd ever seen him in my life," said John, recalling how that same summer, as the United States prepared to send combat troops to Vietnam, the pair labored together to secure draft-age John's forthcoming conscientious objector status. The next summer, as Vietnam turned into a war and tension over civil rights simmered to a boil in cities across the nation, the Garvey family traded the familiar Kansas heat for tropical ocean breezes and desert winds, making their way across Asia, the Middle East, and Europe.

In early June 1965, Willard and Jean, along with her mother, Leota Kindel, and the children — ages 8 to 18 — left for an around-the-world trip that would take them to thirty-one cities in seventy-five days. Although it was essentially a business trip to inspect Willard's affordable housing programs and other potential ventures, the Garveys soaked up everything, from the brilliant blue hues of the sunny South Pacific to the glimmering opulence of Bangkok's Grand Palace. At the same time, they witnessed the immense poverty of Calcutta and passed through areas of intense global unrest, including at least two countries on the verge of war.

The Middle East, even back then, was a dangerous place. Arab-Israeli conflicts over the 1948 land partitions that created the Jewish state were solidifying. On June 4, 1965, the day the family left Kansas, the one-year-old Palestine Liberation Organization announced it was prepared to go to war to take back "usurped land" from Israel. The Garveys were due to arrive in Jerusalem within weeks.

As the younger Garveys frolicked along the black sand beaches of Hawaii, India Prime Minister Lal Bahadur Shastri predicted his country's full-scale war with Pakistan, following skirmishes along a desert border area called Rann of Kutch. Willard and his family intended to spend the early part of July in India, meeting with Shastri to discuss affordable ways to feed and house India's huge population. The Garvey wheat operations were no doubt of interest to Shastri, who helped spearhead India's "Green Revolution," a movement that brought new cultivation techniques to India in the wake of the 1943 Bengal famine, which killed approximately three million people.

Before they left, Jean and Willard had been aware of the world's burgeoning conflicts, but they believed they would be well protected—both physically and spiritually—along the way. "We all just kind of took it in stride," Jean Garvey recalls. "There was a little apprehension, but we were with people with whom we were comfortable."

News of the world trip, on which they traveled 34,250 miles, changed planes thirty-eight times and made twenty-nine overnight stops, made the Wichita newspaper. Pictures of the family meeting with Shastri were distributed to Willard's professional organizations. Every stop, it seemed, held promise for new business opportunities.

In Australia, Willard contemplated plans for a global Holiday Inn franchise and saw potential for a new ranching operation. In Tokyo, he toured a Sony plant producing a "new portable home TV video tape attachment to replay any program" with slow motion, pause, and rewind capabilities. Few Americans could imagine anything other than a new RCA color television in their living rooms in 1965. But what Willard previewed that day was the forerunner to the Sony Betamax home video cassette recorder, which debuted to American consumers a full decade later.

The Sony tour sent Willard's mind churning about the possibilities of morphing technology and media. "Sooner than we think, this may obscure newspaper publishing," he prophetically wrote his mother. And even though it was almost two decades before the U.S. consumer electronics industry yielded itself to Japan, Willard saw enough on that visit to make a determination: "The Japanese will eventually dominate world trade," he wrote. A few years later, he amended that prediction, naming China as the next world trade dominator.

For Jean Garvey, ensuring that six children were well behaved, on time, and presentable to each of their foreign hosts was a bit of a challenge, lessened by the luxury of drip-dry clothes and hotel laundry services. For the Garvey children, the trip created the memories of a lifetime, like the taste of real Swiss chocolate, the stinging cuts of a coral reef, the harmony of a cathedral's bells, and the smell of destitution in India. More important, however, they gained an understanding of the world and their father's place in it.

"We learned about these beautiful countries, and the differences between them," recalled Emily, then just 12. "There was so much begging in Asia. When we got to Jordan, there was no begging, and in Kashmir, people were making things to sell. … Because of that trip, I really understood how if you want to have a stable country you have to have a very strong middle class," she recalled.

"It completely changed me," remembered John Garvey, whose own appetite for travel became even more voracious than his father's. A conversation with John within minutes is likely to stray beyond its objective and on to a travel-related observation such as the historic conflict between the Greeks, the Macedonians, and the Turks, or recent overseas encounters with a Fortune 500 executive or Pulitzer prize-winning author. "A day in a country gives you insights that you don't even realize you have because there is so much data that's coming through all of your senses," he said.

That's exactly what Willard wanted. The meaningful aspects of the trip "could not be measured in dollars," Willard said later. The cost was worth it and then some. "I was able to share a deeply rewarding experience with my family," he recalled. "Each member brought back knowledge of all aspects of life; of man in his universe if you will."

Willard Garvey knew that business wasn't just for the boys in his family. He admired his mother's skill in running the business after his father died, and so the thought of excluding his four girls never occurred to him. When his children were still young, he mapped out a plan—for all of them—although this excerpt from one of his 1964 memos refers to his oldest children John, then 17, and Jim, age 15.

"Someone asked me what my plans in the business for my boys are. I said, 'First, it is a matter of their own decision as to what they desire to go into, whether medicine, law, professions or anything else. Second, I would encourage them to get a complete education including law and probably a business degree, working on weekends and summers starting on Saturday mornings to become familiar with our different departments and operations. Third, they should work at least five years completely independently to see what they can do on their own in order that they can obtain some degree of self assurance and sense of achievement. Fourth, if they desire to return to any of our businesses, they can be put on a project at a time autonomously under our best professional manager to sink or swim, according to their ability, motivation, and judgment and to seek their own level according to results.'"

TO GET HIS young children hands-on experience with business, in 1964 Willard enlisted Bob Page to set up a corporation for them named JAEM, an acronym made up of the first letter of each child's name.

Drawing from the Junior Achievement program, JAEM was designed to teach the Garvey children about the value of entrepreneurship and encourage them to begin business ventures of their own. As part of the exercise, Willard required his children to submit weekly reports—just as he was submitting to his own mother at the time—detailing their interests and activities. Failure to submit a weekly report meant being penalized with no allowance.

"I thought it weird and wonderful to be raised in an environment where business and family are one," daughter Mary Theroux said. JAEM meetings were held Saturdays at noon at the Garvey home, led by Page, who instructed each child to choose from a group of stocks he had identified. The stocks were then purchased for each child, and their share prices were tracked and compared among the group. Julie, then about 13, chose the maker of the Dixie Cup. Mary, at 10, chose a clay company, thinking it was in the Play-Doh family only to discover it manufactured pipes. When Page announced that the firm's plant burned to the ground, Mary cried.

JAEM proved to be more than just a training ground for the Garvey children; it was also their first real business, with income that continued well into the 1980s. Later, the corporation would own real estate, becoming one of the original investors in Colorado's Vail ski resort. JAEM went on to acquire apartment units in Wichita, a ranch in Colorado, and several oil and gas properties. Willard once estimated the unit had a net worth of $6 million and recorded a compounded annual growth rate of nearly 30 percent, the best of any Garvey company.

The insistence that all his children—and not just his sons—learn the lessons of business stemmed in part from the example his own mother was setting, but also from watching his sisters, who were excluded from business lessons when they were young. "For as long as I can remember, we were in business with my dad, attending what sometimes seemed like endless meetings," daughter Mary

Theroux recalled. "But I never remember him expecting that we were anything other than following every financial statement, every manager's report, every analysis, and with as much fascination as he had for it—regardless of the fact that I was a girl … and eight years old!"

Staying well behaved during the dry proceedings wasn't always easy for the young Garveys. Sometimes the children would feign interest, hide in the closet, pass notes, or giggle at their mother napping on the couch during the meeting's dull moments. Yet, in the midst of it all, "There was some decorum," Mary Theroux recalled. "Willard just assumed you could follow along."

Mary also went with her parents to a Garvey, Inc., meeting in Acapulco, where her grandmother, aunts, and uncles hashed out some of their own issues before the final dissolution of Ray Garvey's assets in 1972. Looking back, she recalled how similar that meeting was to one of the many she attended with her own brothers and sisters before they too went their separate ways in business. Disputes and heated discussions seemed to be the norm, she remembered.

"They fought more than—or as childishly as—we did."

THE WORK WILLARD and Jean put into building worldly, capable, and self-assured children created a frightening situation for the family in 1966. During the summer, 16-year-old Jim Garvey accompanied Garvey executive Jack Bode on a seven-week tour of Willard's homebuilding projects throughout Central and South America. The trip took them to Venezuela, Brazil, Argentina, Peru, Ecuador, Colombia, Nicaragua, El Salvador, Honduras, and Panama—places where revolution was frequent, the CIA was active, and violence was a part of life.

Bode was under strict instructions from Willard to travel with Jim on every leg of the trip and to contact the office at designated stops. But when they reached Colombia, the rule didn't hold. Jim ended up taking a side trip with another of Willard's associates to visit a ranching operation in the country's interior, telling Bode he would meet him days later in Nicaragua, where they would pick up a flight to Guatemala.

At 16, Jim was unaware of the perils such a remote jaunt could bring until the driver told him that local banditos were known to jump out onto the mountain roads, commandeer a car, kill its occupants, and take their shoes. "If anybody knew who he was—the son of a rich man in Kansas—he would have been juicy bait," recalled Harvey Childers, the long-time Garvey executive. Fortunately for everyone, the trip to the interior went smoothly and Jim returned safely to Bogota, only to miss his connecting flight to Nicaragua and Bode. Hoping to eventually catch up with his companion, Jim continued on to Guatemala and waited. But Bode waited too, in Nicaragua, where he had to phone Willard and tell him his son was missing.

The news that no one had heard from Jim in almost a week hit Willard hard, causing him to unleash a "total mobilization" of his contacts in the State Department, U.S. embassies, and a host of regional businesses. "Everyone in the office was concerned," Childers said. "It was a real 'red alert.'" Jim, meanwhile, was completely unaware of the international alarm, and when Bode didn't show up in Guatemala, he continued with the itinerary and flew to Mexico City. Arriving at his hotel, the clerk told Jim he had a message and a note to call home.

"I called the office, Dad answered and he was very friendly and said, 'Oh, hi Jim. Good to hear from you!' ... I heard later that he had the world looking for me, and he was really beside himself." Willard was "deeply grateful" for Jim's safety but told his mother he planned to use the episode to teach his children a lesson. He intended to ask all the people involved in the search to bill him for their time and then make Jim pay for it. The punishment never came. "We didn't talk about it ever," Jim recalled. "I did learn a lesson though: If in doubt, call home."

In Guatemala, the unthinkable hadn't happened. And as much as he wanted independent offspring, Willard also wanted to know how to find them in a pinch. "Please, please, please," he later wrote his children. "When you have a problem, your plans change, a change of schedule or whatever, wire or telephone me at home, at the office or whatever necessary so that I can help. … It can prevent misunderstanding, inconvenience and many times more serious troubles and heartaches."

As usual, the children heard him loud and clear. "You never had to learn a lesson from Dad more than once," daughter Julie Sheppard said.

PART OF GETTING exposed to the world also meant getting exposed to work. In their college years, the boys spent part of the summer working in some of the Garvey businesses, where getting dirty was a given. At harvest time in June, Jim worked in the dank, smelly tunnels of Garvey Grain elevators, shoveling putrid rotting wheat off the floors of the mammoth tubular concrete containers. John spent time working on oil rigs, often returning home looking like he had been dipped in an inkwell. Summer jobs for the girls had them working in the office or helping to clean up vacated apartments managed by Builders, Inc.

That early work experience wasn't always as inspirational as Willard hoped. "I wanted to avoid business like the plague until I was in my 20s," said John, who began his career in social work before attending Yale's business program in 1977. In his early 60s, he now presides over Petroleum, Inc., the independent oil company founded by his grandfather Ray Garvey in 1948. Emily Bonavia, who with her son now oversees the Garvey ranching enterprise in Nevada, had similar sentiments. "I don't think I ever looked at any of the businesses as one I wanted to run," she said.

Willard and Jean both hoped the businesses they had helped grow would remain in their family for generations. As their children began to marry and have children of their own, the continuity prospects looked good. Through the 1980s and into the early 1990s, the six Garvey children were involved in the business in some way. John and Ann were in the oil business, and Jim was successfully operating Builders, Inc., where Julie also worked. Emily and her sons had the Nevada ranching operations, and Mary was chairman of Garvey International, the grain and transportation subsidiary based in Chicago. The family's third generation was well entrenched, reporting to their father at the top slot at Garvey Industries.

In 1992, a 72-year old Willard began thinking about his own future, although slowing down was definitely out of the question. Daily swims, business activities, and travel could keep him plenty busy, but there were more projects on his "to do" list. With the family business primed to move into a new era, Willard proposed a new Garvey corporate structure that would allow him to step down and give some children more authority than others. The decision launched the family into a bitter squabble, and the outcome would forever change the face of the Garvey legacy.

The Garvey siblings—all shareholders in the private family company—were required to vote on the plan but balked at yielding control of their future. Although Willard maintained voting control of the shares and could have forced the issue, he wanted his children to agree to his proposal. They wouldn't budge. "He kept pushing and pushing and pushing," daughter Mary Theroux recalled. At every meeting and with each push, tempers flared and civility waned.

Willard called his daughters "The Harpies," dragging out a term he had coined for how they stuck together on business decisions. Jean Garvey tearfully looked on as her family appeared to be tearing itself apart.

Following weeks of contentious meetings, Willard realized he was in the same painful predicament as his mother had been in the years after Ray Garvey's death. Sibling arguments forced Olive to make a choice: break up the family or break up the company. Now it was Willard's turn. He could not stand for both. "This family shall continue forever," Willard wrote to one daughter years earlier. He would stick by his word, even though his hopes of watching the family business grow fourfold as it did between 1959 and 1972, and again from 1972 to 1981, would never come to pass.

Apparently now, another project awaited him. The Garvey enterprises, including its ranching, oil, transportation, building, and real estate businesses, would have to be sold or divided equally. Under a different set of circumstances, this was what he wanted for his children: They were choosing their own future.

"Once he saw that a unified Garvey enterprises could no longer continue, he *immediately* began to work with Bob Page on how to split up the companies and he never said another word about it," daughter Mary Theroux recalls. "He became the quarterback of the whole thing. He worked tirelessly for it to go smoothly. ... I really admired him for that because it was not what he wanted."

At the conclusion of the second-generation business breakup, two of Willard's daughters were bought out of the business entirely. Another sold her company to a long-time employee shortly after. Three other businesses—the ranching, oil, and building companies—are run by Garvey offspring. According to son John, gross assets at Petroleum, Inc., today exceed $100 million, having multiplied several-fold under his management, with net assets exceeding Ray Garvey's empire. Presiding over a growing Builders, Inc., is Willard's grandson, Mike Garvey, who says the company has about $100 million in net assets and has expanded its business to include property management and ownership in five neighboring states. In Nevada, Willard's daughter Emily Bonavia says that Nevada First Corporation enacted several land exchanges with the federal government—which Willard had proposed long ago—creating more contiguous land ownership for both entities. The operation also has consolidated its Nevada lands and added timber and pasture property in northeastern Oregon, while its commercial cattle business commands premium prices. The business progress at these remaining Garvey organizations—and the decisions by other family members to pursue their own personal happiness—would no doubt have made Willard Garvey proud.

Looking back, Jean Garvey believes her husband did the best he could raising six very different and very independent children. "He was a marvelous father," she said. "I know the children thought he was terribly strict, demanding, and not very patient, but I think he was amazingly patient, considering everything."

10

WHEAT FOR HOMES:
EVERY MAN A CAPITALIST

"Property rights are the foundation of individual freedom."–WWG

FROM THE GANGWAY of the M.V. Caronia ocean liner, a squinting 82-year-old Jean Garvey gingerly made her way into the tropical heat of Lima, Peru. It was February—Lima's warmest month—and the intensity of the South American sun strained her vision. As she drew closer to the group of well-wishers who came to the Callao port to greet the ship, Jean scanned the crowd hoping to spot an old friend.

It had been more than a year since Willard's death. And because so much of their life had been spent together traveling, Jean had been "itching to get abroad" for some time. At the suggestion of Seth Atwood, a retired Illinois executive and friend of the Garveys since Willard's days with the Young Presidents Organization, Jean went ahead and booked a 72-day South American cruise on the 700-passenger Cunard luxury liner. The minute the ship pulled out of Fort Lauderdale, Jean began looking forward to this day-long stop in Lima, where she would relive fond memories from long, long ago.

On land, 73-year-old Rodolfo Salinas and his wife, Carmen, anxiously anticipated Jean's arrival. It had been more than 40 years since they first met her as she accompanied Willard on a site visit to Hogares Peruanos, the local arm of Willard's World Homes company. From 1962 to 1971, Salinas was a young manager at World Homes, overseeing the administration, financing, and construction of some of its largest Peruvian projects, including Sol de Oro, a 460-home complex northeast of Lima along the Pan-American Highway.

As he waited, Salinas, an elfin septuagenarian with creased dark skin and warm brown eyes, may have been thinking about how much Lima had changed. What had been a growing capital city of under two million in 1960 had exploded into a giant megalopolis, teeming with more than five million residents throughout. Sol de Oro, the massive, once isolated development outside the city limits, was now engulfed by sprawling development extending directly from Lima. It used to take only 15 minutes to drive from Sol de Oro to the center of Lima. Now—unless you drove like Willard, perhaps—traffic congestion doubled the travel time.

There were other changes too. Over the decades, Peru had suffered at the hands of vicious dictatorships, military coups, earthquakes, and abject poverty. Through it all, Sol de Oro was still thriving, and today, that was something to celebrate. It was why Salinas, his wife, and dozens more waited to see Jean Garvey again.

When the small, brown-haired woman in the green linen dress flashed an illuminating smile his way, Salinas knew her instantly. Barely noticing how the years had unsteadied her gait, he greeted her and two companions from the ship, then whisked them off in two cars. A day of activity awaited them, and Salinas didn't want to waste a minute.

For the 20-minute ride, the caravan made its way east from Callao and then north along the Pan-American Highway, turning left into a grid of streets bearing celestial names such as Jupiter, Saturn, Neptune, and Venus. Out the car window, Jean could see the community of shops, stores, and playgrounds surrounding the development. She saw how many of the original concrete houses were now painted in bright colors and expanded with garages, porches, and second and third stories. It was a clean neighborhood, adorned with shade trees, parks, and a brand new two-story community center. Her mind drifted to Willard: Sol de Oro—which in Spanish means Golden Sun—had turned out exactly the way he envisioned.

In front of the neighborhood community center, Jean and her companions were met by dozens of local homeowners, all cheering at their arrival. A smiling dark-eyed, dark-haired woman in a blue cotton blouse linked her arm in Jean's and led her inside. Beaming with all the excitement, Jean paused and gave a wave to one of the homeowners videotaping the event. The guests took their places on a flower-adorned stage, while the Peruvian and then the U.S. national anthems filled the hall. A young boy gave the group a flute serenade, and Jean thanked him with a hug and a kiss. The Sol de Oro Homeowners Association presented her with a gift, and Jean gladly took the microphone to give the crowd a song of her own. Later she and Salinas walked over to a nearby wall and unveiled a bronze plaque commemorating the man who helped make so much so possible. It read: *In Memoriam, Sr. Willard Garvey, founding businessman of World Homes Inc., Promoter of urbanization, Sol de Oro in Lima, Peru.*

"It was precious," Jean recalled of the surprise festivities. "It was like being the Queen of England or something." Willard would have reveled in such a celebration, despite the financial and bureaucratic setbacks World Homes gave him over the years. "I hope to have World Homes in every country," he once told a Wichita audience. His vision of "every man a homeowner" did not come to pass, but in this corner of the world, for the first 500 families in Sol de Oro, it sure felt like it did.

THE SEEDS FOR what Willard called "his single best idea" were rooted in the economic and geopolitical uncertainty of the late 1950s.

In the second term of the Eisenhower presidency, Americans were still on guard against the spread of communism, which seemed to be moving through the world like a deadly virus. In Germany, Soviet Premier Nikita Khrushchev taunted the United States over control of a divided Berlin, while in Mexico, Cuban rebel Fidel Castro prepared to invade his homeland in a 1959 overthrow that would put the communist threat just 90 miles off the Florida coast. In back yards and basements across the country, Americans—including the Garveys—constructed fallout shelters they hoped would protect them from a hydrogen bomb attack.

Eisenhower the war veteran fully understood the fragility of international borders and chose to fight for worldwide democracy by encouraging private investment overseas. Targeting development in so-called uncommitted nations would introduce the free enterprise system—and a capitalist democracy—to these countries, or so the thinking went.

That kind of talk was right up Willard's alley. Like other tried and true military men, he was alarmed over the prospect of global communism and wanted to do his part to fight it. After hearing Wichita oilman Fred Koch talk about the ominous conditions in communist Russia, Willard took Jean to some of the Koch-sponsored meetings of the conservative John Birch Society, where members discussed ways to stop communism's seemingly growing influence on American life.

Perhaps it was at one of these meetings in the Kochs' large basement, adorned with mounted big game catches from exotic locales, where Willard first heard the phrase "less government, more responsibility, and a better world." And while he did not subscribe to all of the John Birch Society's teachings, the group's motto spoke to Willard directly.

When a national recession and a clampdown on federally financed housing projects slowed business at the Garveys' Builders, Inc., subsidiary, Willard began to think of ways to keep building and help counter the communist threat at the same time.

The result was a new venture that combined his passion for home-building with the Garveys' largesse in the wheat business. He called it World Homes, and for 13 years it brought him the personal high of providing low-cost housing to the working poor in developing countries. It also brought him the frustrating low of dealing with derailing bureaucracies, political upheavals, vast cultural misunderstandings, and employee theft. It never really brought him profits, only the satisfaction that because of World Homes, someone somewhere had a better place to live.

"Willard probably spent millions on it," Harvey Childers said. "Most of the projects were a one-way street. Money went out and very little came back. … The profits on one project would be eaten up before we could get the next project developed."

IN THE MID to late 1950s, U.S. unemployment levels rose right along with the wheat levels in the massive Garvey grain elevators in Kansas and Nebraska. Postwar federal farm subsidies encouraged farmers to plant, so plant they did. By 1958—the year before Ray Garvey's death—the U.S. had a $7 billion agricultural food surplus and a new problem of what to do with it.

Willard watched with great interest in 1954 as Kansas senator and former governor Andrew Schoeppel successfully pushed for legislation to allow the United States to sell excess commodities overseas. His Agricultural Trade Development and Assistance Act (commonly known as Public Law 480, PL 480, and later the "Food for Peace" program) was the foundation on which Willard's idea was built.

In 1957, an amendment to PL 480 filed by North Carolina congressman Harold Cooley required countries buying U.S. grain to keep a portion of the payments within their own countries, where they were turned into low-cost loans for U.S. companies undertaking business development there. These so-called "Cooley loans" were to be managed by the U.S. Export-Import Bank and later the U.S. Agency for International Development (USAID).

This project was exactly what Willard needed to move his world housing program forward. But first he had to convince Congress and the president. To any who would listen, his new battle cry became, "Wheat for Homes" and his goal, "To make every man a capitalist." If Eisenhower truly believed that private enterprise and the free-market system were the best weapons against Soviet economic expansion, housing had to be a part of that mix, Willard believed.

Home ownership, he professed, was the one thing separating communism from capitalism. It distinguished the private ownership of property from the collectivist ideal of public ownership. In a showdown between the two ideologies, a man will always defend his private property first, Willard argued. So what better place to begin developing but in politically and economically fragile Latin American countries, which so desperately needed assistance?

In August 1958, Willard took his platform to Washington, D.C., testifying before members of an Eisenhower-appointed committee charged with investigating ways to counter the Soviet trade offensive, which funneled money to needy, non-communist countries. Food and housing are Russia's weak points, Willard told the panel. "Let's hit them where they live."

Members of the Committee on World Economic Practices, chaired by Harold Boeschenstein, president of Owens-Corning Fiberglas Corp., took note of the 38-year-old man from Kansas who was ready to talk to them for "for five minutes or five hours" about his housing plans. Other panelists, including Stephen Bechtel, president of engineering giant Bechtel Corp., Phil Reed from General Electric, Henry Clay Alexander of J.P. Morgan & Co., Eugene Holman of Standard Oil and Frank Stanton of Columbia Broadcasting System found themselves listening to Willard's pitch.

Since Khrushchev's plan was to make every man a communist, Willard told them, "our aim should be to make every man a capitalist. … When you put a man in a home of his own you make him a capitalist—economically, politically, socially-morally, creatively, and ideologically," he announced.

But first, he said, the United States needed to help these countries create long-term, low-interest mortgage money. Common practice in many countries required homebuyers to pay half the purchase price in cash, with the balance due in two or three years—and annual interest rates of up to 30 percent. In many countries, rapid devaluation of local currencies, which were tied to the U.S. dollar, prevented many banks from making mortgage loans altogether. Homeownership, for the most part, was reserved for the cash-rich.

Latin American leaders were pleading for more housing stock, Willard told the Boeschenstein Committee. In Nicaragua, President Luis Somoza Debayle wanted private builders to construct 7,000 low-cost, privately owned homes on government land, expecting to sell about 500 of these $1,000 units every year. Contractors were available, materials were available, but mortgage money was not, Willard explained.

Using Cooley funds for housing could solve two problems at once, he said. For example, if the money could be used to transform Nicaragua's payments on commodity sales into a revolving fund for affordable mortgage loans, the United States could reduce its wheat surplus, double its exports to that country, and help working Nicaraguans find adequate housing. A similar plan in other countries could put homeownership within the reach of the middle class in Latin America and around the world, he added. Making every man a property owner should be the Cold War goal, Willard said. "Homeownership is our best chance."

The Boeschenstein Committee agreed. In its final report to President Eisenhower, the committee offered a series of recommendations, including tax breaks that would encourage private firms to do business overseas, providing necessary aid to developing countries.

BACK IN KANSAS, Willard's parents and his siblings, each consumed with different aspects of the Garvey operations, were curious about his overseas housing project but concerned about the cost. Willard believed that mass production and volume sales of the low-cost houses had the potential to bring in a 15 percent profit. So why not establish housing operations in almost every country? His family, however, was skeptical. Willard too often was known for letting his big ideas overshadow concern for the bottom line at a time when the finances of the grain, oil, farming, and real estate businesses were all still strongly linked. Shout downs of Willard's lofty proposals were not uncommon during family board meetings, which he once described as "knock-down, drag-out five-day sieges."

Ever the realist and still the boss, patriarch Ray Garvey attempted to size up World Homes' profit potential. "How long are you going to be doing this?" he asked his son in June 1959, as Willard headed overseas to explore building in places like Karachi, Pakistan, where the U.S. government had millions in local currency available from the sale of U.S. wheat.

Willard couldn't remember his exact answer, only that it was the last conversation he and his father ever had. Within weeks, Ray Garvey was dead, and World Homes crept into a special place in Willard's heart, if not for that reason alone.

IN OCTOBER 1959, more than a year after Willard testified before the Boeschenstein Committee and just months after Ray Garvey's death, U.S. funds became available for housing not in Nicaragua, but Peru, a hotbed of economic instability and growing anti-U.S. sentiment. A visit by Vice President Richard Nixon to Lima the previous spring had been punctuated by angry protests. Students pelted the vice president before a speaking engagement at a local university in what the *New York Times* called "a communist barrage of invective and stones, bottles, eggs and oranges."

At the time, Lima was bursting at the seams. Disenchanted immigrants, who came from the mountainous Andes region to the city in search of higher wages and a better life, were finding neither. Securing a place to live was almost impossible, forcing many newcomers to become rustic squatters living in one-room straw huts on undeveloped land in the Andes foothills, seven miles outside of Lima. "People had to build their own houses using what funds they had," remembered Howard Wenzel, manager of the very first World Homes project.

Wenzel, a graduate of Harvard Business School's international management program, was only 28 years old in 1959, when he and his wife left Wichita to head up Hogares Peruanos in Lima, the first Garvey-controlled international housing company. Wenzel met Willard while working for Bill Graham, another Wichita entrepreneur dedicated to promoting capitalism and private enterprise overseas.

Armed with a $143,000 loan from the Export-Import Bank of Washington—the first loan ever made by a U.S. government agency to a private firm for construction of international housing—Wenzel set out to build 72 low-cost homes in a subdivision just north of Lima along the Pan-American Highway. He hired local laborers to construct the single-story, one-bathroom, two-bedroom homes on their 1,722-square-foot lots. The simple concrete homes, which could easily accommodate a small addition or a second story, sold for about $3,000 and sold out before the housing project was completed.

Buyers like Lima taxi driver Francisco Terazona and Max Vera Bravo, an agricultural engineer at the Peruvian Ministry of Development, flocked to purchase the homes, which were a vast improvement from the cramped and unsanitary conditions under which they were living. For the Terazonas, a $600 down payment got them a 10-year, 10 percent loan on a home for less than what they were paying monthly to live in a two-room sub-basement apartment. "Before that time, a clerk or a young professional or somebody who did not have an upper income had no opportunity to purchase anything," recalled Salinas, who was hired by Wenzel in 1962. "To own a house was a dream, and it's a dream that came true."

Poverty, Willard believed, was a frequent thief of what he called man's "five basic wants": food, shelter, clothing, acceptance by peers, and power. His World Homes project was an attempt to restore the most basic of those wants and to forever wipe out a common Spanish phrase in the slums of Lima and elsewhere: "no tiene ni donde va ser muerto" or "He doesn't even have a place where he could die."

FOR MORE THAN a decade, Willard's concept of building low-cost homes with the help of the federal Cooley loans spread to more than two dozen countries, including Brazil, Bolivia, Colombia, Mexico, Taiwan, and India. The effort was helped in part by the swell of political support for foreign aid to Latin America, continuing beyond Eisenhower to John Kennedy's Alliance for Progress program and later Lyndon Johnson's Food for Peace program.

Like his father, who never shied away from dashing off a note to the country's highest-ranking executive, Willard wrote to Kennedy just after his inauguration, urging him to consider making low-cost, private housing "the private property incentive" needed to help foreign countries progress. A month later in an address by Kennedy at the Shoreham Hotel in Washington, D.C., Willard may have been encouraged to hear the president heading in that exact direction. Concerned over the Russians' move to win over developing countries through economic aid, Kennedy had a plan, and he needed America's support to pull it off. "Even in our own hemisphere, communist bloc aid is dangled before the eyes of those who have long been devoted to freedom but have longed for an end to their poverty," Kennedy told the audience at the Conference on International Economic and Social Development, where Willard was a guest panelist.

The president appealed to the group for support of his new Alliance for Progress and other foreign aid proposals. "I therefore urge those who want to do something for the United States ... to channel their agencies behind this new foreign aid program to help prevent the social injustices and economic chaos upon which subversion and revolt feed; to encourage reform and development; to stabilize new nations and weak governments; train and equip the local forces upon whom the chief burden of resisting local communist subversion rests."

It was true that Willard's "deep philosophical sentiment against government and for private production" put him at odds with many elements of Kennedy's political platform. And, perhaps, like his friends in the John Birch Society, he may even have believed Kennedy was too soft on communism. But if Washington rhetoric kept the Cooley funds flowing so that he could keep building houses, that worked out just fine. "I had some of the greatest support of all under Kennedy," Willard recalled later.

By 1966, World Homes had $15 million worth of houses sold and under construction in Ecuador, Colombia, Mexico, Taiwan, Thailand, and India, with another $30 million of homes in the planning stages. Four years later, Willard predicted World Homes would be "one of the 300 major corporations" in the world by the year 2020. In the midst of this rosy forecast, however, World Homes was going broke.

Bob Page, the financial wizard hired by Olive Garvey to help her settle her late husband's affairs and keep the family business from being taxed into extinction, sent out numerous alarms about the profit-eating pitfalls of World Homes.

A caustic character known to pull no punches when rendering any kind of financial opinion, Page immediately took note when a $750,000 investment in World Homes yielded little in return. "I certainly do not intend to depreciate [the] ... pioneering success, in Peru," he wrote a World Homes executive. "But ... success is still measured by monetary units, whether they are in U.S. dollars, soles or rupees. ... Don't you agree that it is reasonable to anticipate some indication of return on this investment in the relatively near future?"

Willard knew Page was probably right. And yet, he couldn't let go. "Sometimes the bottom line and the best project didn't coincide," he said years later. By his own admission, Willard knew the construction of thousands of low-cost homes in needy parts of the world certainly accomplished a great deal from a social standpoint. However, in addition to the financial loss, many of the projects also brought a huge dose of frustration and turmoil for Willard, his family, and his employees.

In Peru, for example, a military coup in July 1962 ousted sitting president Don Manuel Prado. The overthrow so irked the United States, which had invested millions hoping to cultivate democracy there, that President Kennedy cut off all federal funding to Peru, putting Hogares Peruanos in a cash crunch. Days before the junta's Sherman tank crashed through the gate of the presidential palace, Wenzel warned his bosses in Wichita of the potential fallout. "The political situation is fast deteriorating here," he wrote. "If a crisis should occur within the next two weeks to one month, we probably have to count on direct assistance from Wichita to tide us over."

Fortunately for Wenzel and World Homes, U.S. relations with the newly installed junta party were restored within a month, and the flow of government funds eventually began again. Sensing an opportunity for a connection to the new leadership, Willard went to Peru and met with military leader General Ricardo Pérez Godoy, intending to sell him a wheat deal that would create a revolving loan program for residential mortgages. "This money would be continually reinvested in the development of Peru," he told the general.

But that deal never came to pass. As in so many other countries where World Homes operated, shifting political landscapes delivered automatic business setbacks. When Peruvian elections brought civilian leader Fernando Belaúnde Terry into power the next year, World Homes had to put its existing government relationships out to pasture and start forging new ones.

Bureaucratic delays and political coups meant cash problems in other countries as well. In Bolivia, a $1 million loan application to build and finance the sale of 700 houses in La Paz languished for three years. During that time, inflation forced a 40 percent scale-back of the planned project and dried up the availability of long-term mortgage money. When a U.S.-backed overthrow brought General René Barrientos Ortuno to power, first as co-president and then as leader of the Bolivian Revolutionary Front in 1966, many of World Homes's government contacts evaporated, its permitting process slowed, and its flow of funds ground to a halt.

Strapped for cash, the Hogares Bolivianos project manager was, in his own words, "under constant harassment by lawyers, banks, creditors, the Ministry of Labour, [and] homeowners." Court orders were put out for his arrest and imprisonment. There was also an indication that officials at the USAID in Bolivia were sullying World Homes's reputation, hurting the company's development efforts worldwide.

James Van Pelt, the Wichita-based executive vice president of World Homes, pleaded the company's case to American ambassador Douglas Henderson at the U.S. Embassy in La Paz. Rumors about the company were unfounded, Van Pelt wrote Henderson in June 1968.

"World Homes … does not build and run, but endeavors to build housing organizations which grow with the respective countries," he wrote. "You will recall we started developing a housing program in Bolivia at the request of the U.S. government and at a time when Bolivia was one of the least attractive areas in the world in which to invest," he continued. If Henderson could put in a good word for World Homes with the folks at USAID, which managed the Cooley loan distributions, it might counteract the bogus rumors and "silence our detractors" in Bolivia, Van Pelt wrote.

The request must have seemed like small potatoes to Henderson, who months earlier had been tied up with far more pressing communications. In October 1967, the U.S. Embassy in Bolivia was abuzz with news of the death of revolutionary Ernesto "Ché" Guevara, killed in the jungle by members of the U.S.-trained Bolivian army while a CIA official looked on. Henderson, well aware of the CIA's activity in his jurisdiction, was charged with relaying confirmation of Ché's death back to Washington. By comparison, Van Pelt's plea was a simple one, and World Homes continued operating in Bolivia into the 1970s, when restrictive tax laws, building materials shortages and dictatorial governments finally forced it out. "Bolivia was a rat's nest," Willard said later.

World Homes had problems in other areas of the world as well. In Mexico and Taiwan, delays of Cooley loan funds from USAID went on for years. In Colombia, World Homes's Hogares Colombianos built houses in the urbanized Techo neighborhood—renamed Kennedy following JFK's 1963 assassination—but a lack of infrastructure, including water, electricity, and sewer connections, prevented owners from moving in for months. A country of political instability with active pro-Cuban, pro-Soviet, and pro-Chinese factions, Colombia was on the CIA's radar screen throughout the 1960s. So too was Willard, who admitted he would talk with CIA operatives about conditions in global hotspots, but only on his own terms.

"The CIA guy would come down and visit me after I got back from trips," Willard later recalled. "I said, 'I'm pleased to talk to you and I will tell you anything I know, but don't ever tell me anything that you don't want anybody in the world to know because if anybody ever asks me, I'll tell them.' That was fine with them. I wouldn't be co-opted or subservient to any government bureau at any level," he said, adding, "Patriotism and government are two unrelated subjects."

DESPITE ALL THE problems in Latin American countries, India, the world's largest democracy and the country with the most promise—and need—for housing success, brought Willard the most disappointment. "I spent 10 years and a million dollars of my own money there," Willard recalled later.

In 1962, Indian entrepreneur M. C. "Tony" Ray asked Willard to invest in Raymon Engineering Works, a Calcutta-based rail car manufacturing company that could also produce spiral-welded steel pipes, cranes, steel forgings, and metal stampings. Ray—seen as a scoundrel by some and a likable, good salesman by others—needed a foreign investor and partner who could provide access to loans for the company's working capital. Like many Indian businesses at the time, Raymon was gasping for air after a foreign exchange crisis years before left it with no way to fund imports. Substantial U.S. loans through an American co-investor seemed to be just the fix Ray needed. "The partners looked at Willard as a rich uncle from the U.S.," recalled Harvey Childers, who monitored Raymon from his Wichita office.

Willard was enticed by Ray's proposition. He knew India's markets presented unlimited possibilities for housing and other business ventures, and had been trying to break into the market for some time. He had been to India to talk about housing prospects with Prime

Minister Jawaharlal Nehru and his daughter, Indira Gandhi. If he invested in Raymon Engineering Works, it could pave the way for a $4 million Cooley loan large enough to cover a housing project for Raymon's factory workers, Willard thought. The Firestone Tire and Rubber Company had already received a similar loan from USAID for such a project in India. In 1964, Willard purchased 47 percent of Raymon Engineering Works for a little more than $1 million. A $4 million U.S. Cooley loan followed the next year, and the rail car company drew down half the amount for operating expenses. "Nothing but trouble ensued thereafter," remembered one consultant.

In the beginning, Raymon struggled to ramp up production schedules needed to meet a large order of cars for the Government of India Railways. But when the war with Pakistan and famine conditions wiped out government reserves, the country pared back its order in March 1966. Without the cash, Raymon was unable to produce auxiliary parts and equipment the government also said it needed and was hit with steep "non-performance" penalties as a result. Raymon was barely breaking even when its workers went on strike. Meeting payroll became almost impossible.

"It was a real traumatic time," recalls Childers, who spent many a late night in the Wichita office trying to get a call through to Calcutta via international operators in New Guinea, Australia, and Burma (Myanmar). "The (Raymon executives) would tell (Willard) if he gave them more money they could make it happen," Childers said. "Willard put in money to get the thing started … but he didn't have and wouldn't give them more money."

Friction between former owner Tony Ray and the Garvey-appointed production manager Dean Pratt led to Pratt's eventual resignation in July 1966. Then came accusations that Cooley funds were being misappropriated for operating capital, not for an expansion, as expected. USAID officials were up in arms. Pratt was not allowed to leave India, and the U.S. government sued Raymon Engineering

Works and Garvey Industries to recoup the Cooley funds.

Within three years of the heralded arrival of U.S. investors, Raymon had no factory, angry workers, detained executives, and the makings of an extended legal battle. Willard's idea of housing millions of needy workers in India was gone. By 1972, World Homes, too, would be gone, liquidated with no assets remaining, corporate losses of up to $400,000, and personal losses of up to $1 million.

For Willard, World Homes's demise came about as the result of poor business decisions and a shifting political environment, as well some unforeseen and at times insurmountable cultural differences. "We could not adapt American standards to Third World countries," he said. Yet he tried it one more time. Less than five years later, Willard reconfigured and relaunched World Homes as a global acquisition company. Once again, he was drawn to geopolitical hotspots, in 1975 proposing a bartering project with Iran, then an American ally. "We have a major interest in production of food and homes in Iran," he wrote Iranian Ambassador Ardeshire Zahedi, in the waning years of the Shah's monarchy and the early days of the Islamic Republic.

Like a scorned lover's hope for reconciliation, Willard's "best idea" was best left as a memory. By the mid-1980s, World Homes was dissolved once again, leaving Willard with thoughts about how his father might have guided him to deal with the frustrating bureaucracies both in the United States and abroad. "If I were brighter and did it more like my Dad, World Homes would have been a success," Willard said. "I got too emotional about it. I thought wrong was wrong and wanted to change the laws; he would accept them and roll with the punches and operate with them." Willard was 72 years old when he made that observation, more than three decades after his father's death.

"To say that Ray Garvey would have done it better than (Willard), I don't think that's true," said Wenzel, the former World Homes executive in the 1960s. "I think Ray Garvey was good in the U.S.

That's where he got the idea to build the elevators. But I don't think that Ray Garvey had the temperament to be an international operator. Every man a Homeowner: I give Willard a lot of credit for that. … [He] was a guy that wanted to make a difference and I think he really did."

THE DOERS AND
THE THINKERS

"I like to be the doer, performer, creator."—WWG

DEEP IN THE REDWOODS of California, about 70 miles north of the
Golden Gate Bridge, 2,700 acres of thick, ancient forest plays host to
an annual summer retreat for some of the country's wealthiest, most
powerful, prominent, and artistic men. Every July, more than 2,000
members and guests of the prestigious and very private Bohemian
Club in San Francisco flock to club-owned property dubbed "The
Bohemian Grove" where they leave the worries of the world behind
them during a fiery, hooded ceremony called "The Cremation of
Care."

The annual gathering loosely mixes former U.S. presidents, Cabinet members, and congressmen with industrialists, ranchers, financiers, scientists, poets, musicians, and other corporate executives,
who spend a portion of two and a half weeks socializing, attending
lectures, and watching elaborate theatrical performances put on by
fellow Bohemians. An invitation to the Bohemian Grove—women
and families are allowed once in June—is a verified confirmation of
accomplishment.

For Willard, who began visiting as a guest in 1972 and waited 17 years for his own club membership, a trip to "the Grove" was pure bliss, combining his love of the outdoors with a natural draw toward intellect and business acumen. There, he felt at home among the like-minded campers, who would accompany him on a brisk 7 a.m. hike or to one of the daily Lakeside Talks featuring prestigious speakers discussing the economic, social, or political issues of the day. Speakers at Lakeside Talks ranged from Dick Cheney, then secretary of defense under President George H.W. Bush, elaborating on "Defense Problems of the 21 Century," to author Robert Fulghum reiterating the life philosophy outlined in his best-selling book, *All I Really Needed to Know I Learned in Kindergarten.*

For more than a hundred years, the Bohemian Grove has been a sort of isolated hideaway for high-profile businessmen, politicians, and artists ranging from publisher William Randolph Hearst to author Mark Twain and Defense Secretary Caspar Weinberger to musician Bob Weir of the Grateful Dead.

More recently, the annual assembly has become a target of critics. Guests, they say, pay little heed to the club's Shakespearean motto, "Weaving Spiders Come Not Here"—a warning to leave business deals behind—and instead use the exclusive gathering to further their personal agendas. Willard, his friends, and the male members of his family who occasionally accompanied him to the redwoods were likely amused over all the fuss. For them, the Grove was just another adventure together: a high-end Boy Scout camp for well-known overachievers.

"It's purely Bohemian—purely camaraderie," Willard told a group in Wichita after attending his annual summer retreat. "My modus operandi at the Grove is to try to talk with someone new each time." Since his whole life seemed to focus on business—whether it was formulating his next big venture or making his umpteenth tweak to the "GO System"—steering clear of such talk with fellow Bohemians could have posed a challenge for Willard.

Daughter Mary Theroux remembers working summers with colleagues in her father's office while he was off on the July retreat. "We'd wonder, 'What on earth does he talk about when he's there?'" Plenty, Willard thought, as he sat beneath the ancient California trees in the company of so many peers, men who had been in the war, traveled the world, and knew the nooks and crannies of corporate boardrooms. A stroll through some of the Grove's one hundred fraternal camps or along a hilly, mile-long road to the Russian River could yield a joyful visit with any number of interesting executives, like Al Neuharth, the founder of *USA Today*, or Phil Condit, the chief executive at Boeing Co., one of Wichita's biggest employers. Willard's memories of a "delightful afternoon" spent with *National Review* editor William F. Buckley and British actor David Niven, as well as boasted meetings with Richard Nixon or Ronald Reagan "in an atmosphere of equality and camaraderie," stayed with him for a lifetime.

With each meeting, Willard would most likely ask about his companions' ongoing successes and challenges while peppering the conversation with his ideas based in free-market principles. When conservative columnist Robert Novak gave a 1995 Lakeside Talk about the Republican transformation of Washington's tribal society, Willard didn't hold back. His own experience in the years of trying to save his father's estate from being taxed out of existence or with the tribulations of government interference in his overseas building projects taught him otherwise. It didn't matter whether Republicans or Democrats were running the country.

"Government corrupts everybody that is in it eventually," he told friends. "The system makes their word and their actions undependable." Willard's libertarian pronouncements touting privatization over government rule became so well known around the Bohemian Grove that fellow campers came to know his tenets by heart. When congressman and 1996 vice presidential candidate Jack Kemp gave a Lakeside Talk highlighting entrepreneurship and individuality, fellow Bohemians quipped to one another, "That's the same thing Willard Garvey's been saying for 20 years!"

Even if they held opposing political views, many of Willard's companions still found him likable for both his steadfast principles and his contributions to a conversation: the way he could display his knowledge of everything from wild horses in Nevada to New York operettas or Taiwanese culture.

The late Atlanta lumber executive Charles West wrote of being in a group with Willard when someone from Georgia's Cumberland Island approached them and started discussing the wild horse problem there. "None of us knew much about horses. Except Willard," West recalled of the evening encounter. Within seconds, Willard explained how he had wild horses on his "2.5 million acre" ranch in Nevada. The man, clearly awed, looked at Willard strangely. According to West, the conversation for the next hour and a half shifted to "horse breeding, horse racing, horse tracks, horse farms, owners, trainers, jockeys and anything and everything else that you can imagine about horses, and Willard never lost a beat."

"The truth of the matter is Willard would talk to anybody," said David Theroux, whose Oakland-based Independent Institute rigorously promotes individual liberty and an adherence to property rights. As a guest at the Bohemian Grove, David loved to watch his father-in-law in action among strangers. "He had this very populist, down-to-earth respect for people, and interest in people, and he somehow balanced that with this urge to go with people who were winning—the people who were successful," he said. Wherever he was and whatever way he could do it, Willard liked to provoke the doers and thinkers of the world, finding solace, adventure, and a competitive spirit among them.

ALTHOUGH HE LOVED the Bohemian Club and other fraternal organizations, Willard admitted that some of his and Jean's happiest memories involved their participation in the Young Presidents Organization (YPO). Today an international organization of 16,000 members in more than a hundred countries around the world, YPO got its start in 1950 when Rochester, New York, belt maker Ray Hickock invited fifty executives for lunch at New York City's Waldorf Astoria Hotel. Hickock, a free enterprise advocate who took over the reins of his father's belt-making business at age 27, admitted he was often too embarrassed to ask basic questions of his senior executives and sought guidance from others in the same predicament.

From the start, YPO attracted members who seemed destined for greatness. Luncheon attendees included John Templeton, the investment financier and philanthropist known not only for the success of his Templeton Growth Fund but later for the Templeton Prize—the largest individual achievement award (one million British pounds) for contributions to spiritual understanding and development. Other early members went on to build fortunes that launched universities, funded museums, and positioned them for a life in politics.

About a year after the first YPO luncheon, Willard was introduced to YPO through connections with Wichita businessman and chemical engineer Curtis Cannon, president of Vulcan Chemicals. Although Ray Garvey was still calling the shots for the multimillion-dollar Garvey enterprises in 1951, 31-year-old Willard was president of Builders, Inc., one of the city's largest home construction and apartment rental companies. That put him well within the criteria for YPO membership: He was a president before he was 40, and ran a firm with a gross income of more than $1 million and more than fifty employees.

Willard and Jean headed to the organization's first convention in Virginia and became among the first 200 members of the elite organization. Since wives were considered an integral part of YPO,

Jean was an active participant as well. "Jean and I spent a dispro-
portionate amount of our time, effort, and money on YPO activities
during the organization's first 20 years, possibly to the neglect of our
businesses," Willard recalled later. During that time, the Garveys
helped launch a Wichita YPO chapter, entertained YPOers in their
home, and traveled around the world attending YPO events, including a 1971 trip to Africa with the Garvey children.

The YPOers, Willard said, were men and women "of principle
and in intellect, moral fiber and performance far superior to the
presidents I have known." Willard drew energy from the success
of his fellow YPO members, who came to call him "Will." Friends
from the group included Templeton and his wife, Irene, the Wests
of Atlanta, textile heir and former Secretary of Defense Bo Callaway, Motorola president Bob Galvin, Duke University School of
Business benefactor J.B. Fuqua, Tulsa oilman and philanthropist
Walter Helmerich, convenience store owner Dillard Munford, and
publisher John Hartman. For more than 30 years, the men stayed
connected, aging out of YPO and moving on together to become
members of the Chief Executives Organization, or meeting every
few years for a hunting excursion at Garvey's sprawling ranch north
of Winnemucca, Nevada.

Being among some of the wealthiest and most powerful businessmen in the country gave Willard great comfort in knowing he
was not alone; there were other men like him who wanted success
beyond what their fathers could provide. Through them, he would
be introduced to new business prospects, new friends, and even
once, a new country.

SETH ATWOOD WAS fascinated by time. The Rockford, Illinois, executive, who helped turn his father's vacuum company into a diversified

manufacturing, finance, and development firm, was once a collector of time pieces. Sold off to investors in 1999, his collection in the privately owned Time Museum in Rockford included everything from a 3,000-year-old Chinese sundial to the world's most expensive timepiece: a Patek Philippe pocket watch that eventually sold for $11 million.

As a retired horologist and long-time associate from his days with the YPO, Atwood knew Willard Garvey never wasted a minute. "He had boundless energy—absolutely unbelievable energy," said Atwood, who passed away in February 2010. He especially remembered Willard's ability to apply whatever resources were necessary to see a project through to completion. "Willard was willing to do almost anything," he said. "If he'd get an idea, well, he'd just as soon go to the North Pole as he would to eat breakfast."

In February 1969, Atwood was with Willard and Templeton at a Chief Executives Organization gathering in Lima, Peru, where the military government was busy nationalizing businesses, seizing foreign-owned oil fields, and bringing Willard's homebuilding efforts to a halt. Back at home, the American death count in Vietnam was already higher than the totals for the Korean War. Newly installed President Richard Nixon talked publicly of withdrawing troops from Vietnam while secretly sending B-52 carpet bombers into Cambodia.

As they did every time they were together, Garvey, Templeton, and Atwood deliberated on the various ways government interfered in their lives and their businesses around the world. Because of excessive regulations, their ability to expand their businesses was often crushed. Taxes were disincentives for profit, and government spending grew more and more each year. There would be talk of Ayn Rand's *Atlas Shrugged,* Frederick Hayek's *The Road to Serfdom,* or the free-market economics of Milton Friedman.

"What is freedom?" they would ask each other. "What is success?" "What is living a life of value?" In those discussions, the much-admired Templeton, then 57 and well on his way to becoming "the greatest global stock picker of the century," told his friends that in all his travels and research, he had yet to find a country that wanted to maximize a citizen's freedom and minimize the role of government.

Willard became enthused after reading *A New Constitution for a New Country* by Michael Oliver, a Carson City, Nevada, coin dealer, real estate developer, and devoted libertarian who immigrated to the United States from Lithuania in 1947. Oliver was best known for trying to start new countries in the Caribbean islands of Turks and Caicos and in the New Hebrides archipelago of the South Pacific, each time proposing a tax-free, independent state.

"This is the answer!" Willard told Jean as they discussed Oliver's book one evening. Having seen that enthusiasm before, Jean sensed a new adventure in the works. Never one to discourage her husband, she nodded and listened to Willard recount Oliver's premise: a new country without taxes and bloated government would allow individuals to be truly free to pursue their dreams. It was everything Willard had been talking about for years. "It sounded all right to me," Jean recalled. "I wasn't planning to pick up and move anywhere."

In Peru, Willard, Atwood, and Templeton said it out loud: Why not come up with a country all their own—a society where individual freedom was of maximum value to human beings? No sooner had his friend uttered the words than Willard jumped into action, combining the pioneering spirit of his Kansas forefathers with his infamous project-based approach to business. A new country needed a plan, and Willard rolled up his sleeves to make that happen. "Willard was always willing to do almost anything," Atwood said. "Before we went home, we decided to explore the world for a site."

Templeton, who lived in the Bahamas, was charged with looking east of the United States, while Garvey and Atwood planned to look west. Ideally, they would be able to buy land from an established country. Otherwise, they would have to scour the globe for unclaimed land that was 200 miles outside the territorial limits of any other nation, in accordance with international boundaries being considered at the time.

Within a year, Atwood had a line on Palmyra, an uninhabited volcanic atoll about 1,000 miles south of Hawaii. At the time, the mile and a half long coral-reef island was privately owned by a family in Hawaii and embroiled in a lawsuit over the U.S. Navy's use of the property during World War II. Atwood went so far as to meet with one of the family members in Oahu, but concerns over lengthy legal proceedings steered him away from pursuing the deal. That decision was perhaps more fortunate than it seemed. Palmyra may be a dreamy tropical oasis, but it has an eerie—and some say cursed—reputation. Sharks are plentiful in its lagoons, and unsuspecting mariners have been ruined on its razor-sharp reefs. Four years after Atwood inquired about its purchase, Palmyra was the site of a sensational double murder of a yachting couple, depicted in Vincent Bugliosi's best-selling book, *And the Sea Will Tell.*

By the spring of 1970, Atwood had located the atolls of the Minerva Reefs, located about 260 miles southwest of Tonga and 450 miles southeast of Fiji. Bearing the name of the Roman goddess of wisdom and invention, the two atolls of Minerva encompassed 320 square miles, much of which was underwater at high tide. Noted only on maps as a "hazard to shipping," the reefs were unclaimed by any sovereignty and well out of reach for others—or so the men thought. To execute their plan, the men would need to physically claim the territory as their own, write a new country's constitution, and set about creating their New World. They envisioned filling in the reefs and, over time, building out platforms that could accommodate docks, an airport, schools, hospitals, office space, retail areas, utilities, and recreation areas. In a perfect scenario: nirvana for more than 25,000 people.

Willard was eager to put his resources behind the idea. When he heard of Atwood's new find, he offered up laborers, administrative support, and legal expertise to make it happen. "There was total commitment from the word go," Atwood said, "He wanted to be involved." The three opted to keep their project under wraps, lest they jeopardize the effort with unwanted attention. "We agreed we would not talk about what we were doing unless necessary," Atwood said. Still, Willard couldn't resist contacting Oliver and getting him involved. Because Oliver had more experience with this new country business, he took the lead on the project. He created the Caribbean-Pacific Enterprises as the overriding corporate entity and brought in new cohorts, including a mystery man believed to be a one-time international mercenary. To this day, Oliver's name is the one most frequently referenced in association with the Minerva project. "He was not employed by us, but we were his money bank," said Atwood, who estimates the three men put about $100,000 each into the deal.

As Oliver pulled together his own project team, Atwood thought more about the Minerva constitution. It would be a nation of volunteers, with no legal tender. Minerva would attempt to "maximize personal freedom," although too much could bring about "chaos and tyranny," he wrote. To keep their project moving, in August 1971, Oliver and two associates chartered a boat from Fiji and went to the Minerva Reefs to plant in its coral a blue flag emblazoned with a gold torch insignia, pronouncing The Republic of Minerva as a new nation. In January 1972, news of Minerva's "Declaration of Sovereignty" was sent to the U.S. secretary of state's office.

Perhaps U.S. officials, preoccupied with preparations for President Nixon's historic trip to communist China, paid little heed to the one-page communiqué. Officials of the new nation promised to be friendly toward America and build lighthouses, a weather station, and radar equipment to help international shipping routes. There were promises of advancing oceanographic sciences, ecology, and a clean environment amid an increasing world population. The dredging couldn't start soon enough.

For the next several months, Willard and Atwood talked with Oliver and his team several times about the project's finances. They were told that another $400,000 was needed for the development to continue. And one of the first things they needed was a boat. In New Zealand, Willard and Atwood bought the *Ranginui*, a 105-foot dredging vessel that could start work building up the 2,000 acres envisioned around the reefs. They also agreed to lend Caribbean-Pacific Enterprises about $50,000 in exchange for two seats on the board of directors—one for Atwood and one for Templeton. "We worked independently to the extent that we wanted to." Atwood said.

But as Minerva was coming together, so too were the South Pacific island nations. South Pacific leaders, particularly King Taufa'ahau Tupou IV of nearby Tonga, grew increasingly irked with the plan. He went so far as to tell President Nixon that Oliver's group was "either already a front organization or will immediately become one … for large scale international traffic of narcotics." Australia and New Zealand joined forces with Tonga, Fiji, and other nations to stop Minerva's development. The group vowed to urge the U.S. government to "exert pressure" on the American project planners. "We can't have people setting up empires on our doorstep," Tongan Prime Minster Prince Tu'ipeleheke told the *New York Times*.

Within weeks—and some say at the private urging of the U.S. government—King Taufa'ahau Tupou announced that the Minerva Reefs were an important fishing ground to the tiny island nation. A box of emergency rations, clearly marked "Government of Tonga," was dropped on Minerva's shores, establishing a legal "refuge station" there. That wasn't enough for the king, who insisted on creating two new islands of his own at Minerva so that he could claim the reefs as Tonga's once and for all. Just before midnight on Saturday, June 24, 1972, the king, assorted government officials, and members of the public, who agreed to pay $8 in Tongan currency and bring their own food for the pleasure of a 30-hour trip, departed for the Minerva Reefs on the *Olovaha,* a 300-passenger inter-island ferry. A second ship, the *Hifofua,* had gone on ahead with Tonga's minister of police and a crew of prison laborers, who built coral platforms for the "new" islands.

On Monday, June 26, King Taufa'ahau Tupou watched from the *Olovaha* as the Tongan flag was raised on new islands of Teleki Tonga and Teleki Tokelau. The property and "all islands, rocks, reefs, foreshores and waters" within a 12-mile radius of that new flag were firmly in Tonga's hands. As he celebrated his "victory," the king learned that one prisoner working on the reefs was murdered by another brandishing a crowbar. The Tongan "war" against the Minervans had drawn blood.

"The Declaration of Sovereignty blew up the whole project," Atwood wrote.

Several months after the publicized occupation by Tonga, Willard, Atwood, and Templeton were still communicating about Minerva, but they had had enough. Willard paid Atwood his share for the *Ranginui,* and the boat was left to deteriorate in Wellington, New Zealand. Over the next few years, Willard remained in cordial communications with Oliver, who insisted Minerva was still a valid country, minting a collectible gold and silver coin in its name. But by then Willard had moved on. "I hope the idea of minting a Minerva gold coin as a profitable enterprise will bear fruit in 1975," Willard wrote to Oliver after the two visited Garvey's northern Nevada ranch, where Willard was gearing up for a new battle over land ownership rights in the West. Today, Oliver, who still champions the libertarian cause, continues to hold out promise for true independent utopian living.

For Willard, starting his own country had been a grand adventure, a story with which he regaled his children and grandchildren for years. It was a great idea, he told them, if only the government didn't get in the way. "The idea of Minerva wasn't to withdraw from the world," Willard's daughter Mary Theroux said. "It was to create a model to be replicated: an entire country as a proprietary community that others should create around the world in juxtaposition to parasitic states."

For Atwood, the idea of starting his own country was never seen as a true reality, but it was a grand adventure. "The thing to me was an intellectual exercise," he said. "Establishing a new sovereign nation is likely a naïve pipe dream." Still, he said, "I don't think I could have done anything if it hadn't been for Willard."

DON'T FENCE ME IN

"The private property owner will develop his land far better than any professional planner in bureaucracy or government." –WWG

WHETHER HE WAS building new houses or new countries, testifying before Congress or chatting with fellow Rotarians at their weekly Wichita gatherings, Willard never passed up a chance to proclaim his belief in the importance of private property ownership. A 10-minute discussion with him was likely to produce his own version of oft-quoted statements from John Adams or Thomas Jefferson about the fundamental rights of property holders.

"Property rights are the foundation of individual freedom," he could be heard saying. Or, "Ownership is the primary basis for personal responsibility." Willard's espousal of these fundamentals was as inherent to him as the Kansas winds. After all, the Garvey legacy was built on land ownership. Willard grew up watching his father construct an expansive farming operation, shrugging off barbs, negotiating with bureaucracies, and fighting tax battles. He learned that owning land could be an entry into different worlds, often recalling how a 20,000-acre allotment—collective gifts from his parents—earned him an audience with British royalty while a young officer stationed in England during World War II.

He would not hesitate to vigorously defend his role as a developer, no matter how powerful the opponent. When called before a 1954 Senate congressional panel investigating funding irregularities at the Federal Housing Administration, Willard's circuitous answers left him in a stare-down with Senator Homer Capehart of Illinois, who labeled the young Kansan as "evasive" and "cocky."

Like his father, Willard eventually built his own fortune on land, much of it well beyond the Kansas plains in northern Nevada. There, in the confines of the nation's seventh-largest state—where more than three-quarters of the land is owned and managed by the federal government for things such as air bases, nuclear tests, and mining rights—private property is a much-respected asset.

Unromantically, it was the lure of a good tax shelter that first drew Willard to the wide-open spaces of the Silver State. After Ray Garvey's death in 1959, Chief Operating Officer Bob Page, Olive Garvey, and her children fought to keep their assets out of the grips of the Internal Revenue Service, which claimed the Garvey family owed it nearly $80 million. As Page hammered away at retiring the family's outstanding debt and tackling the IRS—eventually earning an estimated $1.5 million refund for each family member—Willard and his siblings looked for businesses that could minimize their tax liabilities.

At the time, the Garvey grain storage business produced heavy cash flow, but not a lot of deductible capital improvements or amortized equipment, which left the Garveys vulnerable to a corporate tax rate of more than 50 percent. Ranching was one way to trim those tax outlays. By operating a capital-intensive business that required big-ticket items such as cattle, feed, irrigation systems, fencing, and trucks, ranch owners were allowed to depreciate equipment at a favorable tax rate, which in turn cushioned land costs and helped the bottom line.

The business not only fit the Garveys' agrarian profile but followed Ray Garvey's path of building assets on large tracts of land. With Page's guidance, in the early 1960s, all four Garvey siblings bought ranches around the country. Brother James focused on Kansas, Colorado, Texas, and Oklahoma, where he purchased a 7,000-acre ranch with Willard in 1961; sister Ruth bought land in Virginia and Oregon; Olivia purchased a big tract in Nevada, as did Willard, who would eventually become the state's largest private landholder.

THE OPEN RANGE of the northern Nevada desert, infused with knee-high sagebrush, emboldened jackrabbits, and the soprano-pitch of coyotes howling under an explosion of stars, drew Willard in like an aromatic perfume. He may have initially invested there for the tax breaks, but over time, the undeniable romance of Nevada's snow-capped mountains, vast sky, and the rugged lifestyle of its people gripped his soul until the day he died.

Never one to do anything halfway, his first stake in the Nevada territory was a big one. In 1962, he made headlines with a $4 million purchase of a spread in Humboldt County, about 200 miles northeast of Reno and about 40 miles north of the tiny western city of Winnemucca. The deal included more than 200,000 acres in a half dozen ranches owned by Frank McCleary, son of a Washington lumber operator for which the company town was named. It also included about 18,000 head of cattle and grazing rights on another two million acres of federal land. Willard's sister, Ruth Fink, who was most likely doubtful of her brother's ability to make money on the mammoth spread, took to calling it "The Tremenderosa," borrowing from the home base depicted in the popular "Bonanza" television show of the 1950s and 1960s.

McCleary, a small-framed, big-drinking, fast-driving character of a man, came to Nevada from Washington and settled in bucolic Paradise Valley, a ranching community founded in the 1860s by a prospector-turned-farmer, lured into the profession by the valley's rich soil. McCleary made his home at the signature Stonehouse Ranch, a handsome three-story clapboard house built in 1941. The ranch house was a beauty against the backdrop of the majestic Santa Rosa Mountains and shaded by a bouquet of hardy Carolina poplar trees.

When Bob Page approached McCleary with an offer for his prime ranching land and all its cattle from the Kansas-based Garveys, McCleary struck what he thought was a hard bargain, asking for $1.5 million up front, with the remainder due in just 10 years. Knowing that the would-be owners were based 1,500 miles away and unlikely to pull up roots, McCleary also threw in a caveat: He wanted the right to live at Stonehouse for the remainder of his life. And then there was the not-so-small matter of a herd count. McCleary's ranch manager assured Page that the 18,000 head count was accurate. But Page worried about being shortchanged and insisted on a deal where McCleary would pay the Garveys a $100-a-head penalty for every cow under the 18,000 tally; the Garveys would pay McCleary $100-a-head for anything over that number. When the final tally came back at 19,000 cows—and the Garvey side had to pay up—Willard was not pleased.

Still, the Kansans couldn't be serious, McCleary thought. Surely, the flatlanders didn't know much about running such a mammoth ranch, and they likely didn't have the deep pockets to keep it going. It was only a matter of time, McCleary bragged, before Willard Garvey and his new Nevada Garvey Corporation would have to give him the money *and* the ranch once again. Catching wind of McCleary's big talk and his bragging that he might even demand a cashier's check for the down payment, Willard traveled to Nevada himself and presented McCleary with a counter check from a Reno bank. When the entire loan was paid off in two and a half years, McCleary was done bragging and lived happily out at Stonehouse for another decade.

Soon after buying the Nevada properties known to the local cowboys as the "Quarter Circle A" after the brand design used on its cattle, Willard came to understand the warnings he had received from Bob Page and others about how owning a ranch and making money on it were two completely different concepts. Serious cash flow problems erupted almost immediately and came close to jeopardizing the final payout to McCleary. Working with Page and getting the ranch on a budget helped stave off big problems, but profits remained elusive.

LARRY HILL AND his wife, Marilyn, live in Orovada, Nevada, a small enclave about 40 miles north of Paradise Valley. The porch of their modest ranch home provides an inspiring view of Sawtooth Mountain, a rocky outcrop on the west side of U.S. Highway 95, the solitary road that stretches from Winnemucca north to the Oregon border. The Hills are northern Nevada natives, and it's clear they love every bit of sage and dust the region has to offer. They are grateful for the 20 acres where they make their home. It was given to them in 1977 as a wedding present by Jean and Willard Garvey, Larry Hill's employers for more than two decades.

Now in his 70s with a smooth bald head, warm eyes, and a melodic cowboy voice that drops its g's and uses *cricks* to describe small streams, Hill was brought up in the cowboy life, "buckarooing" for Frank McCleary's outfit more than 60 years ago. Then, much of the range was wide open, with few fences separating private properties and federal lands. Cattle roamed free on most anyone's grazing land, and ranchers didn't mind tolerating a few stray cows now and then. In 1960, Hill started to fence off McCleary's land, hauling posts and wire across the desert to construct more than 200 miles of fence line that criss-crossed its perimeter. "There wasn't a fence from Paradise Valley to the Owyhee Indian Reservation up there," Hill recalled, describing points of land more than 100 miles apart. "You could go clear to the Jordan Valley (Oregon) and never go through a fence."

Hill met Willard and his brother, James Garvey, just before the McCleary purchase in 1962 and showed the pair around the ranch known as "The UC," near the Oregon border. At the time, Hill couldn't begin to understand the effect the Nevada ranches and their environs would have on Willard; how it would become an antidote to his high-strung, fire-first, aim-later personality, a private oasis and showpiece for his elite group of compatriots, and a draw for family vacations and gatherings for decades to come.

"When he was out here, he was altogether a different person. He was laid back," recalled Hill, who as manager for Nevada Garvey ranches (later renamed the Nevada First Corporation) would head back to Wichita every three months for corporate board meetings, where he witnessed Willard's taste for acrimony, confrontation, and overall restlessness. "He was like a bulldog at those board meetings," Hill said. "Back there he was keyed up and going all the time. Out here, we'd be driving along, and I'd look over and he'd be asleep."

"Nevada is really big, gorgeous, beautiful country," Willard wrote to his mother in an October 1964 weekly report, detailing one of his piloted air tours with World Homes partner Gunter Juncho, who ran a steel fabrication plant in Germany. "I flew Gunter all over the ranch, and we landed at one of the desert air strips, jeeped to our base camp at the Quinn River, rode horseback, and returned to Winnemucca for two nights. ... We did a great deal of walking, exploring, and a minor amount of shooting, although we saw a mountain lion, bobcat, deer, quail, partridge and antelope. … The ranch is really beautiful with many streams, most of which were running, many beaver dams, trees, meadows, mountains, scrub mahogany forest, much sagebrush and thousands of head of cattle, which have not been brought down (to the valley) for the winter."

When it came his turn to drive, the freedom of Nevada's open roads sometimes got the best of Willard and most certainly of his passengers. On at least one occasion, Jean and the children were treated to an in-flight experience in the family's makeshift motor home when Willard's speed clashed unsuccessfully with a cattle guard, a metal grate in the road that keeps cows within their fenced territory. Hill recalled the incident with masterful storytelling.

"Willard hit (the cattle guard) and it absolutely sent that bus airborne! Everybody flew off their seats and chairs and whatever. I think they were playing cards and the cards went all over. … And that was about the last time anyone in that family went with Willard in that motor home." Hill also remembered being called to the rescue when Willard and hunting buddies loaded into a Jeep and headed down a road full of potholes to visit Daveytown, a mining ghost town west of Paradise Valley. It wasn't long before Willard's speed and some tricky road conditions once again made for a bad combination. The Jeep overturned and two of Willard's guests, one an executive from wood products company Boise-Cascade, suffered broken ribs. "I got the call they'd had the wreck," Hill recalled. "I went over, gathered them up, took 'em back to the ranch, pulled the rig back up on its wheels, put some oil back in it, and drove it home."

Word of the close calls got back to family matriarch Olive Garvey, who summoned Hill on the phone. "She told me, 'Absolutely, Willard is not to drive out there.' When he comes out there, you have somebody pick him up in Reno, and don't let him drive any of those people that he's got with him!'" Hill knew better than to cross Olive Garvey and took her directive to heart. From then on, when Willard and his friends came to Nevada for one of their hunting trips, "Either I'd pick 'em up or have one of the guys rent a van and bring 'em up here. Then we'd just put them in four-wheel drives and take them out while they were hunting."

IN THE ARID Great Basin state of Nevada, where most mountain snow runoff travels to creek beds and rivers that never reach the ocean, water is a very precious resource. Season after season, the land bears witness to nature's give-and-take game of moisture-laden bounty, where snowpacks yield to flowing streams later sacrificed by the hot, dry forces of summer evaporation. Rain, always a welcome replenishment, is an infrequent visitor that brings less than 8 inches of annual precipitation to northern Nevada's high desert, twice as much as what arrives in the desiccated Las Vegas region, about 400 miles south.

Stories about journeys to water, finding water, capturing water, dispersing water, and preserving water have been encrusted into the state's history for centuries. After the discovery of gold in California in 1848, the winding banks of the Humboldt River acted as a trail marker and an occasional respite for wagon trains making their way west along the 2,000-mile California Emigrant Trail.

By 1850, small streams east of the Sierras—in what was then the Territory of Utah—proffered small amounts of gold often mired in a bluish sludge that was tossed aside by miners. Years later, when a soil analysis identified the troublesome mixture to be precious silver, Nevada's own mining boom was launched in 1859 at the renowned Comstock Lode near Virginia City. Amid newfound prosperity, Nevada became the thirty-sixth U.S. state in 1864, and its silver helped finance the Union effort in the final year of the Civil War.

Without water, however, Nevada's mounds of metallic riches were of little use to anyone, not the mines that processed the ore or the townspeople who crowded around them. Companies with water rights had a distinct advantage, which didn't always sit well with the locals. In 1864, the Utica Bullion Mining Company claimed water rights for all 330 miles of the venerable Humboldt River and built a dam on the waterway south of Lovelock. Twenty years later, a party of masked men blew up the unpopular structure.

Bold moves to find water also spurred on a host of engineering feats, one of which sent an entire town to the streets in celebration. In the 1870s, California engineer Herman Schussler was tapped to design a long-distance pipeline that would be able to deliver crystal clear water from the Sierra Nevada to the Comstock community around Virginia City. Schussler created an ingenious system of flumes, tunnels, and even an inverted siphon that allowed water to flow first downhill, and then up. The first hydrous surge of mountain runoff reached the parched town of Gold Hill in 1873. Tens of thousands of residents cheered its arrival in a raucous party that lasted well into the evening.

Nevada's first mining boom turned to a bust 20 years later, leaving farmers and ranchers to take up the water cause. With the help of irrigation, pioneered by ancient Pueblo Indians and later the Spanish missionaries in southern Nevada, the state's fertile valleys began producing barley and potatoes and later alfalfa for hay and lush grazing grass for cattle and sheep. Larger irrigation projects sparked controversy that stretched as far back as 1864.

"The great problem in Nevada is not one of land, but one of water," essayist F.L. Peterson wrote in a 1913 volume of *The History of Nevada,* a decade before seven states signed the Colorado River Compact that paved the way for the construction of Hoover Dam, completed in 1936.

TO THE NORTH and the east of Paradise Valley, the land was gifted with two river tributaries that converge at one fortunate spot. Tucked in a desolate desert high country that is more easily traversed by four-legged creatures, the North Fork of the Little Humboldt River begins with the runoff in the Santa Rosa Range and snakes southward between the Calico and Mountain Creek mountains, skirting the southwestern fringe of the Owyhee Desert. From the east, the Little Humboldt's South Fork hails from mountains in neighboring Elko County, winds north through the valleys of the Snowstorm Mountains, and turns southwest to its destination. In their collective 100-mile journey, the rivers' paths cross a huge swath of valleys, ridges, and desert floors owned by the U.S. government. But in a narrow gorge just downstream from their confluence, the land belonged to Nevada First Corporation.

Cowboys like Hill and others familiar with the property had long eyed the land as a good location for a reservoir. They had seen how a healthy spring runoff from the Santa Rosas some years could flood the river creeks and overcome the Garveys' Bullhead ranch and other Paradise Valley ranches located downstream. A dam at an elevation of 4,780 feet would not only prevent flooding by collecting the spring runoff, it would also distribute irrigation water to local ranches, including the Garvey-owned properties. Willard had found his next Nevada project: building what is now the largest private reservoir in the state.

Damming up the local streams for irrigation was not a new idea for Nevada farmers, of course. In 1884, the Nevada Land and Cattle Company built Willow Creek Reservoir in order to irrigate its Squaw Valley Ranch near the gold mining town of Midas. In 1910, ranchers William Pitt and John Taylor began construction on a reservoir and dam in Lovelock, Nevada, that would hold 48,000 acre-feet or about 15 billion gallons of water. In 1935—a year before the completion of Hoover Dam in southern Nevada—the U.S.

Bureau of Reclamation began work on the 21-mile-long Rye Patch Reservoir, located on the Humboldt River northeast of Lovelock. At its prime, Rye Patch would hold between 170,000 and 200,000 acre-feet of water and stretch over 30,000 acres. Construction cost in the 1930s was $1.3 million.

"The idea ... was to change the environment," remembers Garvey CFO Harvey Childers, who worked on the Nevada reservoir project from the Wichita office. "Willard wanted to preserve water for irrigation, and yes, he was the biggest user of water rights in that area." By the spring of 1974, the decision was made. On about 2,100 acres of his private property, Willard was going to do what he loved to do most: build something useful. Other ranchers in the valley weren't so keen on the reservoir idea, however. Some feared that with Nevada First in control, they would end up paying more for their own irrigation, and that if Garvey was damming the rivers, there would be nothing of this critical resource left for them.

Tussles over water rights were nothing new to veteran ranchers like Les Stewart, and he was among those ready to wage opposition. "Water fights in Nevada are not between individual and individual, but generation to generation," he said.

But the Garvey project, dubbed "Chimney Dam" because of the straight, narrow rock wall that harnessed the culminating waters of the Little Humboldt forks, forged on. Garvey hired Galey Construction Company, of Boise, Idaho, to build the project, which would include an earthen dam about a quarter-mile long and 65-feet high across its face. At the heart of the dam would be a 54-inch reinforced concrete pipe, 400-feet long, designed to drain water from the lake above to the irrigation systems below. The Garvey plan was to create a reservoir that could hold about 35,000 acre-feet of water. The total cost was estimated to be about $1 million.

How soon the new reservoir would fill was anyone's guess, even after engineers checked the weather records dating back to 1890 and stream flow records dating back to the 1920s. Some were downright doubtful about its prospects, while others crossed their fingers. "The engineers said there wouldn't be enough to fill it up, or that the ground was too porous," Childers said.

Engineer Kurt Schoufler hedged when a local newspaper pressed a question about how long the county's newest reservoir would take to fill.

"It all depends," he told the reporter. "Well at the maximum—during a dry cycle—what would you guess? Five years?" came the next question. "Could be, I suppose. Or it could fill in a year. For that matter, according to some of those stream flow records, it could fill in a month."

However long it would take, Nevada First planned to create a resource that Humboldt County needed. Since the Garvey outfit was going to pay for the engineering and construction of such a resource, county executives were ready to tap into it. In September 1974, the Humboldt County Fair and Recreation Board agreed to pay Nevada First $200,000 in exchange for the rights to the first 3,500 acre-feet of the water collected at the reservoir. The Garvey ranches would be allowed to access the water only after the so-called "first-claim" had been fulfilled. In addition, the entire surface of the reservoir would have to be available for recreation purposes at all times.

A few years later, Willard took issue with the whole arrangement. Gary Bengochea, the current president of Winnemucca-based Nevada First, remembers being a young accountant for the company when Willard demanded answers about the county deal during a dinner with the ranch managers. "He came in and was raving and raving and raving, asking, 'Who signed that agreement?'" Bengochea said. "Well Willard, *you* signed it," Bengochea told him. "Oh," he answered, and swiftly moved on to other business. A few weeks later, Willard called Bengochea to apologize for the outburst.

At about 4 p.m. on September 27, 1974, a few county officials and a camera-clad newspaper reporter left Winnemucca and drove north, then east, a 60-mile trek to the middle of the desert, where a crew of dust-laden blasting experts had loaded 6.5 tons of explosives into a giant rock bluff that one day would serve as the face of the new dam. Promptly at 5:30, a lone, hard-hatted figure walked across the crest of an adjacent bluff and let out his warning cry to the onlookers: "Fire in the hole!"

In moments, a massive blast sent 10,000 cubic yards of desert rock hurling across the desert and hundreds of feet into the air. Boulder-sized cannonballs flew in all directions, some landing full force onto the construction site, damaging concrete forms that were being used to construct dam outlets. When the dust and smoke began to clear, the bluff face had disappeared, replaced by blue sky and stories-high debris that could fill 500 dump trucks.

Less than two months later, the rivers were dammed and the holding pools completed, all for a total cost of under $400,000, by Hill's estimates, still freshly etched in his mind. That figure was well below the $1 million estimate and included the county financing. "There's 517,000 yards of dirt in that dam. We got it built for $1 a yard, and it would cost over $2 million to get it done today." What was even better, he said, is "the thing filled up plumb-full and was running over the spillway probably about the third year."

In the weeks after construction was complete, Hill joined Willard and Childers on a site inspection at the dam. The trio peered proudly into a 5-foot-wide concrete pipe that angled from the reservoir's floor to a small grassy meadow below. "Just as the first signs of water began to trickle through the pipe, Willard starts walking into the pipe, urging others to join him," Hill recalled. "Them guys walked through it ... I guess the water got clear up to their chests as they were walking through."

Perhaps for the first time, Hill ignored his boss's command and stood firm on solid ground, happy to avoid the potential of being encased in a water-filled concrete tomb. "He could have given me the ranch to go through that thing and I wouldn't have took it."

AS ONE OF THE state's largest private landowners, Willard loved to take up the cause against the behemoth federal government, or even local government, if he saw it growing without reason. Always a voracious newspaper reader, he monitored the goings on in Nevada through a subscription to the Winnemucca newspaper, which circulated to the county's 9,400 residents in 1980. If he saw something he didn't like, a letter to the editor would be quickly in the mail.

"Homeowners should unite to declare war on government waste and controls at every level," he wrote after reading about the local zoning board's involvement in a scuffle between two neighbors. "Establishing laws to pit neighbor against neighbor creates hostility. It destroys mutual self-help, enterprise and initiative." The letter gave Winnemuccans a taste of classic Willard. "Each individual in each community is responsible to restore our economic freedom that politicians have gradually eroded for more than 50 years."

In the 1970s, he was among a group of Western stakeholders behind "the sagebrush rebellion," a movement to return federal lands back to the states, which garnered the attention of President Ronald Reagan, who declared himself a "sagebrush rebel" shortly after his landslide victory in 1980. Willard also joined fellow ranchers in speaking out against federal protection of wild horses, especially in Nevada, where fast-growing herds often starved in the winter and were believed to contribute more to overgrazing than area ranchers accused of putting too many cattle on the range.

A particularly favorite Garvey target was the Bureau of Land Management, the government agency that oversees federal land use. Over the years, the BLM's efforts to restrict and regulate the use of the land so critical to the state's farming, ranching, and mining cultures have turned the agency into a nemesis of fiercely independent Nevadans, who eschew virtually everything about its bureaucracy and regulations. Ask any local about the federal agency's doings, then pull up a chair and be prepared to listen for hours.

Nevadans spoke Willard's language, and he was not shy about vocalizing it. In 1971, Garvey proposed an 18,000-acre land swap with the federal government that gave 1.2 acres of his mountaintop land for every acre of usable valley land held by the BLM. Five years later, the local newspaper reported on what it thought was a new proposal, insinuating that Garvey was pulling some strings in Washington to make it happen.

A letter to Editor Cal Sunderland went in the mail that week. "This story relates to the 'olds,' not the 'news'," he wrote, clarifying that the 1971 proposal was amended in 1973 and again in 1974. Besides, the now two-year-old amendment represented input from three BLM managers and included changes based on their concerns, he added. Willard denied trying to "influence" Washington decisions by calling BLM officers there directly and insisted that local officials were well aware of his efforts.

"The BLM had been so paralyzed by its own procedures and by workloads imposed by Congress, the courts, environmentalists and others, that there has not been a single land exchange processed through to conclusion in the state of Nevada in more than three years," he wrote. The newspaper filed a front-page follow-up on the story later that week.

Garvey critics weren't based only in Winnemucca. In 1987, the *Reno-Gazette Journal* ran a story criticizing the "millionaire businessman" for being a leading tax protester who benefited from taxpayer-supported leases from the BLM. The article accused Nevada Garvey of profiting by subleasing its ranches and their federal grazing rights for far more than what it was paying the BLM. But the article didn't take into account the cost of renting ranch outbuildings, expensive irrigation equipment, the use of private lands, and the debt service that goes with it. As much as he tried to explain it, the story hit home for Willard, who found himself reliving the criticisms in his own father's story almost 30 years later and 1,500 miles away.

IN THE 30-PLUS years he's worked for Nevada First, Gary Bengochea has witnessed a lot of changes at the Garvey ranching operations. The company's land holdings today are smaller, at about 140,000 acres, and the ranching business has become far less profitable. Nevada too has changed, with the state's population growing from about 800,000 in 1980, to more than 2.6 million today. Over the years, Willard's trips to Nevada grew less frequent, and the number of aging men in hunting parties began to dwindle. Willard's daughter Emily Bonavia and her son, Nicholas, own the ranch now and the Paradise Valley's showpiece Stonehouse Ranch was transformed into a popular country inn, complete with a room dubbed "the Garvey Suite." Today, popular hiking and fishing guides with names like "Adventure Guide to Nevada" tout the natural elements of Chimney Reservoir, even though it too suffered the effects of Nevada's 10-year drought and was fully drained for restocking in 2010.

One of Willard's last trips to the land he so loved was in November 1997, when at 77, he traveled to Stonehouse for Thanksgiving with Jean, their six children, spouses, and thirteen grandchildren. The snow-capped Santa Rosa Mountains greeted the family with a breath-taking surprise each morning and gave them a soothing, pink-sky reward each night. Food, card games, and a few good jokes filled the time indoors, while outside, the cattlemen got a hand shipping off a load of cows. Willard took lots of pictures, and family members teased him about the thousands he took in Nevada over the years, often with one hand out the window and another on the steering wheel.

During that special week, Jean Garvey climbed in a car with a handful of grandsons and rode through Paradise Valley, then north along the winding dirt road to the top of 8,471-foot Hinkey Summit in the Humboldt-Toiyabe National Forest. As she rode, she recalled the memorable times she had spent there and a beautiful summer with her children further north at their Rebel Creek Ranch. The road wound further, past the abandoned Bullhead ranch house, and higher still until they spotted the welcome sight of a filled Chimney Reservoir, which for them will forever go by a different name: Lake Willard.

WILLARD'S WICHITA

"We hope to make Wichita a model city to be admired and imitated by communities elsewhere as the best place to live, work, raise our family and enjoy life."—WWG

THE TV CAMERAS were rolling and Willard Garvey was downright fidgety. The bright lights in Wichita's KSN studio irritated his eyes, full of the chlorine flush from his daily swim, and his 65-year-old head was baking beneath the silver toupee he began wearing a few years earlier to replace the brown hair of his youth. He sat, legs apart, behind a coffee table in the middle of the set, flanked by two reporters and two proponents of a proposed new county jail, Sedgwick County Administrator Tim Witsman and citizen advocate Connie Dietz.

Cameras aside, Willard was hot long before he arrived at the TV studio that Sunday morning in March 1986. This time, it was because he and other voters were being asked to approve a $24 million bond issue to finance construction of a new county jail in downtown Wichita. Ballots on the bond issue had been mailed to voters, and a tally was due within weeks. Willard vehemently opposed the jail plan on a number of levels. He took his objections public, saying that the building's design was wasteful and that he could build a suitable, smaller jail for almost half the price. The local newspaper jumped on the story. The "multimillionaire Wichita developer," currently in the throes of building the tallest building in Kansas, was launching a "one-man assault" against the civic powers-that-be. "I just couldn't hold still any longer," he told the paper. "I decided somebody might as well stand up and say that something is wrong here."

It made for good debate, and KSN's "Perspective" program wasn't going to miss out. During the show, Willard was so riled up over the mere thought of taxpayers writing "a blank check" for the jail's construction, he stuttered and squirmed through most of the 30-minute program, tapping his foot, shifting in his seat, and dominating the conversation by rattling off a dizzying amount of facts, figures, and frustration over the building's proposed design, offering up an alternative solution of his own.

"The $25 million (construction cost) to me isn't that important, but the principle is," he told host Nicholas Ramsey, before launching into his explanation of how public spending hurts private sector job growth. "Twenty five million means 2,500 jobs taken away from the private sector. Every million dollars (the government) spends takes away a hundred jobs from the private sector. Ten thousand dollars a job is the capital cost of starting a business. So if you are wasting $10 million on it [the jail's construction], you are wasting a thousand jobs that we'll never have."

For groggy Sunday-morning viewers, Willard's logic may have been tough to follow, until he got to the sound bite. "Garvey's law," he said, "is government is 50 percent counterproductive or wasteful." It was a point he had made hundreds of times before as director of the National Center for Privatization, the organization he founded in 1983, and as a concerned citizen, fighting everything from a taxpayer-funded coal-gasification plant to the inefficiencies of Wichita's public schools. It was a point echoed by the Home Owners

Tax Foundation (HOT), a tax protest organization he launched in the 1950s and resurrected as Home Owners Trust two decades later. HOT, which claimed success just a few years earlier in a 1981 campaign to lower property taxes, had already weighed in on the jail bond issue fight, launching an unsuccessful challenge to the legitimacy of its mail-in ballot.

While Willard was launching the opening salvo in the televised debate, Tim Witsman sat beside him, taking furious notes. The Sedgwick County Administrator was plenty hot, too, only he didn't show it. Overcrowding conditions at the old jail, opened in 1959, violated state and federal standards, and after three years of committee work and public bids, the county felt it had a viable solution in a new jail. Then Willard Garvey showed up, making noise and grabbing headlines about excessive costs, privatization, and exclusionary government procedures. Suddenly, the county's solution was at risk. A war of words had erupted.

The day before the KSN show aired, Witsman was quoted in the *Wichita Eagle-Beacon* saying that Garvey was trying to "bamboozle" voters with an eleventh-hour counterproposal on the jail's design. Later, he told the paper he had no doubt Willard "could build a box cheaper" than the proposed jail, but he asked, "Is the jail going to be built by constitutional standards or by 'Garvey's law?'"

Garvey was on edge, calling county officials "petty tyrants" and "pawns." He told voters, "We have to bring some economic sanity to the table." Willard's argument against government spending was decades old for sure, only this time, it seemed people were listening. In April, the bond issue was rejected, with 58 percent of about 94,000 voters turning it down. Willard took the news "with about as much excitement as a guy whose dry cleaning had come back with all the buttons," the newspaper wrote later.

Standing up to say government was wrong was second nature to Willard Garvey. And he wasn't popular for it. In print, he was once dubbed "a man many Wichitans love to hate." One angry Wichitan said, "If I hear of Willard W. Garvey pontificating on the virtues of free enterprise and the evils of government one more time, I will retch in the lobby of the concrete monument which he apparently built to glorify his image and appease his vanity." The Wichitan's letter to the editor referred to the then two-year-old Epic Center office building. Plenty more Wichitans felt the same way.

"Everybody thought Willard was a pain," said Peg Morrison, a petite, spitfire of an octogenarian who worked as director of community relations for the Garvey companies in the mid-1970s. "And he was, because he was so intent on his belief and his pursuits." Former Deputy Police Chief Bobby Stout recalled, "You couldn't be as visible as Willard Garvey and not have enemies." Stout served as executive director of the Wichita Crime Commission, a local nonprofit organization that every year bestows the Willard Garvey Crime Prevention Awards to a law enforcement officer and a citizen who have worked to deter crimes, not solve them. Willard set up the award with Stout in 1999 because he believed "it was a good investment" for taxpayers to work to stop crime instead of having to support criminals once they were caught. "Willard made enemies by making people look at themselves," said Stout, who like Witsman was a 1986 proponent for the new county jail. "Sometimes they didn't like what they saw, and instead of not liking themselves, they didn't like him."

There were plenty in town who agreed with him too.

"Willard was right on the issues," said Wichita businessman Martin Eby, who recalled sinking into his seat at downtown Wichita Rotary meetings as the loquacious businessman asked a question that turned into a lengthy diatribe against government, bureaucrats, or taxes. "What he believed and what he had to say was so correct, but sometimes he was so long-winded and abrasive in saying it, that it didn't serve his purpose as well," Eby said.

Despite voters' 1986 proclamation against the jail bond issue, a U.S. District Judge ruled the old facility to be unconstitutionally overcrowded, and the new 418-bed Sedgwick County Adult Detention Center opened for business four years later in 1990. The $23.4 million jail was paid for by taxpayers. Just a decade would pass before a $32 million addition doubled the jail's size. Today, inmate overcrowding and calls for a second, $55 million expansion, are still being debated in Wichita.

Somewhere in the midst of it, Willard Garvey's voice can still be heard.

KARL PETERJOHN STILL hears that voice. Every time the Sedgwick County commissioner votes "no"—to property tax increases, a county budget that raises spending, or federal grants—he conjures up a little bit of Willard Garvey. Although he has been characterized as diplomatic and mild-mannered, the registered Republican has been called a warrior in the anti-tax fight, taking on many of the same topics—school budgets, privatization, and property taxes—that brought Willard to the center of the political stage.

An economist by training, Peterjohn, now in his 60s, was elected county commissioner in 2008. When he first met Willard Garvey at a packed Home Owners Trust meeting, he was just 27 and working for Wichita's largest private company, Koch Industries. Watching and listening to more than a hundred people talking informally about government fiscal responsibility was a draw for Peterjohn, then a Wichita newcomer. What may have made it more exciting at the time was that the group was in the throes of a fight against a citywide sales tax, and the meeting seemed to be a "Who's Who" of local business.

"Short of briefly having met Charles Koch when I came to work at Koch Industries, Willard was the second person of prominence in the community that I came across after I moved here," Peterjohn recalled. When he asked people at HOT about some goings on in Wichita, the response was often, "Willard's the guy you need to go talk to." Peterjohn came to know Willard and his family, sharing their small-government/lower taxes stance on a range of issues. In 1992, he became executive director of the Kansas Taxpayers Network (KTN), an anti-tax group established a year earlier and funded in part by Willard's son, Jim Garvey. As head of KTN, Peterjohn spoke out against locally levied property tax hikes, rolled out a taxpayers' scorecard for elected officials, and pushed to get candidates to sign a pledge stating they wouldn't raise taxes.

Over the years, KTN and Peterjohn were accused of being "a self-serving tool of Wichita businessman Willard Garvey." But Peterjohn admits to being his own person, who—like so many others—could have "vehement" disagreements with Willard, but still enjoy a mutual respect. After Peterjohn's election as county commissioner in 2008, KTN merged with another anti-tax group, Americans for Prosperity–Kansas.

"Willard had a sincere love for Wichita and he wanted to make this community an example, not only in the state or in the region, but worldwide," Peterjohn recalled. "Some of Willard's critics thought he was tilting at windmills, but some of the things that he was tilting at needed to be tilted."

DESPITE PURSUITS IN faraway places such as Peru, the South Pacific, and the wilds of Nevada, Willard Garvey did his most influential work in the city alongside the Arkansas River. "Where you are is all that counts," he once said. "You cannot solve problems that are in a vicinity where you are not. If you will solve the problems where you are, if each person will help their neighbor solve the problems where he is, all problems disappear, because they are solved."

From the time he launched the HOT meetings in 1959, Willard fought local officials on everything from the new jail to a downtown tax district to the cost of air conditioning systems for the public schools. In 1990, he launched Total Quality Wichita, a program that urged residents to form neighborhood block groups so they could get together and solve their own problems by helping one another. He fought against government-driven downtown improvement projects and encouraged entrepreneurship at all levels.

A critic of the media, Willard was enamored with them at the same time.

Garvey took the press to task, opposing what he thought was an abundance of stories that were negative or focused too much on government and not enough success stories about what the private sector was contributing. Locally, he toyed with the idea of buying the *Wichita Beacon* in 1960, and then in 1961, he launched *Washington World,* a legitimate weekly tabloid, edited by well-known conservative editor Ralph de Toledano. Years later, he brought the concept to Wichita and for a short time published the *Wichita World.*

Ventures into broadcasting proved slightly more successful. In the 1960s, Willard was one of a handful of investors in the Mutual Broadcasting System, a radio news network that was the largest in the world at the time and later sold to Amway. That same decade, he was a primary investor in the United Network Company, a so-called "fourth network" designed to compete with ABC, CBS, and NBC. The promising network produced *The Las Vegas Show, a* two-hour variety show hosted by comedian Bill Dana. However, the show and the network went dark after only a month. In 1998, Willard launched a UHF community television station called KTQW, which stood for Total Quality Wichita, to broadcast uplifting stories about people, neighborhoods, and organizations tackling problems and solving issues. The station, a precursor to community channels on cable television, won a variety of national and regional awards over the years for its quality local programming.

"Why not go private with City Hall," Willard once proposed. Having private companies sweep city streets, collect trash, and collect parking fees was becoming "a major business opportunity" in the late 1980s, Willard thought. In 1989 he helped push the city to establish a policy for examining those kinds of decisions.

In 1969, Willard told the Kansas City Rotary Club that he wanted the country to prepare for "economic emancipation from government" by the bicentennial year 1976. When that didn't happen, he moved the goal to the twenty-first century. A 1987 treatise written for Willard's National Center for Privatization by historian Craig Miner, entitled "Our Town 2001—A Wichita Countdown," touted the city's tradition of entrepreneurship, which allowed aircraft giants Clyde Cessna, Walter Beech, and Bill Lear to prosper, along with other business heroes such as Koch Industries founder Fred Koch, pizza mogul Frank Carney, and the wheat empire of his own father, R.H. Garvey.

The cover of the dense, ninety-page booklet featured an early rendering of what Willard hoped would be a two-tower Epic Center complex, not the single tower it is today. It prodded readers to think about the possibilities for the future, governed by a set of principles that included morality, individualism, self-reliance, and discipline. The underlying message of the booklet, handed out to graduates of the Wichita Business College in 1987, was: "Our wish is that in the year 2001, Our Town will be changed structurally in three broad areas ... decentralized, localized, and privatized."

Willard had dozens of wishes for Wichita. There were always a host of civic problems he felt needed solving, and he often thought he had the answer—or could encourage others to volunteer their time to find it. A participant with libertarian Richard Cornuelle in a task force appointed by President-elect Richard Nixon to examine volunteerism in the United States and an early member of the National Center for Voluntary Action in the 1970s, Willard believed in the idea of pairing up available volunteers with organizations or groups that needed help, and that Wichita was the perfect place for that idea to thrive. In fact, Wichita was the place where all the good ideas he had seen should come to fruition.

"I've always wanted Wichita to be the best kind of city, so the ideas I have gotten in the rest of the world I always tried to bring back here." Willard said. In his mind all problems were opportunities. In civic issues, problems usually brought opportunities to "reprivatize and manage more effectively." Weighing in on just about any civic issue he would say, "There are only private solutions to public problems."

CHANCES ARE Willard's mother, Olive Garvey, uttered that same affirmation. Mrs. Garvey, who took over her husband's empire in 1959 and held forth as the family matriarch for another 30 years, held strong opinions about the role of government and how the erosion of fundamental economic principals propagated widespread social and business problems. Author of three books, including a 1976 work, entitled *Produce or Starve?*, Olive Garvey lamented the demise of traditional families and public education and was an ardent critic of the welfare state. As a businesswoman, she was confounded by the idea of beneficial tax losses; it was the "utterly irrational system of economics forced on us by our government which makes it more profitable to lose money than to make it … to loaf rather than to work!"

Mrs. Garvey's business savvy was much admired in Wichita, and in 1975, the Wichita Area Chamber of Commerce lauded her with its "Uncommon Citizen" award, citing her business and philanthropic contributions to the city, notably her founding support for what today is The Riordan Clinic, a nutrition-based health center, along with generous donations to the YMCA, Friends University, the Wichita Symphony, the 4-H Foundation, and many more. Her daughter-in-law Jean Garvey received the same award almost 30 years later.

Willard was always "in awe" of his mother, said his daughter, Mary Theroux. "He treated her with enormous respect and propriety. He revered her and was very cognizant of his duty to her and his obligations to her." When 99-year-old Olive Garvey died in 1993, longtime associate Bob Page called her "the best business executive, male or female, I've ever been exposed to." The newspaper—never a favorite of any family member—described her as "skilled at handling opposition, winning people over to her viewpoint without being contrary."

Family members confessed that they always tried to live up to Olive's standards in their lifetimes. "We'll have a tough time doing it," 73-year-old Willard said.

Olive's son may have inherited much of her ideology but certainly not her diplomacy. While beating his drum for privatization, barbs and sarcasm were favorite tools. Willard called politicians "cockroaches," or said "they were nice people to use for ceremonial occasions, but we should not trust them with any more of our money than is absolutely necessary." When the twenty-story Epic Center was under construction, one city manager quipped to others that Willard wanted to build the downtown high-rise just so he could look down on City Hall. Willard's response: "I can look down on City Hall from the sidewalk." It wasn't kind, and the politicians usually bristled. "Willard exerts influence not in the traditional way, and in not a very gracious way," City Commissioner Margalee Wright said in 1982.

Any criticism that came his way was often quickly dismissed. "To me, that's par for the course—people sticking knives in my back. I don't answer it. I ignore it. I won't dignify it with a response. We don't need negative influences," he told a reporter. Despite his irreverent approach, Willard, like his mother, didn't hesitate to put money and efforts behind things he thought could make a positive difference to the city he loved so much.

ON A STEAMY August 11 afternoon in 1976, 55-year-old Peg Morrison was at her desk in Willard Garvey's office on the tenth floor of the R.H. Garvey Building in the heart of downtown Wichita. The boxy, 110,000-square-foot office building at 300 West Douglas opened with great fanfare in 1966 and was the first of four buildings in the Garvey Center complex designed by Sid Platt's Platt, Adams, Braht, Bradley & Associates. With their columned white concrete façades, the buildings are a 1960s interpretation of R. H. Garvey's mammoth grain elevator buildings just outside of town. Willard's office was on the southeast side of the building, looking out onto West Douglas, the Century II Convention Center rotunda just across the street, and beyond that the Arkansas River. There were also views of the adjacent Olive W. Garvey building and the four-story Page Court building just below. Looming just above was the centerpiece of the complex, a 26-story tower, then run as a Holiday Inn.

Having recently been hired as director of community relations for Garvey Industries, Morrison—at Willard's directive—was given a desk in his office. "I want you to see everything I do," he told her. "I want you to see exactly how we operate." For about a year, no matter who was in the office or to whom Willard was talking on the phone, Peg Morrison saw and heard it all. Or so she thought, until about 2:45 p.m. that drizzly Wednesday.

As she and Willard sat at their respective desks, the lull of a high summer afternoon tragically exploded with the sounds of gunfire outside the window. Morrison bolted upright and rushed onto the balcony just outside Willard's office. What she saw has stayed with her, and many other Wichitans, for a lifetime.

Above them, on a twenty-sixth-floor patio balcony of the Holiday Inn, 19-year-old Michael Soles was pointing his bolt-action rifle and shooting. For 11 minutes, the teenager—apparently distraught over a broken heart—fired at anything that moved. Morrison looked down on the roof of Page Court and saw three workers of the Carl Graham Glass Company out in plain sight. The men were just cleaning up after installing six new windows at the top of the office building. They heard the shots but thought they were coming from the street below. When they realized they were in the line of fire, it was too late. "I saw a man running across the roof. I saw an instant burst of blood on the back of his shirt, and he fell," recalled Morrison. "I saw his work partner run over and drag him behind a little ventilator shaft to get him out of the line of fire." In minutes, Elmer "Wally" Hensley, age 57, was dead. His buddy, Arnold Merritt, was shot in the leg.

Morrison stood behind a big round concrete pillar during a fraction of the 11-minute rampage and watched another victim fall. "I saw a car crash because the driver had been shot," she recalled. It was 56-year-old veteran news photographer Joe Goulart, hit through the windshield on his way to the crime scene. Also killed in his car was Mark Falan, a 23-year-old loan officer with American Savings Association, returning with a colleague from a construction site inspection.

Dazed at the unfolding carnage, Morrison drifted back into reality and heard her boss yelling from inside the window, "Peg, get in this office!" She gladly obliged. Away from the windows and safely inside the concrete fortress of the R.H. Garvey building, Willard, one year Morrison's senior, immediately began to voice a familiar theme. "You know," he told her, "the government is going to take this man that is killing these people and they are going to feed him and clothe him, furnish him with medical care, and those people that are falling and dying aren't going to get any help from anybody. … The government ought to … "

Morrison didn't let him finish. "Never mind what the government ought to do," she told him. "What ought *we* to do?"

"Well, somebody ought to start a fund for these people," he told her. "Why don't you start an organization to help these people, and I'll start it off with some money."

At some point, when the shooting had stopped but activity still swirled outside his office building, Willard went ahead with his appointments for the remainder of the day. Morrison started writing a news release announcing a fund to help the victims, a novel idea in a time when random mass killings in America were rare. Later, Garvey workers told them they heard on the radio that police quickly captured the sniper after shooting through a wall in the hotel room next door.

When it was over, Soles had killed three people and injured six, all in broad daylight. Wichita, which had experienced tragedy six years earlier when a plane crash killed thirty-one players, staff, and fans of the Wichita State University football team, was in shock once again.

Willard tried in his own way to buffer the pain. On Friday, August 14, he made a $10,000 contribution launching the "August Eleven Fund" to reward police officers who helped capture the sniper and aid victims of the downtown spree. As part of the effort, an organization called the August Eleven Council was formed to coordinate help for the shooter's victims and later to others in the community. For more than 20 years, the group assisted a variety of Wichitans who needed a little extra help. "The council contacted every victim of crime we knew about, starting with the shooting victims, and we would ask them, 'Is there something you need?'" Money, Morrison said, wasn't always their first answer.

"One time an elderly woman had her purse snatched. She was living month-to-month on Social Security. When the volunteers went out to see her, she had a broken shoulder and said what she really needed was help in her garden. ... Another time, a woman who had been burglarized and raped said she needed help moving to another apartment, so we hired a truck and helped her move. And a lot of people, when they got back on their feet, paid back the fund."

The August Eleven Council was a private solution to a civic problem. It was exactly as Willard would have it.

FOR BOTH WILLARD and Jean, the quality of twentieth-century education was always in question. As far back as the 1950s, when young Jim Garvey came home from school telling his mother he didn't read but correctly "guessed" the word on the flash card at school, the Garveys were on high alert when it came to public education. Jean Garvey believed in phonics, not the sight-reading techniques being taught to Jim. She grew more discouraged when she learned John, then in fourth grade, would not be studying multiplication tables.

The disappointments set Jean Garvey on a course to start not one but two private schools in Wichita. In 1963, Jean, Willard, and a group of other parents, including Bob Love of Wichita-based Love Box Company, got together and in 1963 started what is now Wichita Collegiate School, with Jean serving on the board for more than a decade. Today, more than a thousand preschool through twelfth-grade students attend Collegiate, which boasts that 100 percent of its graduates go on to college. Garvey children were among them.

Willard, meanwhile, kept fighting against what he said was the demise of public education. He scrutinized school budgets and proposed voucher systems, taking swipes at "too much public-school political-economic brainwashing" whenever possible. "Education for our children will continue to fail so long as we worship archaic fetishes, government monopoly, and political bureaucracy," he wrote the *New York Times* in 1976. He argued that giving students a voucher for what it costs to educate them each year would give parents and students the opportunity to fulfill their objectives, whether through public, private, business, or vocational schools or a personal tutor. "The key is to permit these customers—through trial and error, supply and demand—to investigate, test, and retain or reject among competitive educators."

Jean resigned from the Collegiate board in the late 1970s, when her children had moved on to college and out-of-state boarding schools, and she was spending more time out of the state to be with them. But it wasn't long before she decided there was more work that needed doing. "I was on the Salvation Army board and the Symphony board and the kids were hither and yon and we were traveling around seeing them," she said. When she did get back to Wichita, she started to go to school board meetings on Monday night and grew upset over what she saw.

"There were so many unhappy people at these meetings," she recalled. "The teachers were unhappy and the parents were unhappy and they were crying in the hall. I'd sit there and look at that bank of PhDs sitting there telling everybody what they were going to do and I got really distressed. ... I finally just couldn't stand it. The idea then was I would build a little school."

In 1980, Jean started looking at property, including a former public school building that was no longer in use. When the effort to buy that property became too complicated, she looked at abandoned supermarkets, churches, anything that might work. Willard gave his wife some office space at his Parklane commercial strip, and she put an ad in the paper for students. A week before school started, she leased a single-story former nursing home on the city's east side. Eight elementary school students were the first at The Independent School, a place where Jean Garvey hoped children would be encouraged and respected in a learning environment that was truly independent of any school system. Her idea caught on, and in a few short years, the school was running out of space.

One day at home, Jean Garvey walked out of her front door on East Douglas Avenue, eyed the 20-acre hayfield in her front yard, and, like her husband, started dreaming. The Independent School had outgrown its building, and "she was trying to figure out what to do," daughter Mary Theroux recalled. "He said, 'I'll build you a building. We have this field out there. Besides, it's one little building—we won't even see it!'" The first building of the Independent School—built using Willard's preferred, grain elevator-like pre-stressed concrete forms—opened in 1985.

Willard always beamed about his wife's education projects, eventually learning to help Jean only when she said she needed it. "I have a tendency to dominate and interfere," he admitted, "so I stayed off the board and remained on its facilities committee, helping on building, facilities, and grounds." He joked that the school amply filled their empty nest at home. "We got rid of six kids, so we had to get 400 more," he quipped in 1994, the same year he financed The Independent School's $3 million, 68,000-square-foot addition to house a high school. Today, the school in the Garveys' front yard is a hub of activity for more than 700 students, who move between the five buildings of its lower, middle, and upper schools. The property also houses the world-class Wichita Swim Club, built in 1990 with land and financial donations from the Garveys, as well as an athletic field and track.

ALTHOUGH WILLARD COULDN'T be more proud of Jean's efforts in education, his own ideas for a school dated back to the mid-1960s. In 1966, three years after helping to launch Collegiate, Garvey stood before a group of about 350 aircraft industry managers from Kansas and northwestern Oklahoma and announced a plan to start a four-year college in downtown Wichita. As he would throughout his lifetime, Willard went public with a mere spark of an idea, considering the details to be only secondary.

As he envisioned it, the school would allow students to work with local companies for credit one semester and attend classes the other two, a so-called "co-operative" concept accepted in many colleges today. At the time, Garvey saw it as a way to provide Wichita firms with access to an educated workforce. His plan called for presidents of area corporations to sit on the school's board of directors and for local downtown hotels to temporarily house some of its students. In true optimist form, Garvey said he expected the new school would have 500 students at its outset and as many as 10,000 in 10 years.

Such a futuristic concept in 1966 was likely received with doubtful headshakes from his detractors in the audience. At the time, the public's attention may have been on other issues, such as developments in the international space race, or the escalation of the Vietnam War or racial unrest, both locally and across America. Those who knew Willard may have thought that this was just another display of his big ideas and long-winded arguments. But as usual, he stood true to form, not missing an opportunity to drive home his credo. "If we do not find private solutions to these public problems, our property and other taxes promise to double in Kansas in the next 10 years for higher education alone," he told the audience.

In 1966, Olive Garvey was in the throes of preparing for the opening of the new R.H. Garvey building and a corporate reorganization that would divide twenty corporations and almost twice as many trusts into one parent company and four subsidiaries run by each of her four children. A week after the official opening of the R.H. Garvey building, Willard's weekly memo updated his mother on his plans for the new college. The school already had a board of directors and a prospect to head the school, he wrote her. Those interested included representatives from "three banks, the four airplane industries, the three TV stations, the newspaper and John Templeton, an international trustee who is forming the Templeton Christian University, the first college in the Bahamas in Nassau."

But by September 1966, the plans had changed. Willard by then was talking about a two-year business graduate school with a similar work-study semester schedule. He scaled down his attendance projections to 200 students, and that's where the plans seemed to stop. The school had no location or faculty members, just a name: Presidents College. The name would linger in his mind for another three decades.

Looking back, the 1960s probably wasn't the best time to start a U.S. business school. With the Vietnam War raging and popular singers like Joan Baez getting arrested in anti-war protests in California, young people seemed to be turning against the "establishment" that had industrialized America. Many business schools had fallen out of favor.

But Willard kept the idea alive. In 1970, a month after his 50th birthday, he spoke of Presidents College once again, in a speech to the Downtown Wichita Optimist Club. His vision, he told them, was to help "create self-reliant individuals instead of economic illiterates who require Big Brother consumer protection bureaus." His idea for Presidents College would "help fill a worldwide need to create business managers." And there was no better place to do it than Wichita.

Willard Garvey's head was full of ideas, and more often than not, he had the resources to try them out. But Presidents College was one that continued to gnaw at him. In 1994, a 74-year-old Garvey dusted off the idea once more, this time in the form of a law school. In all his 50-plus years in business, Willard believed that some of the best business professionals, including R.H. Garvey himself, were those who understood law. Then why not strengthen the skills of Wichita's own workforce and provide a place to go to school part-time at night and get a law degree?

Once again, Willard came out of the gate with just a concept.

"Millionaire businessman Willard Garvey is trying to breathe life into an idea that is 30 years old," the Wichita paper reported in 1994. Presidents College was a school with no faculty, just a former law instructor trying to drum up local lawyers to help; no staff, as the proposed law instructor was taking calls for the school at another office; no students and no permanent home, save for a little donated space at Garvey's 1950s-era Parklane Shopping Center. But that didn't stop Willard, who had lived through the start-up days of his wife's two successful school launches.

Businessman Martin Eby admits to being "sucked into" Willard's plan for the law school. "I told him, 'We don't need any more lawyers,' but he wouldn't take no for an answer," Eby recalled. Willard shot back: "I'm not going to build more lawyers, I'm going to give businesspeople an opportunity to understand law and be able to fend off those lawyers." So Eby—buying Willard's argument that Wichita deserved its own law school, as it was one of the largest cities in America without one— strapped himself in for the ride and agreed to serve on the school's board of directors. Like most rides with Willard, it was a bumpy one, filled with delays, dents, and derailments due to the accreditation requirements of the American Bar Association.

"Life is a project," Willard always said. As he approached his octogenarian years with the Presidents College School of Law on his agenda, he may have known it would be one of his last.

FINAL CHALLENGES

"I do not plan to retire in the common sense. I notice that people who 'retire' soon die. There are plenty of challenges ahead to occupy many lifetimes."–WWG

"WILLARD THOUGHT HE would live forever," said his sister, Ruth Garvey Fink. Other locals who had watched Garvey for years may have expected him to do just that. Roger Turner, a local assessor and fellow Rotarian who worked on a variety of real estate projects with Willard, remembered coming face-to-face with a buff Garvey—then in or nearing his 80s—in the locker room of a Wichita health club after one of Willard's infamous twenty- to forty-lap swims. "He was the most fit person for his age I had ever seen in my life," Turner said. "I thought to myself, 'That guy is near 80 and he looks like he's 26 years old!'"

But with the new millennium approaching, Garvey's body began to act otherwise. In the early 1990s, as the renewed plans for the Presidents College were about to take shape, Jean's Independent School was expanding, and his businesses were being spun off to his own children, Willard was diagnosed with prostate cancer. The diagnosis was met in true Willard fashion, a matter-of-fact declaration to his children that he might not be around much longer and then a plan to fight it.

For Willard, death was something he feared only as a youngster in uniform, dodging a V-1 buzz bomb on a London street. Like so many wartime veterans who came of age amid great tragedy, he chose to live his life in appreciation of the earthly time he was given. Living was what he concentrated on, not the time and place of his ultimate fate. "Fear of death and dying is an unnecessary waste of time and energy," he said after the diagnosis. He credited his early upbringing at Plymouth Congregational Church with nurturing his belief not only in God but also in immortality. "I have always been and always will be part of God's universe in varying combinations and permutations," he wrote. "This eternal opportunity to experience God's universe in ever-renewed physical form appeals to me and has abated my own concern about physical mortality. … I really believe that the mortal experience can and should be 'heaven on earth.'"

The cancer found a formidable foe in the health-conscious Willard, who engaged the holistic treatment of Dr. Hugh Riordan at what was then called the Center for the Improvement of Human Functioning. "The Center," as it is known locally, is a complex of eight geodesic domes on a bucolic 90-acre site just northwest of downtown Wichita. It was funded in large part by Olive Garvey in 1975. Riordan was an advocate for treating cancer and other diseases with large intravenous doses of vitamin C. In addition to the local help, Willard and Jean sought out alternative treatments in Costa Rica and Australia, staying Down Under for up to a month at a time. For nearly a decade, the cancer came and went, never slowing Willard down, but keeping him aware that he wasn't going to live forever, as perhaps he once thought.

CANCER OR NO cancer, the 1990s held their share of celebrations for Willard and Jean, even amid heavy personal losses as both of their mothers died in 1993. Jean's mother, Leota Kindel, 91, died six months after Olive Garvey, who was two months shy of turning 100. Jean's brother Jim died in 1996, and long-time associate Bob Page followed in 1998.

There were quiet celebrations over things like the 1994 opening of the Presidents College School of Law, with eight students and a space in Parklane Shopping Center. There were excursion celebrations, like the 1995 family reunion at Tall Timber Resort in Durango, Colorado, the first all-family, non-business meeting since Willard and Jean spun off 95 percent of their assets to their six children.

The grandchildren who gathered around him at the Colorado resort—fourteen grandsons and one granddaughter—may not have known what to make of the aging Willard. To some, he was the grand patriarch versed in the manliness of war, ranching, politics, and reckless driving. To others, he was simply an aging relative who snored too loudly, couldn't hear well, and conducted rip-roaring throat-clearing episodes. Yet they were all devoted to Willard and "Granny Jean" and appreciated the legacy the couple would leave behind. "The most valuable asset we have is our children and their children," he told them at the Tall Timbers gathering. "You are our first and nearest and dearest priority. If there is anything we can ever do to help you, we will."

There were public parties, too. In April 1996, Willard and Jean officially celebrated their 50th wedding anniversary at a party at The Independent School, where the Big Band music of their courtship filled the hall and a debonair 75-year-old Willard entered the room comfortably wearing his major's uniform from half a century earlier. He smiled as he had so many times at his ever-stunning wife and displayed agility on the dance floor. Long-time friends, some wearing

1940s-era clothing, joined the Garvey children, nieces, nephews, and grandchildren to fete the couple.

There were also celebrations of service and legacy. Willard was deeply touched in 1999 when he was honored with a plaque in the lobby of the YMCA South, one of the city's six active Y branches, after his son Jim donated the site's 58 acres in his father's name. The athletic fields outside the facility are also named for Willard, who attended a YMCA camp when he was eight years old and joined the Y's board of directors at 28. Over the years, Garvey helped raise funds to build Wichita's Central Branch YMCA. He also was instrumental in establishing two other branches on the city's east and west sides. Willard's grandson Mike, the fourth generation of Garveys to run Builders, Inc., continued the family's philanthropic relationship with the YMCA in 2011 by deeding a Garvey-named, nine-court youth basketball arena to the organization.

Through his cancer treatments and remissions, Willard maintained a relatively active business schedule, too, campaigning for privatization and volunteerism at talks at the Wichita Petroleum Club, the Downtown Y Men's Club, East High School luncheon, and the 21st annual meeting of the August Eleven Council. He served on Wichita Mayor Bob Knight's Long-Range Task Force in 1996, even though the two often clashed on a host of civic issues. He worked on a plan to turn the vacant 26-story hotel at the Garvey Center into downtown apartments and focused on getting the law school a new building, a library, and what proved to be the elusive goal of accreditation from the American Bar Association.

Friends and family say that during this time he even started to mellow. "He became a gentler presence," Craig Miner said. "I think God informed him he was human, and so he got a little shot of compassion," said Gillenwater, who moved from being Willard's administrative assistant to program manager of the KTQW television station before it was sold in 2006.

"The last 10 years, he was real easy to deal with," said his son John, who enjoyed weekly lunches with his father during those later years. Willard's receded hairline is one of the few traits that a full-maned John Garvey did not inherit from his father. The resemblance between the two was evident from childhood, however, and John's appearance at a downtown Rotary meeting will still make Willard's colleagues do a double take. "He sounds like him, he walks like him, talks like him, gestures like him," says Elton Parsons, a former Builders, Inc., executive.

THE TURN OF THE century was certainly a milestone for Willard, who by this time was seeing many of his economic, political, and social forecasts come to pass. Japan, and then China, became world economic leaders as he predicted. Consumers turned away from newspapers, seeking out electronics and specialized media outlets with their preferred points of view. Spending on public education skyrocketed, yet vast percentages of America's children were still underperforming. Private "virtual" universities had yet to take the country by storm, but the concept of school vouchers and privatizing street cleaning services were no longer considered radical. "I was a voice in the wilderness for 50 or 60 years," Garvey said. "To me, I was almost always right, and it took the rest of the world that long to catch up."

"Dad wasn't an ideologue," daughter Mary Theroux said. "He dealt in tangibles. When he built houses in Wichita after the war, he saw how that created community; World Homes was his extension of that. He and Mom were always drawn to people, readings, and ideas that expressed much of their own experience as entrepreneurs." Willard Garvey turned 80 on July 29, 2000, and a party with about a hundred friends and colleagues was held that week in his honor. Willard had foregone his toupee years earlier but still looked vibrant, just older. The party yielded recollections from dozens of associates, many of whom poked fun at the ever-changing "GO" System, his YPO antics, and the way he could simply get things done. Eight decades of living had been good to Willard Garvey, and the people in the room were better off for it.

"I have had all the freedom in the world—through my parents and my good fortune in my life—to do whatever I want to do whenever I want to do it," he once said. "So my only problem has been to find what is most important to me and try to pursue it and see where I can do the most good and where I can help people the most."

THE PRESIDENTS COLLEGE School of Law was Willard's last big challenge. By 1999, the night school was budding with promise. About fifty students attended its classes held in a former downtown bank building and taught by practicing local attorneys. However, the school's success faced a major roadblock in that it did not have degree-granting authority from the Kansas Board of Regents and it was not accredited by the American Bar Association. That meant that, first, the school didn't have authority to grant a law degree to its students and, second, even if it did, graduates would not be able to take the bar exam or practice law.

Looking back, board member Martin Eby says Willard's inattention to these issues sealed the school's fate from the start. "He had *not* researched it, and he did *not* know the full requirements of the American Bar Association," he said, shaking his head. According to Eby, the ABA requires a school to have a comprehensive, fully staffed law library, a full-time faculty, and millions in funding before it will consider accreditation.

"He could have spent a few thousand dollars or done a little research to find out that the ABA is an absolute monopoly," Eby said.

"They don't want more law schools, they don't want more lawyers." Although the college eventually secured authority from the Kansas Board of Regents to grant the *juris doctor* degree in 2001, the lack of ABA accreditation kept the school in peril of closing permanently.

From 2001 to 2003, new college dean Dixie Madden and the school's board members exhausted every possible option to move forward with ABA accreditation, including collaboration with various local colleges, the state's accredited law schools, and the city and county government. Consultants told the board it needed a minimum of $25 million to move forward, money that probably couldn't be found anywhere but from the Garveys themselves. Willard had already put about $5 million toward the school, and that was about all he could risk.

IN THE SPRING of 2001, Willard had been feeling poorly, yet accompanied Jean on a bus trip with the Wichita Art Museum. When they reached their destination, the ever-speedy Willard didn't get off the bus. He blamed his lethargy on what had been a pesky infection. At home, he got chills and grew faint. John Garvey called an ambulance.

Willard was taken to St. Francis Hospital, where his condition worsened, and he grew disoriented. Yet when a doctor came into the room to evaluate him and asked how he was, Willard's distinctive manners took hold and his head shot up, saying with a grin, "I'm fine. How are you?" After a slew of doctors looked Willard over, the Garveys learned that Willard had a heart virus for which there was no cure. He received a cardiac catheterization to confirm the diagnosis and assess the damage. It was the first hospital stay of Willard Garvey's life.

A month later, Willard was moved to a rehabilitation center, where he slipped into cardiac arrest, his heart stopping for about 10 minutes. As the doctors worked to revive him, the usually acquiescent Jean Garvey gave him some no-nonsense orders: "Willard, don't go." Like the dutiful husband he was, Willard hung on. He went home at the end of June 2001.

Willard lived for another year, but it wasn't an easy one. His athletic, vibrant, quick-footed, logical, and challenging self with the sharpest memory in the room was now diminished. He was weak, but somehow, he kept moving. And he kept swimming, even if he couldn't feel his legs.

In April 2002, the downtown Wichita Rotary Club honored its long-time member with its annual "Service Above Self" award, the highest honor bestowed on an individual Rotarian. Willard was on hand to enjoy the accolade, but struggled as he rose from his chair to receive it. As he walked toward the podium, Wichita school superintendent Winston Brooks, all too familiar with Willard's assessment of the city's "obsolete, bloated, bureaucratic, socialistic school system," jumped to his feet, offered his hand for congratulations, and walked the unsteady Garvey up the stairs to the podium. Family members cried at the recognition.

In May, Willard and Jean flew to California for a grandson's college graduation, and in June, a weakening Willard proudly handed diplomas to the first graduates of Presidents College School of Law.

Jean Garvey turned 80 in the winter of 2002, and that spring her family pushed for a family get-together in Nevada. On Memorial Day weekend, a group of about twenty children, spouses, and offspring traveled to Willard and Jean's beloved Stonehouse to celebrate. In the 40 years he had been going to Nevada, Willard's deep passion for the ranch was always effusively transparent. But on this trip he was quiet, spending most of the time sitting in the living room gazing out its wide windows and across the cattle-strewn valley. Paradise Valley was just that to him: a place where he could absorb the desert's vastness and listen to the silence only it could offer. Willard had vast memories at Stonehouse too, remembering the warmth of sitting with dear friends in the living room and standing before its white fireplace to deliver the hand of his daughter Julie in marriage.

After a few days' stay at the ranch, the Garveys returned to a relatively mild summer in Wichita, devoid of its incessant triple-digit heat. At the end of June, Willard attended his 65th high school reunion, and in mid-July, he spent a memorable day visiting with son Jim Garvey and two of his boys. "Dad needed help getting around," Jim recalled. "He was in pain occasionally, but he didn't complain." As Willard reclined in a chair, he gestured to his son to look at some nearby papers; they were the plans for a new, 80,000-square-foot building for the Presidents College School of Law. "He was looking forward to the next building he could build," Jim said.

The next day, Willard was back in the hospital. Again, doctors didn't expect him to live. Again, his family took him home. For four more days, Willard Garvey lay in a hospital bed in the glass-walled sunroom at the far end of the spacious ranch home he built for his family in 1957. The room's raised beamed ceilings and southern exposure encouraged the huge palm tree greenery but diffused the heat of a mid-summer afternoon. Its adornments, like the oriental rug hanging on the beam overhead, were reminders of a lifetime's travels. Although he was slipping away, Willard could rest knowing that beyond the windows in his front yard, contractors had just finished installing the track for the students at Jean's beloved Independent School. The project was one of his last, transforming the last big chunk of land the school site had to offer.

Willard's children John, Jim, Ann, Julie, and Emily took turns staying with him over the next few days. Daughter Mary spent a few days there but returned to her home in California when it seemed uncertain how much longer he might live. As the days wore on, Jean Garvey clung hard to both her husband and her Christian Science values. She didn't ask for an intervention from God to spare him, but she accepted with faith that Willard's spiritual journey on earth was nearly over. It had been almost a year since his near death in the rehabilitation center, and watching his decline was difficult.

Still there were moments of levity among conversations and quiet contemplation as the families shared stories over card games during those long, last sad days. In the early evening hours of Thursday, July 25, and just four days before his 82nd birthday, Willard Garvey's life was over. Daughter Julie Sheppard got the news on her cellphone. Moments before, she had left her parents' house, then quickly turned around and pulled back in the driveway. As she got out of the car, she looked up. "I saw Dad swimming through the sky, gliding, with the greatest of ease. It was such a wonderful feeling; more than a wonderful sight."

The next day at The Independent School, receptionists greeted an older man who asked to leave a few roses at the desk in Willard's memory. He never gave his name, only a card that read, "Goodbye to a friend I never met."

"WICHITA WITHOUT Willard Garvey? Unthinkable."

The editorial in the *Wichita Eagle* said it all. Over the years, the newspaper may have taken its shots at Willard and disagreed with him wholeheartedly, but in the end, it could not deny his impact. "Unlike few others in the city's history, Mr. Garvey helped shape how Wichitans think—or at least challenged them at every turn to give his vision of limited government and privatized services a chance," the editors wrote at his passing.

For some, it wasn't just what he was saying that was so important; it was that he took the time to say anything at all. Seven-term Republican Mayor Bob Knight certainly withstood his share of ire from Willard Garvey, in person and in print, as evidenced in this, one of his last Letters to the Editor, the volume of which could fill a book all its own:

"Why does Wichita Mayor Bob Knight, as the person responsible and accountable for City Hall, confirm again and again that City Hall is a cheat," Willard wrote to the newspaper in March 2001 in protest over the plan for a new downtown tax district.

"We didn't agree on fundamental political values," Knight said, and yet, years after Willard's death, he believes both he and Wichita have lost something significant. "Willard had enormous resources, and he could have taken an easier path," Knight recalled, noting that Garvey purposefully chose to focus on the "minutia" of local government. The former mayor can still recall Willard's voice at countless meetings; how he pressed him and other candidates to sign no-tax pledges; how he always, always spoke up about his mistrust of government and was a passionate defender of his freedoms.

"His commitment level was extraordinary," Knight said. "He took his responsibility to be a steward of the community very seriously."

That may have been Olive and Ray Garvey's doing. "We didn't grow up saying we were going to change the world," Willard's sister Ruth Fink remembered of her late siblings. "And none of us changed the world, but you do what you can."

What is Wichita without Willard Garvey?

"Blander," said Karl Peterjohn. "He was part of the spice in this community in my opinion. ... For some people he was the anchovy on the pizza and the garlic in the stew. For other people, who like anchovies and garlic, he was part of what made Wichita what Wichita was, and part of what it is today too." Hundreds of people turned out for Willard's memorial service at Wichita State University's Metropolitan Complex, as Big Band music filled the hall. Although a somber occasion, it was full of much laughter, as Jean's children and grandchildren recounted the quirks, pleasures, and perils of being a part of Willard's epic life. Business associates, including

Harvey Childers from Wichita, Bob White from Illinois, and Gary Bengochea from Nevada, joined in the tributes. Somewhere perhaps, Willard was laughing right along with them. "Humorously enough," he told Craig Miner in 1993, "I now feel like I've been everywhere. I'm not aware of anything worthwhile I have missed."

A YEAR AFTER Willard's death, the Presidents College School of Law closed, as Garvey financial support alone couldn't sustain it. But by August of 2003, Jean Garvey and others had a new solution intended to keep Willard's dream alive. They turned to Wichita's Friends University, home to the Olive White Garvey Business and Technology Building and the Garvey Physical Education Center. Using a $2 million Garvey-funded endowment, the school launched the Garvey Institute of Law, a graduate-level law program for students who want legal knowledge for their business careers. Dixie Madden, who saw through the Presidents College closing, now serves as the Willard W. Garvey Distinguished Chair in Law and directs the business law graduate program.

"This end result is precisely what Willard wanted," Madden said. "He didn't want to produce more lawyers; he believed that individuals with legal knowledge added great value to business."

There are plenty of people who believe that Willard Garvey was no more than a fortunate son of Ray and Olive Garvey, true giants of entrepreneurship who helped shape Kansas history. Willard likely understood that, but he traveled the world and came back again to Wichita, where he could be forever devoted to his family and the place they all once called home.

"He was an amazing citizen," an emotional Bob Knight said. "Wichita was lucky that Willard called it home. ... It's a different community because he lived."

THE GARVEY LEGACY

WILLARD GARVEY

"Kansan of Achievement Award" – Topeka Capital Journal (1971)

International Swimming Hall of Fame Gold Medallion Award (1987)

Willard Garvey Citizen Crime Prevention Award

Willard Garvey Athletic Fields

Willard Garvey Law Enforcement Officer Crime Prevention Excellence Award

Garvey Institute of Law

Garvey Lectureships in Law

Willard W. Garvey Distinguished Chair in Law

Twelve Apostles of Justice Award," Wichita Crime Commission (2000)

YMCA Hall of Fame (posthumous 2003)

GARVEY FAMILY

Wichita Sports Hall of Fame inducted (2010)

Garvey Branch YMCA

The Garvey Center, Wichita, Kansas

Garvey Sports Center (YMCA basketball)

Ruth Garvey Fink: Distinguished Kansan of the Year, Native Sons and Daughters of Kansas (2003)

Ruth Garvey Fink Convocation Center, Washburn University

Olive White Garvey Business and Technology Building (Friends University)

James Sutherland Garvey International Center, Wichita State University

Garvey Competitive Scholarships, Washburn University

Olive W. Garvey Center for Healing Arts

ABBREVIATIONS

FDR – Franklin Delano Roosevelt

JKG – Jean Kindel Garvey

JBS – John Birch Society

KHS – Kansas Historical Society, Olive White Garvey and Ray Hugh Garvey Papers, 1922-1993, Ms. Collection no. 809, Library and Archives Division

OWG – Olive White Garvey

RHG – Ray Hugh Garvey

WSU – Wichita State University

WSU-WH – Wichita State University Ablah Library, Special Collections, Willard and Jean Garvey World Homes Collection

WWG – Willard White Garvey

ENDNOTES

PROLOGUE

xv   "Pursuit"—WWG interview with Craig Miner, October 7, 1993.

CHAPTER ONE: Epic on the Plains

1   **"Why Kansas?"**—WWG interview with Craig Miner, October 7, 1993.

2   **In 1928**—Description of roads in Jones, Billy Mack, *Olive White Garvey: Uncommon Citizen,* p. 81; Vehicle identified in Garvey, Olive White, *Once Upon A Family Tree,* p. 232.

2   The aircraft industry—Described in Wings Over Kansas. http://www.wingsoverkansas.com/features/article.asp?id=306; http://www.wingsoverkansas.com/features/article.asp?id=209.

4   **Sid Platt**—Comments from Sid Platt interview, May 2007.

4   **devastating recession**—*Time* magazine, "He Could See for Miles," June 14, 2004, p. 94. Until 2008-2009, the 1982 downturn had been called "The worst recession since the Great Depression."

5   **largest single development**—*Wichita Eagle-Beacon,* "Epic Center's Design Reflects 'Scale' of City," August 28, 1983, p. 1G.

5   **"centralized elites"**—Family papers, WWG speech, "Full Gospel Business-man," Wichita City Hall, August 28, 1987.

6   **At Builders, Inc.**—Alex Dean interview, April 2007.

6   **"I might regret"**—Jim Garvey interview, February 2007. Executives and Garvey Industries board members voted to approve the Epic project. Bob Page, the family's financial adviser, was against it. After the go-ahead vote, Jim

Garvey went to his father and said, "Dad, I guess you could lose everything if Epic doesn't fly." Willard said, "Back before we had Builders there was nothing. I don't mind if we end up that way."

6   **For five years**—Progress on the project is described in a series of newspaper articles: *Wichita Eagle-Beacon,* "Epic Center to take bow to its public," November 6, 1987, p. 1B. *Wichita Eagle-Beacon,* "Epic Center Delayed by Matter of Acre on Block," October 22, 1983, p. 1C. *Wichita Eagle-Beacon,* "Epic Center is Getting Off Ground," September 22, 1985, p. 1G. *Wichita Eagle-Beacon,* Special Advertising Section on Epic Center, November 9, 1987, p. 4.

7   **sense of security**—*Wichita Eagle-Beacon,* Special Advertising Section on Epic Center, November 9, 1987, p. 5

7   **"Sneers and snickers"**—*Wichita Eagle-Beacon,* "Epic Center is Getting Off Ground," September 22, 1985, p. 1G.

8   **King Kong**—United Press International, "Quirks in the News," November 8, 1987, describes, "At 22 floors, the $28 million Epic Center is scarcely the Empire State Building, but Garvey Industries officials will still have an actor dressed in a King Kong suit atop the 22nd floor to pose for pictures with guests."

8   **"a festive air"**—Bonnie Bing interview, November 2007

8   **The celebration**—Vacancy rate reported in *Wichita Business Journal,* "Garvey may walk away from Epic Center project," August 21, 1989, p. 1, and "Firm representing bondholders buys Epic Center from Builders Inc.," December 25, 1989, p. 3; also, Builders, Inc. records per Brad Smisor and Alex Dean. Flooded market described in *Wichita Eagle,* "Wichita Landmark is Sold – Epic Center's Price less than $12 million," February 12, 1993, p. 7B. Monthly shortfall reported in Alex Dean and Brad Smisor interviews, April 2007.

9   **"In hindsight"**—*Wichita Eagle,* "Wichita Landmark is Sold, Epic Center's Price Less than $12 million," February 12, 1993, p. 7B.

CHAPTER TWO: DOWN ON THE FARM

11   **"Most fortunate"**—Family papers, "Everyone an Entrepreneur," WWG speech to Wichita State University Entrepreneurs Teachers Class, 1990.

11   **thirteen flying schools**—Miner, Craig, *Kansas: The History of the Sunflower State,* p. 267.

11   **Even the rivers**—See Homer Harden photograph of Riverside Boat Company, circa 1928, Historic Wichita photos online, www.wichitaphotos.org/graphics/wschm_M1-2.3.4.jpg

12   **"It was a big deal"**—Family papers, WWG speech, "Intro to Study Group," May 3, 1989.

12   **chigger infestation**— Garvey, Olive White, *Once Upon A Family Tree,* p. 234.

12   **"lobbying for a move**— Garvey, Olive White, Olive White Garvey, *Once Upon A Family Tree,* p. 239.

12   **"Well, we went along"**—Ruth Garvey Fink interview, July 2006.

12   **"a scrawny, peevish baby"**— Garvey, Olive White, *The Obstacle Race,* p.8.

13   **At the time**—Civil War deaths: History of the Public Schools, Wyandotte County, Kansas, 1884-2006, http://www.kckps.org/disthistory/publications/mcguinn-kcks/mcguinn_civilwar.htm; Public Broadcasting Service, "Africans in America: Bleeding Kansas," Part 4, http://www.pbs.org/wgbh/aia/part4/4p2952.html.

13   **$1.25 per acre**—http://www.nathankramer.com/settle/article/homestead.htm.

13   **Ray Garvey's grandparents**—Garvey, Olive White, *The Obstacle Race,* p. 6.

13   **Seth became**—Descriptions of schools developing during the time, Stratton, Joanna L., *Pioneer Women: Voices From the Kansas Frontier,* p. 157-170; 1883 salary, p. 161.

14   **"Nettie" Post**—Garvey, Olive White, *The Obstacle Race,* p. 7, calls Nettie "nearly sixteen, a pert little lass with a sassy tongue, coal black hair swept back from a widow's peak and deep blue eyes. . . . They were married soon after the beginning of the next school term."

14   **A few years**—"Drought and depression:" Miner, Craig, *Kansas: The History of the Sunflower State,* p. 148. Six-room house: Garvey, Olive White, *Once Upon A Family Tree,* p. 10-11. Reed Larson, who grew up in Agra, Kansas, remembered that the Garvey place was "on the south side of Rt. 36, right opposite Gretna. On Highway 36, there was a real gooseneck in those days, a real sharp bend around a creek. What I always understood to be the Garvey place was right there on that road on 36. About 6-8 miles east of Phillipsburg."

14   **$45 a month**—Garvey, Olive White, *The Obstacle Race,* p. 19; Family papers, RHG letter to WWG, October 7, 1944: "35 years ago this week I started my first monthly job for pay at $45 teaching school."

14 **At school**—Paper routes: Garvey, Olive White, *The Obstacle Race*, p. 26. "Prettiest smile": Ibid., p. 227. Olive Garvey writes that in his will, Ray Garvey gave Washburn enough money to set up an annual "Olive White Garvey Award for the junior with the prettiest smile." Engagement: Garvey, Olive White, *Once Upon A Family Tree*, p. 200.

14 **Olive was born**—"Prosperous implement dealer": Jones, Billy Mack, *Olive White Garvey*, p. 24. Number of children: Ibid., p. 24; Garvey, Olive White, *Once Upon A Family Tree*, p. 85.

15 **Arkansas City**—Ibid., p. 85.

15 **Oklahoma land rush**—Ibid., p. 95-97. On September 16, 1893, when Olive was three months old, her father and uncle participated in the land run for the Cherokee Strip. She describes the influx of 65,000 people and the start of the rush.

16 **Olive learned**—Garvey, Olive White, *The Obstacle Race,* p. 25, on their meeting and engagement. See also, Garvey, Olive White, *Once Upon A Family Tree,* p. 191.

16 **Law work**—Garvey, Olive White, *The Obstacle Race,* p. 63. Also, RHG letter to WWG, November 20, 1945: "When I was your age 27 years ago, the other War was just ending, and I was quitting the law business after three years to go exclusively into real estate which was paying much better and which I had been following for almost the same length of time. I had been making a few thousand a year out of law and twice as much out of real estate." KHS, Box 21, Series 2, Folder 5.

16 **Ray Garvey often**—Timing and conditions "forced" him: Family papers, RHG letters to WWG, November 1945.

17 **But his timing**—Garvey, Olive White, *Once Upon A Family Tree,* p. 220.

17 **constant motion**—Ibid., p. 224. "Since well before his birth he had been hyperactive."

17 **"red-headed lad"**—Family papers, RHG letter to WWG, July 3, 1944, names "Bethl Hospital," actually "Beth-El," now the site of Memorial Hospital Central.

17 **Ole Olson**—Agricultural depression reported in Family papers, RHG letter to WWG, July 29, 1943.

CHAPTER THREE: Training Ground

19 **"on-the-job training"**—Family papers, WWG speech, "Entrepreneurs and the Competitive Free Market," to the Association of College Entrepreneurs, November 3, 1984.

19 **$3 a bushel**—Family papers, RHG letter to WWG, November 20, 1945, describes how wheat was $2.70 a bushel in June 1920 and six months later it was $1.10 a bushel.

20 **But as the decade**—Falling wheat prices: Miner, Craig, *Next Year Country,* p. 170-180.

20 **dog named Beans**—Garvey, Olive White, *Once Upon A Family Tree,* p. 232.

20 **"All through my years"**—Family papers, WWG speech, "Entrepreneurs and the Competitive Free Market vs. Marxist Mentality," to entrepreneurship class at Wichita State University, June 24, 1980.

20 **"a particularly fine lot"**—Family papers, RHG letter to WWG, July 3, 1944.

20 **"cried yourself to sleep"**—Ibid.

21 **"the human Univac"**—Family papers, WWG speech, "Entrepreneurs and the Competitive Free Market vs. Marxist Mentality," to entrepreneurship class at Wichita State University, June 24, 1980.

21 **"He kept all"**—Family papers, WWG speech at Ray and Olive Garvey's induction into the Kansas Business Hall of Fame.

21 **The Garvey youngsters**—Garvey, Olive White, *The Obstacle Race,* p. 64. "It was all hustle and bustle and a lot of jostling around the countryside in Model T touring cars. The partners bought and sold and optioned land." Cars acquired in lieu of land: Ibid., p. 229.

21 **"touring car"**—Garvey, Olive White, *Once Upon A Family Tree,* p. 229.

21 **Environmental and economic**—Craig Miner interview, February 2007.

22 **Still, the attacks**—Extent of dust bowl: Egan, Timothy, *The Worst Hard Time,* p. 9.

22 **"My mother and father"**—Ruth Garvey Fink interview, August 2006.

22 **And that's what**—"Electric winds": Garvey, Olive White, *Once Upon A Family Tree,* p. 227-228. Anyone who managed: Some Garvey Land Company newspaper ads are reprinted in *The Obstacle Race.* On p. 85, RHG discusses

"Practical Economics," saying, "The man who can regulate his expenditures to his income, and save something besides is pretty apt to get along all right." Also, "We should pay very little, if any attention to the overproduction propaganda, and keep busy raising all the crops and other products we can, for . . . a farmer or community that raises a lot of products is busy, happy and prosperous." Also, Craig Miner interview, February 2007.

22   **"was forced into"**—*Southwestern Miller*, "The World's Largest Grain Elevator Operator," December 9, 1958. OWG also refers to this in a 1989 taped interview, as does Craig Miner on several occasions.

23   **"He was always busy"**—Jones, Billy Mack, *Olive White Garvey*. In preparation for his book, Jones conducted extensive interviews with Olive and the Garvey children. While the bibliography states that the interviews are with the Wichita State University Center for Entrepreneurship Collection, they are not there, nor are they with the author or the WSU Special Collections staff.

23   **In a winter photo**—Unbuttoned coat: Garvey, Olive White, *Once Upon A Family Tree,* p. 233. Scarf and gloves: Interview with Cheryl Gillenwater, WWG's administrative assistant, September 2006.

23   **The children went**—Sunday school: Garvey, Olive White, *Once Upon A Family Tree,* p. 101, and family papers, WWG college paper, "Why I Attend Church," December 11, 1939.

24   **kinetic activity**—Garvey, Olive White, *The Obstacle Race*, p. 103. "All parts of his body were probably never completely still during his waking hours, with the possible exception of when engrossed in reading."

24   **a toy taxicab**—Ibid., p. 232.

24   **"almost always right."**—Jones, Billy Mack, *Olive White Garvey,* p. 100.

25   **Right about Wichita**—Garvey, Olive White, *Once Upon A Family Tree.* p. 239. "I was always harping": Family collection, OWG video interview, spring 1989.

25   **Her pleas**—Amortibanc Investment Company: Garvey, Olive White, *Once Upon A Family Tree,* p. 241. "Issued guaranteed first mortgage bonds, with agreement to repay the investors in amortized or divided payments." Third major business venture: Garvey, Olive White, *The Obstacle Race,* p. 84. After farming and the service stations, RHG got into oil exploration in 1948, home building in the early 1940s and grain elevators in the late 1940s and '50s, although he acquired his first grain elevator for his own use in 1928.

25 **Almost immediately**—"Hog heaven": WWG interview with Craig Miner, January 23, 1995. "terrific competitor": Jones, Billy Mack, *Olive White Garvey*, p. 100.

25 **In the water**—Family papers, WWG speech, "Innovation & Enterprise in a Comprehensive Organization," at the University of Michigan, November 21, 1987.

26 **Black Tuesday**—In famous week around "Black Tuesday," stocks lost more than 10 percent of their value. About $30 billion was lost in one week. http://www.sniper.at/stock-market-crash-1929.htm.

26 **"He laughed"**—Family papers, WWG speech at Plymouth Congregational Church, January 13, 1985. On cattle investments: Garvey, Olive White, *The Obstacle Race*, p. 84.

26 **"poor reader"**—Jones, Billy Mack, *Olive White Garvey*, p. 100.

27 **"competitive nature"**—Ibid., p. 102.

27 **Unlike his efforts**—Colorado church trip: Family papers, WWG college paper, "Why I Attend Church," December 11, 1939.

27 **"eternity and immortality"**—WWG interview with Craig Miner, February 28, 1994.

27 **"I do not believe"**—Family papers, WWG college paper, "Why I Attend Church," December 11, 1939.

28 **Between 1929 and 1933**—"One in four:" Egan, Timothy, *The Worst Hard Time*, p. 132. Between 1929 and 1933, 10,763 of the 24,970 commercial banks in the United States failed. http://www.econlib.org/library/Enc/Great-Depression.html. 1932 dust storms: Public Broadcasting Service, American Experience series, "Surviving the Dust Bowl," http://www.pbs.org/wgbh/amex/dustbowl/timeline/.

28 **John Kriss**—"met him with tears": Family collection, OWG video interview, spring 1989. "total failure": Miner, Craig, *Harvesting the High Plains: John Kriss and the Business of Wheat Farming, 1920-1950*," p. 107.

29 **For the most part**—Circle Drive house: Garvey, Olive White, *Once Upon A Family Tree*, p. 249 for 1932 date. Garvey, Olive White, *The Obstacle Race*, "large but not pretentious house," p. 102. Sedgwick County property registry, C0199 S-2-2/1243, house built in 1920. "bake oven": Garvey, Olive White, *Once Upon A Family Tree*, p. 254.

29 **Bank holiday**—Federal Reserve Bank of Boston, "Closed for the Holiday." Also see Fearon, Peter, *Kansas in the Great Depression*, p. 54-55; *Atchison*

Daily Globe, March 14, 1933. Banks were closed Monday, March 6, 1933, through Monday, March 13, 1933, when some were allowed to open depending upon their viability. Some remained closed longer. "dying by inches." FDR Fireside Chat, May 7, 1933.

29   **That same year**—Percentages from Miner, Craig, *Harvesting the High Plains,* p. 72.

29   **Ray Garvey was not**—For Garvey's allotment program: Ibid., p. 72-94. The methodology used by the federal government to set quotas on farm acre production severely restricted Garvey output during this time. It defined the universe of available farmland as land that had been recently sowed. Because Garvey let half his land recuperate for one year in order to yield larger than average crops the next, more than 12,000 acres, or about 50 percent of his holdings, were not even considered in the equation. By government standards, they didn't exist. Production limits were then placed on his 13,000 remaining acres.

30   **The locals**—"suitcase farmer": Hewes, Leslie, *The Suitcase Farming Frontier: A Study in the Historical Geography of the Central-Great Plains,* p. 4. "The typical suitcase farmer is conceded to be a man who farms so far away from home that he has to carry his suitcase to his farm work, but he has some brothers who live close enough to carry a dinner pail." "in effigy": Garvey, Olive White, *The Obstacle Race,* p. 89-90.

30   **FDR and his policies**—Garvey, Olive White, *The Obstacle Race,* p. 88. "When you take their handouts, you submit to their tender disciplines." WWG on FDR: Family papers, WWG speech at Plymouth Congregational Church, January 13, 1985.

30   **Despite bureaucratic aggravation**—RHG farm purchases: Garvey bought land owned by the Farm Credit Administration, a New Deal agency that restructured farm mortgages and provided financial assistance to farmers. Amortibanc buys banks: Garvey, Olive White, *The Obstacle Race,* p. 97. Also see KHS.

30   **"We operate"**—*Time* magazine, "Garvey's Gravy," June 6, 1959, p. 21.

31   **on his first ride**—WWG driving: Garvey, Olive White, *Once Upon A Family Tree,* p. 255.

31   **"I put his bicycle"**—WWG tells a version of James's accident in the May 3, 1989, "Intro to Study Group." OWG tells her version of it in *Once Upon A Family Tree,* p. 255.

32   **Later interests**—WWG interview with Craig Miner, November 18, 1993.

32   **"I can match"**—Family papers, 1939 letter to WWG from Venora Layman.

32   **In the summers**—WWG interview with Craig Miner, September 9, 1993.

33   **"All walks"**—Ruth Garvey Fink interview, July 2006; "sleepless nights": Jones, Billy Mack, *Olive White Garvey*, p. 102.

33   **Unlike the more dismal**—Hourly wage and full story of this anecdote about picking peaches in California: Jones, Billy Mack, *Olive White Garvey*, p. 102. Also see Steinbeck, John, "The Harvest Gypsies," one of a series of articles he wrote for the *San Francisco News*, October 1936.

33   **By the time**—"Pretty Boy" Floyd: WWG interview with Craig Miner, September 9, 1993. "Beat-up old cars": Ibid.

34   **"smart remark"**—Ibid.

34   **After two months**—"dirty, smelly object": Jones, Billy Mack, *Olive White Garvey*, p. 102; "Mother let it go": Ruth Garvey Fink interview, July 2006.

34   **"a wonderful experience"**—Jones, Billy Mack, *Olive White Garvey*, p. 103.

CHAPTER FOUR: RECIPE FOR WAR

35   **"It is better"**—Family papers, WWG college paper, "Why I Attend Church," December 11, 1939.

35   **With some life**—Enrolling in WSU: Family papers, WWG speech, "Intro to Study Group," May 3, 1989. "Dad thought I would go to Wichita U for a couple of years." Clark Ahlberg: Family papers, WWG speech, "Entrepreneurs and the Competitive Free Market vs. Marxist Mentality," to entrepreneurship class at Wichita State University, June 24, 1980.

35   **Financially, the Garveys**—Miner, Craig, *Harvesting the High Plains*, p. 117, letter from John Kriss to RHG.

36   **Willard, his family**—"lithe young body": Family papers, RHG letter to WWG, July 3, 1944; Dating Kathleen: Family papers, clip from unknown 1942 newspaper calls her "member of the dean's honor list and a 1942 Women's honor graduate."

37   **"helpless with laughter"**—Garvey, Olive White, *The Obstacle Race*, p. 106.

37   **By the time**—Family papers. Letters from November 1939 are addressed to WWG at the 303 Allen Rumscy House.

38   **"Keeping busy"**—Family papers. This six-page treatise is found among WWG's college papers. It is not dated, yet references Ann Arbor.

38   **"You sound like"**—Letter from Betty Ann Bassett: Family papers, personal letters from friends to WWG, 1939.

38   **In his first semester**—Grades: Family papers, report card for February 1940, which was end of first semester.

38   **"You, sir"**—While there was no date on this note, it was included with WWG's college-era papers. Other personal references in the note indicated that this was in fact Willard's memo.

39   **"Defend our own land"**—Family papers, WWG English essay, "Let Them Beg Their Bread," September 29, 1939.

39   **"Multiple elements"**—Family papers, WWG English essay, "To Be a Rationalizer," October 20, 1939.

40   **That summer**—Camp Custer described: https://www.mi.ngb.army.mil/ ftcuster/default.asp. ROTC workouts: Family papers, WWG college paper, Reserve Officers Training Corps. This describes the likely scenario he went through in ROTC. Company C: Family papers, See roster accompanying photo from Camp Custer.

40   **"The higher the officer"**—Family papers, WWG college paper on ROTC.

40   **"Roosevelt had been"**—Family papers. WWG oral history, April 13, 1993.

41   **Europe's War**—Family papers. Undated poem with WWG's University of Michigan papers. On the original version, there are asterisks inserted in pen before "America issues treaties through dictation."

42   **As Willard**—War reports from: *New York Times,* "1,500 Nazi Planes Bomb London; Industry and Services Damaged," September 8, 1940; *New York Times,* "Nazis See Battle as Fight to Finish," September 11, 1940. Death tolls to end of November per BBC report, http://www.bbc.co.uk/ww2peopleswar/ stories/30/a6655430.shtml. That report also states that "The raids on London continued until May 1941, by which time 40,000 civilians had been killed and 46,000 more seriously injured." Wendell Willkie: Madison, James H., *Wendell Willkie: Hoosier Internationalist,* p. 24.

42   **"You are surely"**—Family papers, Ruth Garvey letter to WWG, October 12, 1940.

42   **"gay, sensible, vivacious birdie"**—Family papers, RHG letter to OWG, January 1941. This letter was written later than the time described but is illustrative of how RHG felt about Olivia.

42 **Despite his father's**—"better get Bs": Family papers, postcard from RHG to WWG, October 16, 1940. Daily routine: WWG interview with Miner, September 2, 1993.

43 **"Rewrite. Too vague"**—Family papers, WWG's college journalism paper, March 17, 1941. "verbal gymnastics": Family papers, WWG college report, "Transition in Superstition," about mistletoe, December 13, 1939 (WWG's junior year).

43 **Ray and Olive**—Family papers, RHG letter to WWG, December 20, 1940, conveying to him two parcels of land. "One, the S/2 of 9-11-36, Logan County," which he described as "a good level half section . . . not in wheat but probably will be put to wheat this fall, which would give you a half section of wheat each year if continued that way. . . . It is rented to G-K farm for ¼ of the crop." The other was "the SW of 35-9-33 Thomas County, which is a mile north of your other land and subject to a lease to Mary Franz for 1/3, I believe, and to a Land Bank loan on which there is an unpaid balance of about $1,400. This should give you some good experience in paying off indebtedness. . . . I hope you keep them a long time and enjoy good returns on them." RHG's wheat report: Family papers, RHG letter to WWG, October 8, 1940. John Kriss was managing the family farming operation out of Colby.

43 **"Mr. R"**—Family papers, RHG letter to WWG, November 4, 1940.

44 **"While I favor Britain"**—Family papers, RHG letter to WWG, February 14, 1941.

44 **"Judge Alexander and I"**—Ibid.

44 **"You have done"**—Family papers, RHG letter to WWG, November 3, 1940. Comments are an amalgamation of notes.

44 **In the city**—50,000 planes: Miner, Craig, *Kansas: The History of the Sunflower State,* p. 309. Traffic downtown: Family papers, OWG letter to WWG, December 5, 1940. New homes: Family papers, OWG letter to WWG, November 6, 1940.

45 **Armistice Day storm**—Minnesota Public Radio, http://minnesota.publicradio.org/display/web/200011/10_steilm_blizzard-m/. See Armistice Day Blizzard reference.

45 **Community Chest drive**—Family papers, OWG letter to WWG, November, 24, 1940.

45 **"Fingers in my ears"**—Family papers, OWG letter to WWG, October 28, 1940.

46 **"Quite frankly"**—Family papers, OWG letter to WWG November 6, 1940.

46 **"I hope you are not"**—Family papers, OWG letter to WWG, March 20, 1941.

47 **"War on the ground"**—Family papers, OWG letter to WWG, May 29, 1941.

47 **Willard succeeded**—Fort Lauderdale pool described: 1941 *Michiganesian* Yearbook, p. 210. College Swim Forum: http://www.fortlauderdale.gov/flac/events.htm.

47 **The trip gave**—"Ruth is giving up": Family papers, OWG letter to WWG, December 16, 1940. "Blitzkrieg Battalion": 1941 *Michiganesian* Yearbook, p. 210.

47 **"A woman from Chicago"**—Family papers, OWG letter to WWG, October 22, 1940, discusses "Coupe Sedan."

47 **Afterward**—Family papers. Story was a combination of letters from OWG, January 7, 1941, and WWG's sister Olivia, January 12, 1941.

48 **"The future looks"**—Family papers, David Jackman letters to WWG, January 16, 1941 and May 13, 1941.

48 **"Give us the tools"**—Gilbert, Martin, *Churchill: A Life*, p. 690.

48 **Colonel Lindbergh**—"another step away": Goodwin, Doris Kearns, *No Ordinary Time,* p. 212. RHG was likely a member or supporter of the America First Committee. "police the world": Berg, Scott A., *Lindbergh,* p. 450-453. Lindbergh's September 1941 America First speech in Des Moines, Iowa, entitled "Who Are the War Agitators," referred to three groups that were pressing the United States toward war: Roosevelt, the British, and the Jews.

48 **"Did you see"**—RHG letter to WWG, March 1, 1941.

49 **Last truck for civilian use**—http://www.hsmichigan.org/pdf/timelines/Historic_Dates_Calendar.pdf.

49 **Williard's sister Ruth**—Family papers, Ruth Garvey Fink letter to WWG, June 12, 1941. "I am writing the Delta Gamma House now."

49 **"Congratulations"**—OWG letter to WWG, June 17, 1941.

49 **Class of '41**—University of Michigan Archives, 1941 Commencement Speech, "Our Moral Heritage."

CHAPTER FIVE: WE'RE IN IT. LET'S WIN IT.

51 **"The war and the military"**—Family papers, WWG remarks to ROTC graduates, May 16, 1981.

51 **"fatherly discipline"**—Miner, Craig, *Harvesting the High Plains,* p. 125. The book says that James and Willard were in Colby "off and on in 1940 and 1941 working with John [Kriss]."

51 **"I enjoyed the day"**—Ibid., p. 125.

52 **2,400 Americans killed**—*New York Times* on Americans killed. http://www.fpp.co.uk/online/01/11/WTC_DeathRoll1.html.

52 **"Wichita won't like"**—Family papers. In this December 8, 1941 letter, this "Margaret" with no last name says, "I hope you are winding your affairs up satisfactorily, or with the meaning made clearer, winding up some of your affairs period." It is unclear if she, as a potential romantic interest, is urging WWG to break it off with Kathleen, or more simply talking about his plans for going into the service.

52 **"We're in it"**—Family letters, RHG letter to WWG, September 3, 1942. "You're 'we're in it, let's win it' is the only attitude now of course." The family's Christmas card that year was a photo of Willard in his uniform and his quote underneath; per RHG letter to WWG, December 26, 1942.

52 **"We hadn't raised"**—Garvey, Olive White, *Once Upon A Family Tree,* p. 262.

53 **"More money"**—Family papers, WWG interview with Melody Phillips, April 13, 1993, p. 15.

53 **"What shall I do"**—Family papers, OWG letter to WWG, January 14, 1942.

53 **"I hope you"**—Ibid.

53 **"There are no words"**—Garvey, Olive White, *Once Upon A Family Tree,* p. 262.

54 **"I wish you"**—Family papers, November 23, 1942. WWG is stationed in Westover AFB in Chicopee, Massachusetts. "deeply grateful": Garvey, Olive White, *Once Upon A Family Tree,* p. 269.

54 **Despite their son's**—Ruth's engagement: Jones, Billy Mack, *Olive White Garvey,* p. 94. "This makes it perfect": Family papers, RHG letter to WWG, February 19, 1942.

55 **Racial segregation**—"This is the army": WWG interview with Miner, April 21, 1994. Invitations to weddings: Ibid.

55   **"You will go"**—Family papers, RHG letter to WWG, August 14, 1942.

55   **write about business**—Scarcity of materials: Family papers, RHG letter to WWG, October 16, 1942. Scarcity of labor: Family papers, RHG letter to WWG, August 2, 1943. Labor force: "Most of it is over 50 and under 19, such as it is," he wrote.

56   **"You mentioned once"**—Family papers, RHG letter to WWG, October 16, 1942.

56   **Westover Air Force**—Allied troops in French North Africa: Kearns Goodwin, Doris, *No Ordinary Time,* p. 386. "300,000 Allied Soldiers": *Lowell Sun,* "300,000 Allied Soldiers Thunder into Tunisia," November 19, 1942.

56   **"would behave better"**—Garvey, Olive White, *Once Upon A Family Tree,* p. 264.

57   **"I was shocked"**—Family papers, RHG letter to WWG, July 3, 1944.

57   **one-year anniversary**—*New York Times,* "City at War Marks Pearl Harbor Day," December 8, 1942.

57   **HMS Queen Mary**—Statistics: www.queenmary.com.

57   **Carrying about**—hundred pounds of gear: Butler, Daniel Allen, *Warrior Queens: The Queen Mary and Queen Elizabeth in World War II,* p. 129. Willard's bunk: Family papers, WWG oral history, April 13, 1993. "From my main deck inside stateroom . . . we were stacked five high and I was on the top." Holland Tunnel clearance: Butler, *Warrior Queens,* p. 83.

58   **safe arrival**—Family papers. WWG's "Certificate of Service" marks arrival date as December 14, 1942.

58   **"tossed like a cork"**—Family papers, WWG oral history, April 13, 1993.

58   **rogue wave**—Butler, *Warrior Queens,* Height of wave varies, but 75 feet seems the average. Butler's full description of the incident is on p. 97.

58   **"Everyone had abandoned"**—Family papers, WWG oral history, April 13, 1993. Also, WWG interview with Craig Miner, September 21, 1994.

59   **"most interesting wartime job"**—Family papers, WWG "Intro to Study Group," May 3, 1989.

59   **During the day**—Willard's Sunninghill job described: Family papers, V-mail from WWG, September 6, 1943.

60   **100-yard freestyle trophy**—*Stars & Stripes,* "Swimmers Take Chelsea Trophy," July 19, 1943, p. 5.

60 **Willard's brush with British royalty**—According to Willard's notes, this was the home of Sir William Ernest George Archibald ("Sir Archie") Weigall and Grace Emily Baroness von Echardstein ("Lady Weigall"), only child of furniture magnate Sir John Blunden Maple. In one story, Willard was leaving a party and turned to Lady Weigall, mocking the comic George Burns, and said, "Goodnight Gracie." But fortunately for him and others, Lady Weigall did not hear. "landed gentry": Family papers, WWG V-mail to family, April 1943. The formal names are Princess Marie Louise of Schleswig-Holstein; Princess Helena Victoria of Schleswig-Holstein. "port and roulette": WWG V-mail to family, November 19, 1944.

60 **Elizabeth Letner**—De Rothschild, Edmund, *Edmund de Rothschild: A Gilt-Edged Life,* p. 175-177. Husband EDR says Elizabeth was 25 in 1948. She lived with her grandmother and her parents returned to Czechoslovakia in 1939. Her father died of a brain tumor there in 1939, after Hitler marched into the country. Her mother caught the last train out of the country and landed in America. Perhaps that is why they formed a bond: Willard may have been an American connection to her mother, who returned to live with her at the Berystede.

60 "**rather settled in**"—Family papers, WWG letter home, September 2, 1943.

61 "**I want to see**"—Family papers, WWG V-mail, July 29, 1944.

61 "**Nothing could be farther**"—Family papers, WWG letter to family, July 29, 1944 (Willard was stationed in France with the First Allied Airborne Army headquarters shortly after the invasion).

61 "**We had a letter**"—Family papers, RHG letter to WWG, August 2, 1943.

64 "**A lot of things**"—Family papers, RHG letter to WWG, December 27, 1943.

64 **A hardy man**—Family papers, RHG letter to WWG, December 18, 1944. Letter also talks of "pie a la mode and cherry pie, peach cobbler and cream on March 15, 1945." "little wise-cracking": Family papers, RHG letter to children, October 15, 1944 is the notation made on the second page. 100,000 acres: Miner, Craig, "RH Garvey, Operations Are Interesting," in *John Brown to Bob Dole: Movers and Shakers in Kansas History,* edited by Virgil Dean, p. 260.

64 "**You boys can come home**"—Family papers, RHG letter to WWG, December 31, 1944.

66 "**I shall write**"—Family papers, OWG letter to WWG, June, 29 1943.

66 **Wichita . . . was changing**—Boeing shifts: Family papers, RHG letter to
WWG, January 1, 1944: "Boeing has gone on a two shift, 10-hour work
period from a three shifter. Pretty long hours, but the employees make lots
more money." "people applaud": Family papers, RHG letter to WWG,
August 23, 1944.

67 **"They are having a service"**—Family papers, RHG letter to WWG, December 12, 1944.

67 **"war is now personal"**—Family papers, WWG letter to family, March 6,
1944.

67 **"150,000 men"**—*Time* magazine, "D-Day in Europe, The Forge of Victory,"
June 8, 1959. Ken Burns' *The War* says 11,000 war planes, more than 5,300
ships and 176,000 men went across the English Channel.

67 **"I am a little bored"**—Family papers, WWG V-mail to family, May 31, 1944.

67 **Sainte Mère Egliese**—http://www.helium.com/tm/217170/
similar-versions-article-author.

68 **Willard remembered**—"tragically impressive day": WWG interview with
Craig Miner, April 21, 1994. A neighbor boy: WWG interview with Miner,
April 5, 1995: "I had to check out and find missing in action paratroops. . . .
I did not return for the 50th anniversary of Normandy because the cemeter-
ies sadden me too much." WWG interview with Craig Miner, September 2,
1993: "One of them looked like my neighbor on Circle Drive."

68 **"I notice the casualties"**—Family papers, RHG letter to WWG, August 23,
1944. "17,000 houses per day": Family papers, RHG letter to WWG, August
26, 1944.

69 **summer of 1944**—move to France: Family papers, WWG letter to friend
named "Charlie," December 13, 1944 saying, "Spent June, July and part of
August in France." "mild apprehension": Family papers, WWG letter from
France to family, July 23, 1944.

69 **"hundreds of searchlights"**—Family papers, WWG letter to family, August
13, 1944. Guards Chapel bombing: Irving, David, *The War Between the Gen-
erals*, p. 180.

70 **Operation Market-Garden**—Ryan, Cornelius, *A Bridge Too Far*, p. 11, 599.

70 **"If we fought"**—Headquarters infighting: WWG interview with Craig
Miner, September 2, 1993. Hotel Royal: Details of this headquarters estab-
lishment are in unclassified documents, "History of Headquarters of the First
Allied Airborne Army."

71 **"select and train men"**—Family papers, WWG letter to family, October 28, 1944.

71 **"FDR was short"**—Family papers, RHG letter to WWG, January 6, 1945. RHG expansion to Colorado: Miner, Craig, *Harvesting the High Plains,* p. 139-163. RHG acquired at least 19,000 acres in Cheyenne County, south of Kanorado, bringing his totals to expand his farming operations to more than 100,000 acres in two states and launching "one of the largest crops ever harvested by an individual."

71 **While the U.S. casualty count**—Casualties include killed, wounded or missing in action http://www.battleofthebulge.org/. "Quite pleasant": Family papers, WWG letter to Elizabeth Letner, February 1945. "Lovely old town": Family papers, WWG letter to brother James, May 21, 1945.

71 **Russians moved westward**—Beevor, Anthony, *The Fall of Berlin 1945,* p. 11. 7,000 prisoners: http://www.ushmm.org/museum/exhibit/focus/auschwitz/.

72 **"It appeared"**—Family papers, RHG letter to WWG, April 17, 1945.

72 **Now a major**—Family papers, WWG oral history, April 13, 1993.

73 **Newspaper pictures**—London celebration: Family papers, Elizabeth Letner letter to WWG, May 24, 1945. V-E Day in Kansas: Family papers, RHG letter to WWG, May 25, 1945.

73 **"Be prepared"**—Family papers, WWG oral history, April 13, 1993.

73 **Willard picked up**—Family papers, WWG speech at Berlin CEO seminar, April 20, 1992, and WWG oral history interview, April 13, 1993. There are some contradictions in these documents. WWG mentions that he was "billeted in the houses surrounding the Schlectensee [*sic*]." But it is more likely that he was near Lake Griebnitz. Also see *Chicago Daily Tribune,* "Big 3 Parley Begins Today," July 15, 1945. "Maj. General Floyd L. Parks, commander of the American troops in Berlin."

73 **Berlin was still smoldering**—WWG letter to RHG, July 25, 1945, KHS. Also see Beevor, *The Fall of Berlin 1945,* illustration no. 36.

74 **first three U.S. officers**—Family papers, WWG speech at Berlin CEO seminar, April 20, 1992.

74 **The real damage**—Russian brutality: Beevor, Anthony, *The Fall of Berlin 1945*, p. 419. Beevor provides a chilling description from a German woman's perspective on p. 409- 419. Baby carriage filled: Family papers, WWG speech at Berlin CEO seminar, April 20, 1992, and WWG oral history, April 13, 1993. See also McCullough, David, *Truman,* p. 414.

74   **"important international conference"**—*Los Angeles Times*, "Secrecy at Potsdam Meeting Disappointing," July 18, 1945. A detailed description of the Potsdam conference can be found in McCullough, David, *Truman*, p. 409-436.

75   **led to the Cold War**—Mee, Charles, *Meeting at Potsdam* (thesis).

75   **residences for visiting dignitaries**—McCullough, David, *Truman*, p. 407. Leave in an hour: Ibid., p. 407. Quotes letter to Truman that describes Russian occupation and orders to leave.

75   **Willard witnessed**—"cleaning up the houses:" Family papers, WWG speech at Berlin CEO seminar, April 30, 1992; a cultivated house: McCullough, David, *Truman*, p. 408.

75   **Preparations for conference**—WWG letter to family, July 24, 1945, KHS. Conference table description: McCullough, David, *Truman*, p. 420. Menus served: *Wall Street Journal*, "Potsdam Blackout," July 25, 1945, p. 8.

76   **Willard's role**—Family papers, WWG speech at Berlin CEO seminar, April, 23, 1992. Missouri visitors: Ibid.

76   **"all the high brass"**—Family papers. WWG's Berlin CEO seminar speech on April 30, 1992 details "high brass" and late nights. Other details, *Chicago Daily Tribune*, "Big 3 Political Military Chiefs Sign at Potsdam," July 16, 1945, p. 5. "practically walked over": WWG letter to family, July 25, 1945, KHS, Box 21 FF7.

76   **"I happened"**—Encounter with Stalin: Family papers. WWG describes Stalin incident in 1993 oral history interview. Also see details in 1992 Berlin CEO seminar speech, WWG saying Stalin was "about 25 feet away." "a vivid reminder": Family papers, WWG speech at Berlin CEO seminar April, 30, 1992.

77   **"The atom bomb"**—Family papers, WWG oral history, April 13, 1993.

77   **After Potsdam**—Family papers, WWG letter to family, August 28, 1945.

77   **Allied Kommandatura**—Family papers, WWG speech at Plymouth Congregational Church, January 13, 1985.

77   **World War II exposed**—French hospitality: WWG letter home, October 8, 1944, talks about French inviting him in for what little they had to eat.

77   **"They were accumulating"**—WWG speech to the National Conference on International Economic and Social Development in Washington, D.C., June 1961. WSU-WH, Box 96 FF2-FF4. "ready to be a civilian." Family papers, RHG letter to children, August 28, 1945.

78   **"Don't be discouraged"**—Family papers, Ruth Garvey Cochener, September 9, 1944.

CHAPTER SIX: A LIFETIME DEVOTION

79   **"most fortunate association"**—Family papers, WWG speech, "Innovation & Enterprise in a Comprehensive Organization," to University of Michigan American Institutions, November 5, 1987. In same speech, he calls JKG "my first successful project."

79   **After Japan's surrender**—Family papers, RHG letter, October 6, 1945. "We had a 40-page letter from Willard dated Sept. 23 yesterday, telling about his trip to Frankfurt, Vienna, Switzerland, Rome, Marseille, Paris, Frankfurt, and Berlin."

79   **"I can just see you"**—Family papers, RHG letter, September 28, 1945.

79   **end of October**—Return to Circle Drive: WWG service papers say that he left for the continental United States on October 29, 1945, and arrived in the United States on November 7, 1945. "A happy day": Garvey, Olive White. *Once Upon A Family Tree,* p. 266.

80   **A lot had changed**—Population change: Miner, Craig, *Kansas: History of the Sunflower State,* p. 315; Wichita population change 1940-1945, http://www.kgs.ku.edu/Publications/Bulletins/79/04_geog.html. Postwar wage shifts: Family papers, RHG letter to WWG, March 15, 1945. "Reclaimed rubber." Giffels, David, and Steve Love, *Wheels of Fortune: The Story of Rubber in Akron,* p. 106. Access to natural rubber had been cut off since the war, and new synthetic rubber tires developed as a result were still reserved for military use. Civilian rubber products were "turned into civilian tires, but they were not quality products." Stalled cars: Family papers, OWG letter to WWG, August 28, 1945.

80   **"Is the girl"**—Criteria in family papers, WWG letter to his brother, James Garvey, May 31, 1945. The letter comes as James is contemplating his own marriage to a woman he had met in the army.

81   **Ray Garvey's businesses**—Clarence Drake: Family papers, WWG speech, "Intro to Study Group," May 3, 1989. Also, World Homes 1961 Annual Report states: "In 1941 Builders, Inc. built approximately 20 $350 houses in suburban Wichita to sell to war workers for $15 a month. These houses had a WPA outdoor toilet, pitcher pump and water and city electricity. They were outside the city limits on gravel roads. . . . By 1946, these houses had

been annexed to the city. Paved streets, sewers, plumbing, wings and annexes added." Home values double: Family papers, RHG letter to family and WWG, April 17, 1945. "Wichita may have lost": Ibid.

81   **"go build some houses"**—Family papers, WWG speech, "Intro to Study Group," May 3, 1989.

81   **Across town**—Family collection, JKG video interview.

82   **When the war** Swallow Aircraft: Ibid. University of Kansas: Ibid.

82   **Jean Kindel**—Olivia's recollection: Garvey, Olive White, *Once Upon A Family Tree,* p. 266. "All fixed up." Family collection, JKG video interview.

83   **"extremely suspicious"**—Garvey, Olive White, *Once Upon A Family Tree,* p. 266.

83   **As she watched**—Formal winter uniform: Stanton, Shelby, *U.S. Army Uniforms of World War II,* p. 17-31. Includes "olive-drab shade 3 mohair necktie," or "pinks and greens," named for the rose-colored hue in the pants and shirt. "Most interesting man": Family collection, JKG video interview. "came home in a daze": Garvey, Olive White, *Once Upon A Family Tree,* p. 266.

83   **"Willard came back"**—Family collection, JKG video interview (two quotes combined into one).

83   **Getting Jean**—Family papers, WWG letter to JKG, January 6, 1945.

84   **"I left school"**—Harvey Childers interview, July 2006.

84   **At 11 a.m.**—Family papers. Wedding outfit: Family papers, newspaper clipping, "Garvey-Kindel Vows Exchanged This Morning," date unknown.

85   **The first leg**—Muehlebach Hotel: Truman Library.org, www.trumanlibrary. org/places/kc11.htm. "dinner and relaxation:" Family collection, JKG video interview.

86   **family dog**—Family interviews. Many dogs in the family. Major, a collie, (1957); Franz, a poodle; Missie, a wire-haired terrier; Clown, a mix-breed spaniel.

86   **Jean and Willard**—City's largest homebuilder: Family papers. National Housing Hall of Fame application states, "Builders, Inc. was the largest homebuilder in Wichita during the building boom, constructing 2,400 houses, 1,800 apartments, and developing 20 subdivisions." Community play: Family collection, JKG video interview.

86 **Within months**—Children's births: John (1947), Jim (1949), Ann (1951), Emily (1952), Julie (1954), Mary (1957). "Nice, young wife": Family papers, WWG speech, "Intro to Study Group," May 3, 1989.

87 **"He did have a temper"**—Cheryl Gillenwater interview, September 2006.

87 **"a big smooch"**—Mary Theroux interview, June 2007.

88 **"Unabashed, Willard"**—Family papers, Bud Beren 80th Birthday wish to WWG, July 31, 2000.

88 **"When Willard was with Jean"**—Alex Dean interview, April 2007.

CHAPTER SEVEN: FATHER AND SON

89 **"He was a dreamer"**—Family papers, "Kansas Business Hall of Fame Induction of R.H. Garvey," February 9, 1992.

89 **The early 1950s**—Baby boom: *American Demographics,* September 1995, p. 2. "The original baby boom lasted from 1946-1964, produced 77 million people in the U.S. Also, Kallen, Stuart, *A Cultural History of the United States Through the Decades, The 1950s,* p. 53. Record production: U.S. Bureau of Economic Affairs, "Mobilizing Production for Defense: A review of 1951," http://fraser.stlouisfed.org/docs/publications/SCB/pages/1950-1954/9072_1950-1954.pdf. Output of goods and services rose 8 percent to a record total.

89 **By 1951**—RHG memo to his children, April 3, 1951, KHS. Four years earlier, RHG became known as "the largest wheat farmer in the country," having produced a crop of 1 million bushels.

90 **With profits**—Oil exploration: Family papers, WWG speech, "Entrepreneurs and the Competitive Free Market," to the Association of College Entrepreneurs, November 3, 1984. Willard helped his father get into oil exploration. After the 1947 bumper crop, Ray suggested that the company try to spend $300,000 in oil exploration. In December, Ray, struck with diabetes, was resting in Colorado. While he was gone, Willard took the challenge seriously. Willard talked about completing sixty-five deals in three months. "We drilled 12; hit six and two are still producing." In March, he called his father to tell him the $300,000 was gone. Ray responded by telling his son the instructions should have been to spend the money "intelligently." Petroleum, Inc. drilled more than 6,000 wells by 1984. 1951 tax rates: http://www.truthandpolitics.

org/top-rates.php#data-source. Tax worries: RHG memo, April 3, 1951, KHS, Box 25, Series 2, Folder 7.

90 **Willard was**—firmly in charge: Garvey, Olive White, *The Obstacle Race,* p. 143. "The dinner table conversations often dealt with business and there was general discussion. Without effort the family became a business unit with no formal rules. That the father's dealings and decisions were final was accepted without question. And seldom, if ever, was there room for criticism." "To be acquainted": Ibid., p. 228.

90 **"out of mischief"**—RHG memo, April 3, 1951, KHS, Box 24, Series 2.

90 **Working with**—Grain elevator capacity: Miner, Craig, "RH Garvey, Operations Are Interesting," in *John Brown to Bob Dole: Movers and Shakers in Kansas History,* edited by Virgil Dean, p. 253-264. The Jayhawk: RHG memo, November 3, 1951, KHS Box 24, Series 2.

91 **"Willard thinks"**—RHG letter to family, April 3, 1951, KHS, Box 24, Series 2. "Ramrod in there": RHG memo to WWG, September 15, 1956, KHS, Box 30, Series 2.

91 **In the mid 1950s**—Bonnie Brae and subdivisions: Family papers, WWG speech, "Entrepreneurs and the Competitive Free Market," to the Association of College Entrepreneurs, November 3, 1984. Also, WWG nomination to National Housing Hall of Fame, courtesy of Elton Parsons. 1956 interest rates: Bureau of Economic Analysis, "Changing Patterns in Economic Expansion: A Review of 1956," http://library.bea.gov/index.php, p. 4. Rising construction costs: Ibid., p. 24. "The year's 5 percent rise in construction costs was the highest since 1951."

92 **Words of disagreement**—"Needling him": WWG letter to RHG, September 20, 1956, KHS, Box 30, Series 2. "Management by Generalities": RHG letter to WWG, September 15, 1956, KHS, Box 30, Series 2. "You cannot appoint": WWG letter to RHG, September 20, 1956, KHS, Box 30, Series 2.

92 **"copy all of the peanuts"**—Ibid.

93 **"a small emancipation proclamation"**—WWG letter to RHG, October 3, 1956, KHS, Box 30, Series 2.

93 **"constantly upsetting"**—RHG letter to WWG, December 5, 1956, KHS, Box 30, Series 2.

93 **He attacked**—"deflated morale": Ibid. "Too many businesses": RHG letter to WWG, November 26, 1956, KHS, Box 30, Series 2. "Jack of all trades":

RHG memo to WWG, November 26, 1956, KHS, Box 29, Series 2. RHG writes, "We have made most of our construction money, you know, on GI houses and fourplexes to rent. They might still be good ones to pursue."

93 **"Dad was right"**—WWG interview with Craig Miner, October 7, 1993. "Gently leading": Family papers, WWG speech at Plymouth Congregational Church, January 13, 1958.

93 **That guidance**—Builders, Inc. history: Family papers, John Garvey letter to Robert Buck, nominating Willard for the "Rotary Service Above Self Award," November 15, 2001. "Willard's involvement": Elton Parsons interview, October 26, 2007.

94 **Having witnessed**—Truman on Stalin: Mee, Charles, *Meeting at Potsdam*, p. 263. Superpower showdown: Halberstam, David, *The Fifties*, p. 63-77. At Potsdam, Truman asked Stalin for Russia's help in defeating the Japanese, although the atomic bomb (dropped three weeks after the conference) effectively ended the war and halted the need for Soviet assistance. Still, the Russian army began moving into Korea through Manchuria, agreeing to stop at the 38th parallel. Russia built its army in North Korea, while the U.S. presence grew weak. By June 25, 1950, the Russians crossed the border.

95 **36,000 American lives**—*Time* magazine, "The Military," June 12, 2000. Pentagon revises death toll downward from 54,246 to 36,940.

95 **Richard Nixon**—Halberstam, David, *The Fifties*, p. 312. "If there was a politician in America who reflected the Cold War and what it did to the country, it was Richard Nixon," Halberstam writes. "He himself seized on the anti-communist issue earlier and more tenaciously than any other centrist politician in the country. In fact, that was why he had been put on the ticket in the first place."

95 **McCarthyism**—Garvey, Olive White, *The Obstacle Race*, p. 206.

95 **tongue-in-cheek letters**—Ibid.

95 **his own brand of letter-writing**—Cheryl Gillenwater interview, September 2006.

96 **"the most dangerous menace"**—*Time* magazine, "Opinion: Brotherly Blow," August 3, 1953.

96 **"I hope that"**—Family papers, Craig Miner manuscript, p. 29.

96 **Jean Garvey heard**—"right to work" movement: WWG was an early supporter of the "right to work" movement, offering the organization free use of

office space in downtown Wichita. For more on right to work in Kansas, see Miner, Craig, *Kansas: History of the Sunflower State*. Protested bidding practices: Family papers, Miner, Craig, p. 31. WWG "wrote Washington asking about the FHA eliminating the provision that the Secretary of Labor should set minimum wages on federally-supported low-income housing."

97 **"Youth today"**—*Time* magazine, "The Younger Generation," November 5, 1951, cover story.

97 **Ray Garvey . . . health problems**—Garvey, Olive White, *Once Upon A Family Tree*, p. 273.

97 **Garvey Grain elevators**—Ibid., p. 289.

98 **"Garvey's Gravy"**—*Time* magazine, "Garvey's Gravy," June 8, 1959. "In the last four years, Garvey has received $791,488 in support loans for wheat he raised, plus $405,647 in cash from the federal soil bank program for the acreage he left idle."

98 **"He was starting"**—John Garvey interview, February 2008.

99 **Ray Garvey was dead**—Describing car accident: *New York Times*, "Wealthy Kansan Dies In Car Crash," July 2, 1959, reports the car "ran into the bed of a truck that had stopped to make a left-hand turn." OWG's *Once Upon A Family Tree* says "a heavy truck pulled out of a service station into the direct path of the car, and the impact sheared off the right-hand side of the car." (p. 294). A July 2, 1959 report from The Associated Press headlined "Raymond Garvey Killed in Crash" says the truck driver was charged with making an illegal left turn.

100 **"the meal's leftover wishbone"**—Jim Garvey interview, June 2008.

100 **Two hours before**—Funeral services described: *Wichita Eagle*, "Ray H. Garvey Funeral Held," July 4, 1959. "restless energy": Garvey, Olive White, *The Obstacle Race*, p. 229-230.

100 **"valued health above wealth"**—*Topeka Daily Capital*, "Garvey Was Millionaire Who Didn't Act Like Tycoon," July 3, 1959.

100 **a place in Kansas history**—Miner, Craig, "RH Garvey, Operations Are Interesting," in *John Brown to Bob Dole: Movers and Shakers in Kansas History*, p. 253-264.

101 **"You always wonder"**—Family papers. A compilation of two quotes: "You always wonder," interview with Craig Miner, November 20, 1994, and "I

wish…", from WWG speech, "Entrepreneurs and the Competitive Free Market vs. Marxist Mentality," to entrepreneurship class at Wichita State University, June 24, 1980.

CHAPTER EIGHT:
OUR FELLOW OF PERPETUAL MOTION

103 **"Happier in the pursuit"**—WWG interview with Craig Miner, October 7, 1993.

103 **"Before and after"**—WWG interview with Craig Miner, February 24, 1994.

103 **"Mother decided"**—Ruth Fink interview, September 2007.

104 **James Garvey**—Garvey, Olive White, *Once Upon A Family Tree,* p. 297.

104 **$10 million estate**—*Wichita Beacon*, "R.H. Garvey Estate Totals $9,748,424," July 31, 1960.

104 **Bob Page**—Miner, Craig, *Garvey, Inc.,* p. 10. This book details the Garvey family operations in the 14 years after RHG's death.

104 **"Mother and Page"**—Ibid., p. 42.

105 **As Page worked**—IRS disputes: Ibid, p. 7. Pizza Hut: Bob White interview, August 2006. Accounts vary of the actual offer from the Carney brothers. This one is from WWG's November 1987 speech, "Innovation & Enterprise in a Comprehensive Organization," at the University of Michigan. Willard claimed in that speech he asked the Carneys, "What is pizza?" White said the original offer may have been $150,000 for half of the company.

105 **James "Harvey" Childers**—Harvey Childers interview, July 2006.

106 **Jeffersonian individualism**—*Washington World*, Statement of Purpose, October 11, 1961, p. 1.

106 **"Willard would get a thought"**—John Lewis interview, June 2008. Lewis is a Kansas publisher of legal newspapers. He traveled with Willard in the early 1980s.

106 **"Let's double-time"**—Harvey Childers interview, July 2006.

107 **"life like a cavalry charge"**—Martin Eby interview, January 2007.

107 **"What's new?"**—Harvey Childers interview, July 2006. "Willard's motivation was to get people engrossed in things that are productive and to make a better person out of them," Childers said.

107 **"Personally committed"**—Family papers, WWG speech, "Full Gospel Businessman," August 28, 1987.

108 **The opportunities came**—Swimming regimen: Harvey Childers interview, July 2006. "He'd keep anybody waiting to go swim." "Swimming is my drug": WWG interview with Craig Miner, November 18, 1993.

108 **Wet bathing suit**—Harvey Childers interview, July 2006, Cheryl Gillenwater interview, September 2006.

108 **Evenings with Jean**—Alex Dean interview, April 2007.

109 **John Birch Society**—Jean Garvey interview of February 4, 2007 confirms they were at meetings with Koch in his basement.

109 **Mother as standby**—Family papers, WWG speech, "Innovation & Enterprise in a Comprehensive Organization," University of Michigan, November 21, 1987.

109 **"He was curious"**—Mary Knecht interview, February 2007.

110 **"Energizer Bunny"**—Gary Bengochea interview, August 2007, and remarks at Willard Garvey Memorial Service, July 2002.

110 **"Start something new"**—Craig Miner interview, February 2007.

111 **Successes and losses**—Family papers, WWG speech, "Innovation & Enterprise in a Comprehensive Organization," University of Michigan, November 21, 1987.

111 **Solving persistent problems**—*Wichita Eagle,* "She seeks to share small-town spirit with her neighbors in the big city" (Total Quality Wichita), August 12, 1992, p. 1A.

111 **Education vouchers**—WWG letter to *New York Times,* "To Educate Our Children," December 29, 1976.

111 **Downtown arena**—World Homes 1965 Memo, December 20, 1965, WSU-WH Box 96 FF1.

111 **"10,000 more ideas"**—Herb Bevan interview, October 2007. Bevan worked for Bob Page, the trusted chief financial officer of the Garvey enterprise.

111 **Page loses patience**—Miner, Craig, *Garvey, Inc.,* p. 31. "I certainly do not intend to depreciate [the] . . . pioneering success in Peru," Page wrote to a principal in Willard's World Homes project, "but Willard's comment about 'reinforcing . . . successes' gives me somewhat concern since I am sure you,

Willard and I all agree that success is still measured by monetary units, whether they are U.S. dollars, soles or rupees."

111 **"My job each month"**—Nation Meyer interview, September 2006. Page and Willard were attending a local YPO meeting, and each man was asked to introduce himself and his main role.

112 **"Create a bigger pie"**—Family papers, WWG speech, "Entrepreneurs and the Competitive Free Market," to the Association of College Entrepreneurs, November 3, 1984.

112 **"Ideas are cheap"**—WWG weekly memo, January 10, 1966, WSU-WH Box 96 FF6.

112 **GO system**—WWG remarks on "Project Manager Concept and Wichita's Future" to Air Capital Management Conference, February 5, 1966, Wichita. WSU-WH, Ms. 94-09 Finding Aid Intro File. "Project GO" memo 4/12/82 Box 94-09 Box 97 FF24.

113 **"Overcome my shortcomings"**—WWG interview with Craig Miner, November 20, 1994.

113 **GO as recordkeeping system**—Julie Sheppard interview, November 2007.

113 **"Perfect form"**—Mary Theroux interview, June 2007.

113 **GO as mantra**—Family papers, Emily Bonavia interview with Craig Miner.

113 **"Entrepreneur, not an operator"**— Bob White interviews, August 2006 and September 2006.

114 **"A lot of yelling"**—Charlotte Weidman interview, August 2006.

115 **Executive locks horns with Willard**—Letter exchanges between WWG and executive, January 1982, WSU-WH, Ms. 94-9 Box 97 FF15, FF18.

117 **"Could *not* have worked"**—Ruth Fink interview, July 2006.

117 **"Very, very wrong"**—Craig Miner interview, February 2007.

117 **"Drag me into his office"**—Julie Sheppard interview, July 2008.

119 **"Needle. Ball. Airspeed."**—Stanley O. "Bud" Beren interview, March 2007. Beren said the meeting was in the 1960s or 1970s. Beren died on September 2, 2007.

CHAPTER NINE: Growing Up Garveys

145 **"My mother thought"**—Family papers, WWG's remarks to children and grandchildren at his and Jean's fiftieth wedding anniversary party, June 1995.

145 **"Military fashion"**—Family collection, JKG video interview.

146 **Emily left behind**—Emily Bonavia interview, July 2008.

146 **Housekeeper recollections**—Anderson, Dorris Easley, *The Wind in Our Face and For More Than Wages,* p. 83-84.

146 **1952 trip to Europe**—Jean Garvey interview, September 2008.

147 **Souvenirs**—WWG memo, October 6, 1964, WSU-WH Box 96 FF4.

147 **Assigning chores**—Family papers, "This Man," essay by Jim Garvey, 1962.

147 **Compensating for absences**—WWG memo, October 6, 1964, WSU-WH Box 96 FF4.

148 **"She wasn't crazy"**—Mary Theroux interview, June 2007.

148 **Compassionate traits**—Garvey children interviews: Ann (movies), Emily (shoes), Julie (skiing).

149 **To former son-in-law**—Family papers, WWG letter, April 9, 1985.

149 **Children on business trips**—WWG memo, August 4, 1965, WSU-WH Box 96 FF5.

149 **Wishes for children**—Family papers, WWG speech, "Innovations & Enterprise in a Comprehensive Organization," University of Michigan, November 21, 1987.

150 **JKG open-fire cooking**—Family collection, JKG video interview.

150 **To South America**—Anderson, Dorris Easley, *The Wind in Our Face,* p. 83.

150 **1964 itinerary**—WWG memo, November 30, 1964, WSU-WH Box 96 FF4.

150 **Nick Bonavia**—Video of WWG memorial service, July 2002.

150 **1964 trip to Berlin**—WWG memo, November 30, 1964, WSU-WH Box 96 FF4. Also, Jean Garvey interview, February 2008.

151 **Around-the-world trip**—Family papers, itinerary, "Willard Garvey & Family 'Round the World Trip, 4 June-15 August, 1965."

152 **"Usurped land"**—*New York Times,* "Arab Group Pledges War," June 5, 1965, p. 11.

152 **War in India**—*New York Times,* "India-Pakistan War Feared By Shastri," June 7, 1965, p. 6.

152 **Bengal famine**—*The Times of India*, "Winston Churchill to Blame for Bengal Famine," September 9, 2010. Under Shastri, India launched its "Green Revolution," which eventually made the nation self-sufficient in wheat production.

152 **Photos with Shastri**—*Wichita Beacon*, "Returned from World Tour, Garvey Reveals New Plans," August 19, 1965.

152 **Sony Betamax introduction**—Museum of Broadcast Communications, http://www.museum.tv/archives/etv/B/htmlB/betamaxcase/betamaxcase.htm.

152 **"Japanese will dominate"**—WWG weekly memo from Bangkok, Thailand, July 2, 1965. WSU-WH Box 96 FF5 (quote altered for grammar).

153 **"We learned about"**—Emily Bonavia interview, January 2007.

153 **"It completely changed"**—John Garvey interview, February 2008.

154 **WWG on world trip**—*YPO Enterprise,* January 1966.

154 **Plan for children**—WWG memo, November 4, 1964, WSU-WH Box 96 FF4.

155 **Penalties for no weekly report**—WWG memo, December 11, 1967, WSU-WH Box 96 FF7.

155 **"Weird and wonderful"**—Family papers, Mary Theroux letter to her parents, September 25, 1992.

155 **JAEM investment selections**—Julie Sheppard interview, November 2009. Julie also recollects Mary's tears over the fire at the clay company.

155 **JAEM and Vail**—Hauserman, Dick, *The Inventors of Vail.* Appendix C lists all original investors (JAEM Inc.: $3,750).

155 **JAEM net worth**—Family papers, WWG speech, "Entrepreneurs and the Competitive Free Market," to the Association of Collegiate Entrepreneurs, November 3, 1984.

155 **Sisters excluded**—Family papers, RHG letter to WWG, August 26, 1941. "I have no plans for Ruth. I hope she develops some plans of her own."

156 **Children at business meetings**—Mary Theroux comments at WWG Memorial Service, July 2002.

156 **Dissolution of RHG assets**—For more on how Page and the family dissolved RHG's assets, see Craig Miner's *Garvey, Inc.*

156 **Jim Garvey in South America**—Jim Garvey interview, October 2008, and Harvey Childers interview, July 2006.

157 **"Total mobilization"**—WWG memo, August 6, 1966, WSU-WH Box 96 FF6, and Anderson, Dorris Easley, *The Wind in Our Face*, p. 90.

158 **"Please, please, please"**—Family papers, Craig Miner manuscript, p. 43.

160 **Growth in family business**—Family papers, WWG letter to family, January 14, 1982. "The total original capital of all our companies prior to 1980 was less than $360,000. Growth quadrupled between 1959-1972, and quadrupled again from 1972-1981."

CHAPTER TEN:
WHEAT FOR HOMES: EVERY MAN A CAPITALIST

163 **"Property rights"**—Family papers, World Homes Annual Report, quoting WWG remarks to the National Conference on International Economic and Social Development in Washington, D.C., June 16, 1961.

163 **"Itching to get abroad"**—Jean Garvey interview, February 2007.

165 **"In every country"**—Family papers, WWG speech to Downtown Optimist Club, August 5, 1970.

166 **"Single best idea"**—Family papers, WWG speech to Downtown Y Men's Club, December 6, 1996.

166 **Fallout shelters**—*Life* magazine, "H-bomb Hideaway," May 23, 1955, p. 169, and *New York Times* editorial, "Shelter – Right Now," March 13, 1955, detail how Civil Defense Administrator Val Peterson testified before the Senate Armed Services subcommittee and urged citizens to build underground shelters "right now." Willard and Jean's new home on East Douglas included a room that could serve as a bomb shelter.

166 **Eisenhower overseas investment**—Kaufman, Burton I., *Trade and Aid: Eisenhower's Foreign Economic Policy 1953-1961*. In his conclusion on p. 207, Kaufman argues, "Concern with communist expansion continued to be the major motivating force behind the nation's policy toward the Third World as administration officials remained persuaded that economic development would lead to the type of government the United States desired." On p. 208: "The administration's determination to wean Third World countries away from international communism and toward the West, particularly following

the launching of the Soviet economic offensive in the mid-1950s, had largely determined the White House's foreign economic program."

166 **John Birch Society**—Jean Garvey interview, February 2007. Jean remembers going to the Kochs' castle-like home for JBS meetings in a large basement room adorned with big-game mounts. The meetings were not secret; however, "people were very suspicious" of the John Birch Society, she remembered. "They thought they were plotting against the government," she said. "They were trying to save the government really. People are suspicious of you when you're trying to straighten out the government—they think you are subversive."

166 **JBS motto**—JBS founder Robert Welch, a former New England candy maker, once wrote to friends that Eisenhower was "a dedicated, conscious agent of the communist conspiracy." Welch expounded the ideas in his 1963 book *The Politician*, saying he believed the president was more of a communist tool and perhaps unwitting sympathizer. See also Griffin, G. Edward, *The Life and Words of Robert Welch*, p. 225 249. The group changed its motto to "Less government, more responsibility – *and with God's help* – a better world."

167 **Clampdown on housing finance**—In 1954, the U.S. Senate Committee on Banking and Currency investigated irregularities in rental housing financing programs administered by the Federal Housing Administration. Willard testified before the committee in Chicago in September about the financing on several of Builders' projects and was criticized for receiving loan amounts that were above 90 percent of the construction costs. Congressional testimony p. 2332-2343. By 1955, the federal government enacted selective credit controls on VA and FHA loan terms. According to Willard, in 1955 the VA put a limit of twenty units per builder. For more details on the housing slump and subsequent regulations, see Grebler, Leo, "Housing Issues in Economic Stabilization Policy 1960, p. 37-68. www.nber.org/chapters/c2411pdf.

167 **Employee theft**—Howard Wenzel memo to Lee Thayer, "Random Comments on My Experience in Peru," February 25, 1963. Wenzel states that "the first employee I hired turned out to be a swindler" who took about $10,000 from the company. WSU-WH Box 1 FF2.

167 **"spent millions"**—**Harvey** Childers interview, November 2008.

167 **"little came back"**—Harvey Childers interview by Jerome Waltner, July 27, 1993, WSU-WH Box 100.

167 **Grain elevator capacity**—Miner, Craig, *Kansas: The History of the Sunflower State,* p. 340, states that in 1958, Ray Garvey's Wichita elevator had a capacity of 23 million bushels, and was "expanding as fast as tanks could be added." Ray Garvey also benefited from federal incentives to grow and store grain. The *Time* magazine article, "Garvey's Gravy" (June 8, 1959), reported that Garvey received an accelerated five-year tax write-off to build the grain elevators, as well as support loans for the wheat he grew on his own farms, along with $14 million annually to store government surpluses and, later, additional cash incentives to leave land unfarmed in an effort to reduce surpluses. Willard and his father's participation in these types of programs were often the crux of long-standing criticism.

167 **1958 food surplus**—WWG estimate per testimony to Boeschenstein Committee, August 28, 1958, Richard Nixon Pre-Presidential Collection: General Correspondence Series 320, Richard Millhouse Nixon Presidential Library, Yorba Linda, California.

168 **Cooley amendment**—Family papers. Harvard Business School case study includes explanation of how when wheat or rice was sold in countries such as Peru or India, the U.S. government was allowed to accept local currency in return so as not to aggravate the balance of payments problems in underdeveloped countries. As a result, large reserves of local currency belonging to the United States built up in the banks of the underdeveloped countries. The Cooley amendment allowed 25 percent of the funds for loans to American companies making investments in that country. See also Congressional Record, May 4, 1966, p. A2414-16. re: The Cooley Loan Program American Free Enterprise Abroad, extension of remarks of Hon. Harold D. Cooley. Later the program extended to U.S. banks, urging them to re-lend to local enterprises. Cooley said in the testimony, "I am proud that it has planted the flag of American free enterprise in many foreign places."

168 **Soviet economic expansion**—Kaufman, Burton I., *Trade and Aid*, p. 155. Russia was providing generous credits and grants to undeveloped countries around the world. In 1958, the Soviet economy grew by 7 percent a year compared to a 3 percent annual increase in the U.S. economy.

168 **"hit them where they live"**—Statements about WWG's feelings toward capitalism and communism were read into the Senate Congressional Record on May 2, 1960, p. 8401.

168 **Boeschenstein Committee testimony**—Nixon Pre-Presidential Collection: General Correspondence Series 320, Richard Millhouse Nixon Presidential

Library, Yorba Linda, California. The testimony was also an endorsement for giving "government clearance" to Private Enterprise, Inc., an organization founded by Bill Graham of Graham Oil Company in Wichita to promote private investment in India.

169 **Latin American home loans**—Atkeson, Tim, "Aid for Latin American Housing," *The George Washington Law Review*, Vol. 31, No. 3, March 1963.

169 **Unavailability of mortgage loans**—Howard Wenzel interview, March 2009.

170 **Boeschenstein final report**—*New York Times*, "Overseas Investments Urged," October 19, 1958. The article is a brief summary on a preliminary report by the Committee on World Economic Practices, headed by Harold Boeschenstein.

170 **Homes for every country**—*American Builder*, August 1960.

170 **"Five-day sieges"**—Ruth Fink interview, July 2006. "Nobody held anything back," Ruth said. See also, WWG weekly memo, May 20, 1968, WSU-WH Box 96 FF8.

170 **Pakistan currency available**—Howard Wenzel interview, March 2009.

170 **Last conversation with RHG**—WWG interview with Jerome Waltner and Mark Unruh, WSU-WH Box 100.

171 **Nixon visit to Lima**—*New York Times*, "Nixon is Stoned by Peru Rioters Headed by Reds," May 9, 1958, p. 1. Hoping to draw some of the much-needed U.S. economic help, the Peruvian government later painted the incident as an isolated one and distanced itself from the protesters. For his own account of the events surrounding his weeklong mission to Latin America, see Nixon, Richard, *In the Arena*, p. 178-181.

171 **Lima population**—A 1958 World Homes video reported that Lima's population grew from 800,000 in 1940 to 2.3 million in 1958. In actuality, population was more like 600,000 in 1940 and 1.9 million by 1960, according to http://www.inei.gob.pe/biblioineipub/bancopub/Est/LIb0002/cap0101.htm.

171 **"People had to build"**—Howard Wenzel interview, March 2009.

171 **Bill Graham**—Bill Graham ran a successful oil company, but a great deal of his attention went to Private Enterprise, Inc., the organization promoting private investment in India. Jim Donaldson, another employee Willard hired away from Graham, was tapped for the Peru assignment; however, he died suddenly while exploring options in Pakistan weeks before Ray Garvey's

death. According to Wenzel, "Willard decided to put Pakistan on the back burner and I was sent to Peru."

171 **First loan by U.S.**—Thayer, Leo, *Hogares Peruanos SA. A 1960 Study of Private U.S. Enterprise in Foreign Housing*. Thayer, an assistant professor of administration at the University of Wichita, prepared an International Case Study for classroom discussion by the Harvard University Graduate School of Business Administration.

172 **Cost of Lima homes**—*Wichita Eagle*, "Local Builders Look Abroad," April 11, 1961.

172 **10 percent loans**—Reports of interest on these loans range from 8 to 12%. Tim Atkeson says 10 percent in his March 1963 *George Washington Law Review* article.

172 **"To own a house"**—Rodolpho Salinas interview, November 2008.

172 **World Homes federal financing**—The federal financing was a combination of things at various times, including grants from USAID, and assistance from Father Dan McClennan's savings and loan, which operated on funds from the Inter-American Development Bank (see August 1962 memo from Howard Wenzel). WSU-WH Box 58 FF23.

173 **"private property incentive"**—WWG to President John F. Kennedy, May 9, 1961, White House Central Name File, Box 955, John F. Kennedy Library, Boston.

173 **JFK's Alliance for Progress**—World Homes 1961 Annual Report quotes WWG's remarks as a member on a panel on housing at the Eighth National Conference on International Economic and Social Development, June 1961. See WSU-WH Ms. 96-09 Finding Aid Intro File.

173 **"I therefore urge"**—http://www.jfklink.com/speeches/jfk/publicpapers/1961/jfk244_61.html.

173 **"deep philosophical sentiment"**—WWG interview with Jerome Waltner and Mark Unruh, July 21, 1993, WSU-WH Box 100.

173 **Kennedy support**—Ibid.

173 **World Homes in 1966**—WWG remarks to World Homes' First Annual Seminar, November 14, 1966, WSU-WH Box 96 FF6.

173 **World Homes in 2020**—Family papers, WWG speech before the Downtown Optimist Club, Wichita, August 5, 1970.

174 **"do not intend"**—Miner, Craig, *Garvey, Inc.,* p. 31.

174 **"Sometimes the bottom line"**—WWG interview with Jerome Waltner and Mark Unruh, July 21, 1993, WSU-WH Box 100.

174 **Construction totals**—World Homes built at least 2,000 homes, including approximately 800 in Peru, 474 in Colombia, 160 in Mexico, and 464 in Bolivia. Hearings before the Committee on Agriculture, U.S. House of Representatives, February 28-March 1966, put the total at the time at 1,670.

174 **Peru coup, 1962**—Keen, Benjamin, and Mark Wasserman, *A Short History of Latin America,* p. 394-395.

174 **junta tank**—Rabe, Stephen G., *The Most Dangerous Area in the World: John F. Kennedy Confronts Communist Revolution in Latin America,* p. 120.

174 **"situation is fast deteriorating"**—Howard Wenzel memo to Floyd Baird, July 12, 1962, WSU-WH Box 58 FF23.

175 **Meeting with General Godoy**—WWG memo, August 22, 1962, WSU-WH Box 7 FF27.

175 **LaPaz, Bolivia**—Bolivia manager T.R. Hawthorn memo, "Review of the San Miguel Housing Project," August 14, 1970, courtesy Bob White.

175 **Bolivian Revolutionary Front**—Zunes, Stephen, "The United States and Bolivia," *Foreign Policy in Focus,* September 18, 2008.

175 **"under constant harassment"**—T.R. Hawthorn memo to Terrence McDonald, June 26, 1970, WSU-WH Box 5 FF4.

176 **"least attractive areas"**—James Van Pelt letter to Douglas Henderson, June 13, 1968, WSU-WH Box 4 FF12.

176 **Ché death**—Airgram to the State Department, "Official Confirmation of Death of Che Guevara," October 18, 1967, George Washington University National Security Archive Book No. 5.

176 **"rat's nest"**—WWG interview with Jerome Waltner and Mark Unruh, July 21, 1993, WSU-WH, Box 100.

176 **Delays of Cooley funds**—James Van Pelt letter to Senator Frank Carlson, December 11, 1964, WSU-WH Box 2 FF3.

176 **Delays in Colombia**—Van Pelt memo to Agency for International Development executive Fred Kayser, July 10, 1963, WSU-WH Box 1 FF7.

176 **Colombia and CIA**—*CIA Weekly Review,* "Cuban Subversive Activities in Latin America 1959-1968," February 16, 1968. CIA Freedom of Information

Act report released February 12, 1997, and available on CIA website under FOIA Electronic Reading Room. See also "A Survey of Communism in Latin America," November 1, 1965, approved for release June 2007.

177 **"Patriotism and government"**—WWG interview with Jerome Waltner, February 23, 1994, WSU-WH Box 100, Tape 2.

177 **"10 years and a million dollars"**—WWG interview with Jerome Waltner and Mark Unruh, July 21, 1993, WSU-WH Box 100.

177 **Raymon Engineering Works**—Precis, REW—Garvey Grain Company Collaboration, Matthew J. Kust, WSU-WH Box 85, FF4. An expert on India, Kust served as legal counsel to U.S. Embassies in South Asia and Southeast Asia from 1951-1954.

177 **"rich uncle"**—Harvey Childers interview, November 2008.

179 **"We could not adapt"**—WWG interview with Craig Miner, May 12, 1994.

CHAPTER ELEVEN: The Doers and the Thinkers

181 **"doer, performer, creator"**—WWG interview with Craig Miner, September 9, 1993.

182 **Bohemian Grove memories**—Family papers, WWG speech at Plymouth Congregational Church, September 6, 1995. Details of his activities and various talks made during the July 1995 Bohemian Grove encampment are included here based on interviews with family and friends.

182 **Lakeside Talks**—*Sonoma County Free Press*, "Bohemian Grove Encampment Highlights of Lakeside Talks over Time," July 2003. According to this list, Cheney spoke in 1991.

182 **"My modus operandi"**—WWG interview with Craig Miner, June 9, 1994.

183 **"We'd wonder"**—Mary Theroux interview, June 2007.

183 **"delightful afternoon"**—WWG interview with Craig Miner, September 11, 1995.

183 **"Government corrupts everybody"**—WWG interview with Craig Miner, September 6, 1995.

184 **"Jack Kemp speech"**—Nation Meyer interview, September 2006.

184 **"2.5 million acres"**—Although Willard may have been the largest private landowner in the state of Nevada, the 2.5 million number he liked to bandy

about included land leased from the federal government. The closer estimate on his land acreage was somewhere around 200,000 acres.

184 **"never lost a beat"**—Family papers, Charles West letter to Craig Miner, Miner manuscript.

184 **"talk to anybody"**—David Theroux interview, June 2007.

185 **YPO history**—YPO.org and family papers, WWG essay, "YPO Early Years (1950-1970), 1999.

186 **"far superior to the presidents"**—WWG interview with Craig Miner, February 17, 1994.

187 **Patek Philippe pocket watch**—The Time Museum Collection, Caretaker of the World's Timepieces. www.timemuseum.com, Forbes.com

187 **"boundless energy"**—Seth Atwood interview, July 2006.

187 **Minerva idea**—Family papers; Atwood, Seth, "The Republic of Minerva: Adventures of Seth G. Atwood, Willard Garvey and John Templeton." This was distributed to members of the Garvey family in 2004, two years after Willard's death.

187 **Nationalization efforts**—Rodolfo Salinas interview, November 2008.

187 **Cambodia bombing**— Karnow, Stanley. *Vietnam,* p. 591.

188 **"Greatest stock picker"**—*Money* magazine, January 1999, http://www.templetonprize.org/sirjohntempleton.html.

188 **"This is the answer!"**—Jean Garvey interview, February 2007.

189 **Palmyra**—In 2000, The Nature Conservancy bought Palmyra from the Fullard-Leo family for $37 million, and its shores are now a National Wildlife Refuge managed by the U.S.

190 **Caribbean-Pacific Enterprises**—Oliver's group is also referred to as the Ocean Life Research Foundation. *Barron's,* "Utopia on the Rocks, Or, the Short, Unhappy Life of the Republic of Minerva," March 26, 1973.

190 **Minerva investments**—Associated Press, "Republic of Minerva Will be Heard From," December 1972, mentions that seven stockholders invested a total of $250,000 in Minerva. However, an April 1972 contract from Caribbean-Pacific Enterprises estimated it would need at least $425,000 for "the continuation" of the project. Atwood said he himself put about $100,000 into it.

190 **"chaos and tyranny"**—Atwood, Seth, "The Republic of Minerva:

Adventures of Seth G. Atwood, Willard Garvey and John M. Templeton," p. 16, Exhibit 8.

190 **Minerva as a new nation**—Horn, Lawrence, "To Be or Not to Be: The Republic of Minerva; Nation Founding by Individuals," *Columbia Journal of Transnational Law*, 520, 1973. Published accounts indicate two different dates for the flag planting. *Ocean Science News* of April 7, 1972 gives the August '71 date, as does Horn's treatise, which cites a letter from a New Zealand lawyer. The *San Francisco Examiner*, "A Nation, From Pacific Depths," March 5, 1972, mentions the August date. However, *Barron's* "Utopia on the Rocks" has it as January 1972.

190 **Declaration of sovereignty**—Family papers, Atwood, Seth, "The Republic of Minerva," p. 10, Exhibit 4a, is copy of the January 19 letter from Minerva's Secretary of State to U.S. Secretary of State.

191 **Another $400,000 needed**—Family papers, Morris Davis memo to WWG, April 26, 1972.

191 **Land creation**—Estimates range from 15 acres, per Strauss, Erwin S., *How to Start Your Own Country*, p. 115, to 2,500 acres, *Ocean Science News*, April 7, 1972.

191 **$50,000 loan to Caribbean-Pacific**—Family papers, May 1, 1972. Also, a July 26, 1972, letter that has WWG paying $29,751.79 for a 45 percent interest in the *Ranginui*.

191 **Tongan king and Nixon**—March 22, 1972 letter to President Nixon from Tongan king, White House Central Files, [Ex] CO 151, Tonga, Kingdom of, 1/1/71 [Box 69].

191 **"empires on our doorstep"**—*New York Times*, "Pacific Islanders Fight Reef Plan," February 27, 1972.

191 **"refuge station"**—*San Francisco Examiner*, "A Nation From Pacific Depths," March 5, 1972, p. 1.

192 **Tongan flag raising**—Family papers, *Tonga Chronicle*, "King to Lead Flagraising on Teleki on Monday," June 22, 1972.

192 **Minerva gold coin**—Family papers, WWG letter to Michael Oliver, December 31, 1974.

CHAPTER TWELVE: DON'T FENCE ME IN

195 **"The private property owner"**—WWG Letter to the Editor, *Humboldt Sun,* September 8, 1981.

195 **"foundation of individual freedom"**—Family papers, WWG remarks to the National Conference on International Economic and Social Development in Washington, D.C., June 16, 1961. Willard was speaking as a member of a panel on housing. This is a paraphrase from a John Adams quote: "Property is surely a right of mankind, as really as liberty," or Thomas Jefferson's belief that "Property is the foundation of all civilized society."

196 **Federal land in Nevada**—Nevada Division of Forestry, Department of Conservation and Natural Resources, "State Natural Resource Assessment 2010." This source was one of several reviewed that stated that 86.1 percent of Nevada lands are controlled by the federal government. Many sources use 87 percent, but that number has since come into question. See Myers, Dennis, "The 87 percent deception," *Reno News & Review,* April 1, 2010. http://www.newsreview.com/reno/content?oid=1397212.

196 **$80 million IRS debt**—Miner, Craig, *Garvey, Inc.,* p. 43.

196 **Deductions**—Ibid., p. 56.

196 **U.S. tax rate data**—U.S. Department of Revenue, "Corporate Income Tax Brackets and Rates 1909-2002." http://www.irs.gov/pub/irs-soi/02corate.pdf.

197 **Oklahoma ranch**—*The Lawton Constitution,* "Large Oklahoma Ranch is Sold," October 25, 1961.

197 **Sibling ranch purchases**—Miner, Craig, *Garvey, Inc.,* p. 60.

197 **1962 Paradise Valley purchase**—*Nevada State Journal,* "Paradise Valley: Century-old Garden Spot," January 27, 1963.

197 **18,000 head of cattle**—Miner, *Garvey, Inc.,* p. 43.

197 **"Tremenderosa"**—Ibid, p. 62.

198 **19,000 cows**—*Humboldt County News,* April 19, 2006. Story confirmed with Larry Hill. "If they left it alone, (Willard) would have ended up with more than he guaranteed," Hall said.

199 **Presented McCleary with a check**—Miner, Craig, *Garvey, Inc.,* p. 61.

199 **Payout to McCleary**—Miner, Craig, *Garvey, Inc.,* p. 90.

199 **No fences**—Larry Hill interview, August 2007. The Owyhee Indian Reservation lies to the east on the Idaho border, about 80 miles and a few mountain ranges away from Orovada and more than 200 miles by car. Jordan Valley is north of Nevada on the Idaho border, about 170 miles from Paradise Valley.

200 **"gorgeous beautiful country"**—Family papers, WSU-WH Box 96 FF4.

202 **Gold in 1850**—Thomson, David, *In Nevada: The Land, The People, God and Chance*, p. 24. Thomson calls it "sludgy blue-black sand." Laxalt, Robert, *Nevada: A History*, p. 36, calls it "heavy black mud."

203 **Fate of Humboldt River dam**—Nevada Division of Water Planning, Humboldt River Chronology—Part II, p. 23. http://water.nv.gov/WaterPlanning/humboldt/PDFs/hrc-pt2.pdf.

203 **Comstock water**—Davis, Sam B., *The History of Nevada Vol. 1*, (1912) Chapter 16, "Water Supply of the Comstock," courtesy of The Nevada Observer, www.nevadaobserver.com. The chapter describes San Francisco hydraulic engineer Herman Schussler's efforts to install a pipeline to Virginia City from the high Sierra Nevada 35 miles away.

203 **Residents cheered**—Nevada State Engineer's Office, "Water for Nevada: Nevada's Water Resources," State of Nevada Water Planning Report, No. 3, October 1971, p. 3.

203 **Early irrigation**—Nevada Division of Water Planning, Humboldt River Chronology, Part II, p. 23-24. http://water.nv.gov/WaterPlanning/humboldt/PDFs/hrc-pt2.pdf.

203 **Nevada crops**—Laxalt, Robert, *Nevada: A History*, p. 115.

203 **"The great problem"**—Davis, Sam B., *The History of Nevada Vol. 1*, (1913) Chapter 40, "Water Supply and Irrigation" by F.L. Peterson, p. 756-770, courtesy of The Nevada Observer, www.nevadaobserver.com.

204 **Willow Creek Reservoir**—Nevada Division of Water Planning, Humboldt River Chronology, Part II, p. 61. http://water.nv.gov/WaterPlanning/humboldt/PDFs/hrc-pt2.pdf.

204 **Lovelock Reservoir capacity**—One acre foot, or the quantity of water needed to cover one acre to a depth of one foot, is equivalent to about 325,850 gallons. 48,000 x 325,850 = 15,640,800,000.

205 **Rye Patch construction**—Nevada Division of Water Planning, Humboldt River Chronology, Part III, p. 18.

205 **"change the environment"**—Harvey Childers interview, July 2006.

205   **2,100 acres**—Nevada Department of Wildlife, http://www.hcnv.us:1403/
cadocs/08_02_10/NDOW/Chimney%20Res%20Proposal%207_15_10.pdf

205   **Local ranchers' fear**—Julie Sheppard interview, 2009.

205   **Water yield from streams**—*Humboldt Sun*, "Public Meet on Humboldt Water
Plans Set May 16," May 8, 1974, p. 1.

205   **"water fights"**—*Humboldt Sun*, "'Prior Water Rights Will Be Protected,'
Westergard Says," May 22, 1974.

206   **Engineer Kurt Schoufler**—*Humboldt Sun*, "Trip to Chimney Dam," October 2, 1974.

206   **Humboldt County Fair and Recreation**—*Humboldt Sun*, "County Board
Buying Water," September 18, 1974.

206   **"raving and raving"**—Gary Bengochea interview, August 2007.

207   **Massive blast**—*Humboldt Sun*, "Trip to Chimney Dam," October 2, 1974.

208   **"Homeowners should unite"**—*Humboldt Sun*, November 5, 1981, WSU-
WH Box 97 FF 24.

209   **18,000-acre land swap**—*Humboldt Sun*, "Garvey Proposed Land Exchange 5
Years Ago," October 7, 1976.

209   **"millionaire businessman"**—*Reno Gazette-Journal*, "Ranchers wrangle over grazing fees," May 11, 1987, p. C1.

210   **140,000 acres**—The Land Report, "100 Largest USA Landowners," Fall
2010. Emily Garvey listed at No. 63 on p. 50.

210   **Drained for restocking**—*Silver Pinyon Journal*, "NDOW presents proposal
to drain Chimney Reservoir," August 4, 2010.

CHAPTER THIRTEEN: Willard's Wichita

213   **"a model city"**—Family papers, WWG comments to Eagle Scout Court of
Honor, Plymouth Congregational Church, August 19, 1991.

214   **"one-man assault"**—*Wichita Eagle-Beacon*, "Garvey Ideas on Jail Will Be
Heard," March 20, 1986, p. D6.

214   **Jail debate**—Family collection, tape of KSN "Perspectives," March 23, 1986.

215   **HOT**—*Wichita Eagle-Beacon*, "HOT Hit Paydirt With Campaign to Keep
Tax Lid," p. 1A, November 19, 1981 (WSU-WH Box 97 FF24); "HOT's
Grund May Challenge Voting by Mail," p. 1C, February 24, 1986.

215 **"bamboozle" voters**—Ibid., "Garvey's Pitch for Smaller Jail Angers Witsman," March 22, 1986, p. 1B.

215 **"constitutional standards or Garvey's law"**—*Wichita Eagle-Beacon,* "Garvey, County Get Testy Over Proposal for Jail," March 27, 1986, p. 1B.

215 **"petty tyrants"**—Ibid.

215 **"economic sanity"**—Ibid., "Public Could End Debate Over Jail," March 16, 1986, p. 14A.

215 **"guy whose dry cleaning"**—Ibid., "Decision Encourages Jail Critic," April 11, 1986, p. 9A.

216 **"Wichitans love to hate"**—*Wichita CentreCity News,* "Willard Garvey: His 'EPIC' Achievement Downtown," November 1987, p. 2.

216 **"If I hear of Willard"**—*Wichita Eagle,* Letter to the Editor, signed by Patrick Blanchard, January 18, 1988.

216 **"Willard was a pain"**—Peg Morrison interview, April 2007.

216 **Willard Garvey Crime Prevention Awards**—Bobby Stout interview, June 2011.

216 **"long-winded and abrasive"**—Martin Eby interview, January 2007.

217 **Jail opening**—*ichita Eagle,* "Judge Gives Stamp of Approval to New Jail; Overcrowding, Rats, Things of The Past," January 9, 1990, p. 10D.

217 **$23.4 million jail**—*Wichita Eagle,* "Bonds Proposed for Financing Jail; County to Hear Plan Tomorrow," February 13, 1990, p. 1D. Background on the history of Sedgwick County Jail: http://www.sedgwickcounty.org/SHERIFF/CJCC_Master_Plan.pdf.

217 **$32 million addition**—Minutes, Regular Meeting, Board of County Commissioners, Sedgwick County, February 9, 2000, http://www.sedgwickcounty.org/countyclerk/2000/regular/reg02-09.pdf.

217 **More jail expansions**—*Wichita Eagle,* "County Commission Candidates Weigh In on Jail Overcrowding," July 3, 2010, p. 1A.

217 **Karl Peterjohn voting record on federal grants**—*Wichita Eagle,* "Grant vote won't save tax dollars," August 13, 2010; on county budget: Ibid., "There are limits to funding of Project Access," April 26, 2011, p. 7A.

218 **"Willard's the guy"**—Karl Peterjohn interview, March 2007.

218 **Peterjohn and no-tax pledge**—*Wichita Eagle,* "Board OKs Compromise on LOB," December 9, 1997, p 1A.

218 **KTN and Garvey**—Ibid., "Best Election Races Are in Wichita," October 7, 2000, p. 7A.

218 **"tilting at windmills"**—Karl Peterjohn interview, March 2007.

218 **"All that counts"**—Family papers, WWG speech on "Goals for Wichita," January 1973.

219 **Tax levies**—*Wichita Eagle,* "Downtown Tax Plan Rejected," March 4, 1998, p. 1A.

219 **Air conditioning in public schools**—*Wichita Eagle,* "Can Schools Be Cooled for $10 Million?" February 20, 2000, p. 1A.

219 **Total Quality Wichita**—*Wichita Eagle,* "She Seeks To Share Small-Town Spirit with Her Neighbors in the Big City," August 12, 1992, p. 1A.

219 **Buying Wichita newspaper**—Miner, Craig, *Garvey, Inc.,* p. 51.

219 **KTQW**—*Wichita Eagle,* "KTQW-TV49 Wins Five National Awards," October 23, 2004, p. 4F.

220 **"private with City Hall"**—Family papers, WWG speech, "Declaration of Independence for 1976," Kansas City Rotary Club, September 18, 1969.

220 **"major business opportunity"**—Family papers, "Go-4-It," WWG speech to Wichita Business College Commencement, July 17, 1987.

220 **Privatization in Wichita**—*Wichita Eagle-Beacon,* "Panel Pushes City to Use Private Firms," January 9, 1989, p. 1C.

220 **"economic emancipation"**—Family papers, WWG speech, "Declaration of Independence for 1976," Kansas City Rotary Club, September 18, 1969.

220 **A Wichita Countdown**—Family papers, "Our Town 2001—Wichita Countdown," National Center for Privatization, 1987.

221 **Task force on volunteerism**—Family papers, "What is a Volunteer?" WWG speech to the National Society of Fundraising Executives, October 26, 1989. In this speech, Garvey said he was part of the 1968 Presidential Task Force on Volunteerism. An earlier draft of the remarks said "Richard Cornuelle, chairman, invited me to join his task force on volunteerism." Garvey's appointment to National Center for Voluntary Action, National Center for Voluntary Action, 6/3/69-12/28/70, Box FG 259, Nixon Presidential Returned

Materials Collection, White House Central Files. Richard Nixon Presidential Library and Museum, Yorba Linda, California, National Archives and Records Administration. See also "Mr. Nixon's Volunteerism," *Commonweal*, January 16, 1970. Article describes how Richard Nixon formed "The Cabinet Committee on Voluntary Action in 1969" with George Romney serving as Chairman of the Cabinet Committee.

221 **"best kind of city"**—Family papers, WWG interview with Craig Miner, June 9, 1994.

221 **"manage more effectively"**—Family papers, WWG speech on "Declaration for Independence for 1976," Kansas City Rotary Club, September 18, 1969.

221 **"private solutions to public problems"**—WWG speech, "Project Manager Concept and Wichita's Future," to the Air Capital Management Conference, February 5, 1966, WSU-WH Finding Aid Intro File.

221 **"to loaf"**—Garvey, Olive White, *Once Upon A Family Tree*, p. 310.

222 **"in awe of"**—Mary Theroux interview, June 2007.

222 **Olive Garvey death**—*Wichita Eagle*, "Olive Garvey Gave Range to New Ideas, Decorum," May 5, 1993, p. 1A.

222 **"cockroaches"**—Interview with Mary Knecht, February 2007, and Cheryl Gillenwater, September 2006.

222 **"ceremonial occasions"**—Family papers, "Thinking the Unthinkable," WWG speech to Pachyderm Club, September 30, 1988.

222 **"look down on City Hall"**—Family papers, WWG speech, "Entrepreneurs and the Competitive Free Market," to the Association of Collegiate Entrepreneurs," November 3, 1984.

222 **"exerts influence"**—*Wichita Eagle-Beacon*, "Garvey says time at hand for his ideas," January 14, 1982, p 1D.

223 **"par for the course"**—*Wichita Eagle-Beacon*, "Vision now towering reality," November 11, 1987, p. 12A.

223 **Garvey Center details**—See Miner, Craig, *Garvey, Inc.,* p 63-68, for more on Garvey Center history.

224 **August 11 shooting details**—*Wichita Beacon*, "Motive in Sniper Attack," April 12, 1976, p. 1A; "Sniper's Movements Traced," p. 1A; and "Sniper Sights Trio on Roof," p 3A. Also, Peg Morrison interview, April 2007.

225 **$10,000 contribution**—*Wichita Eagle and Beacon,* "Fund to Cite Police, Aid, Sniping Victims," August 15, 1976, p. 16A; "August Eleven Council to Aid Crime Victims, Reward Valor," December 5, 1976 p. 1A.

226 **"guessed" on flash card**—Family collection, JKG video interview.

227 **"economic brainwashing"**—*Wichita Eagle-Beacon,* "Time to say no to tax wasters," WWG Letter to the Editor, May 13, 1985.

227 **"archaic fetishes"**—*New York Times,* WWG Letter to the Editor, December 29, 1976.

228 **Outgrew that building**—Mary Theroux interview, June 2007.

228 **"tendency to dominate"**—WWG interview with Craig Miner, October 7, 1993.

228 **"got rid of six"**—Ibid.

228 **Independent school addition**—*Wichita Eagle,* "Independent Addition Inspires Pride: Public High Schools Gain New Competitor," March 15, 1994, p. 1D.

229 **1966 college plan**—*Wichita Eagle and Beacon,* "New Four-Year College Urged for Downtown," February 5, 1966; "Core Area Will Double As Campus if Plan OKd," February 6, 1966.

229 **Olive Garvey in 1966**—Miner, Craig, *Garvey, Inc.,* p. 81.

230 **John Templeton's Christian University**—WWG weekly report, May 16, 1966. WSU-WH Box 96 FF6.

230 **"self-reliant individuals"**—Family papers, WWG speech, "20/20 Foresight, or What do I know now Charlie Brown," Downtown Optimist Club, Wichita, August 5, 1970.

231 **30-year-old idea**—*Wichita Eagle,* "A law school in Wichita may soon become a reality," April 14, 1994, p. 1D.

CHAPTER FOURTEEN: Final Challenges

233 **"retire in the common sense"**—Overview to Directors and Managers, Garvey Industries, October 31, 1981, WSU-WH Box 97 FF24.

233 **"live forever"**—Ruth Fink interview, July 2006.

233 **"most fit person"**—Roger Turner interview, May 2007.

234 **"Fear of death and dying"**—Family papers, letter to Craig Miner, February 28, 1994.

234 **Holistic treatment**—*Wichita Eagle,* "Physician, Iconoclast Riordan Dies at 72," January 9, 2005, p. 1B.

235 **"most valuable asset"**—Family papers, video, Tall Timbers Talk, July 1995.

236 **Family support of YMCA**—*Wichita Eagle,* "Greater Wichita YMCAs celebrate 125 years," January 10, 2010, p. 1B. See also, *Wichita Eagle,* "YMCA honors program pioneers," September 29, 2003, p. 1B; Family papers, Introduction by Dick DeVore, South Branch dedication, September 1, 1999; and *Wichita Eagle,* "Former Biddy courts get new life as home for Y basketball," June 29, 2011, p. 1B.

236 **Garvey Center apartments**—*Wichita Eagle,* "Downtown Landmark Faces Rebirth," January 22, 1999, p. 1A.

236 **"a gentler presence"**—Craig Miner interview, February 2007.

236 **"shot of compassion"**—Cheryl Gillenwater interview, September 2006.

237 **"The last 10 years"**—John Garvey interview, February 2008.

237 **Children underperforming**—U.S. Department of Education, National Center for Education Statistics, http://nces.ed.gov/pubsearch/pubsinfo. asp?pubid=2000062.

237 **"voice in the wilderness"**—Family papers, WWG to family in Tall Timbers Talk, July 1995.

237 **"almost always right"**—Family papers, WWG speech, "Entrepreneurs and the Competitive Free Market," to the Association of Collegiate Entrepreneurs, November 3, 1984.

238 **"all the freedom"**—Family papers, video, Tall Timbers Talk, July 1995.

238 **"About 50 students"**—*Wichita Eagle,* "New site bought for law school," January 24, 1996, p. 7B.

238 **Presidents College School of Law**—Dixie Madden interview, February 2007, and notes, July 2011.

240 **Kept swimming**—Andy Garvey interview, November 2007.

240 **Service Above Self Award**—Mary Knecht interview, February 2007; *Wichita Eagle,* "School Building Projects Trimmed," January 16, 2000, p. 1A.

241 **"Dad needed help"**—Jim Garvey remarks at WWG Memorial Service, July 30, 2002.

242 **"Dad swimming through the sky"**—Julie Sheppard interview, July 2007.

242 **"Goodbye to a friend"**—Jean Garvey interview, February 2007.

242 **"Wichita without Willard"**—*Wichita Eagle,* "Builder Willard Garvey's Legacy is His Civic Ideology," July 30, 2002, p. 6A.

243 **"City Hall is a cheat"**—*Wichita Eagle,* "Different Rules," Readers Views, March 30, 2001.

243 **"We didn't agree"**—Bob Knight interview, February 2007.

243 **"none of us changed"**—Ruth Fink interview, July 2006.

243 **"Blander"**—Karl Peterjohn interview, March 2007.

244 **"Humorously enough"**—Family papers, WWG interview with Craig Miner, September 2, 1993.

244 **"this end result"**—Correspondence with Dixie Madden, July 2011.

244 **"an amazing citizen"**—Bob Knight interview, February 2007.

INDEX

ACKNOWLEDGEMENTS

I'D LIKE TO EXTEND a sincere thank you to all those who helped this project and this writer along the way.

Dear old friends, many of them talented journalists and writers, did me a favor by searching a database, an archive or a library stack, hosting me in their guestroom, or offering encouragement on a variety of levels. They include: Sandra Block and Denny Gainer, Kathleen Sullivan, Janet Moore, Melanie Payne, Geoff Gevalt, Leslie Lombino, Sy Montgomery and Howard Mansfield, David Bauder, Jacqui Salmon, Bob Paynter and Anita Silvey.

Newer friends were cheerleaders who urged me to keep going or led me to resources that permitted it: Nadine Boughton, Hannah Grove, Carolyn Cichon, Judith Nies, Valerie Wall, Peg Leary, Dee Morris and Mark Ziady. Doug Shoop of DSA Architects offered a Medford office and his expert computing support. In Wichita, Elizabeth Winterbone (WWED) provided personal assistance and guidance, while a lucky bid led me to gracious author Robert Beattie.

Scholars Elizabeth and Kenneth McEnaney, my loving and brilliant niece and nephew were always at the ready to help their auntie from the campuses of Columbia University and MIT.

Researchers Matthew Hogan, Daran Doolcy, Rita Sevart and Ben Jenkins dug up the details that made for a better story. In beloved Nevada, Mike and Suzie Quilici did the same. The good folks at

Stonehouse Country Inn welcomed me back. Mary Nelson of Wichita State University Libraries' Department of Special Collections was a consummate professional.

Jean Garvey trusted me to tell her husband's story, as did her children. Sons John and Jim gave me their truth and emotion. Daughters Ann showed me love and Emily sent beautiful notes at exactly the right moment. Mary and David were honest, professional and wonderful hosts, and lifelong friend Julie made it all happen. Also thanks to grandchildren Mike and Andy Garvey, Abby Sheppard and Nick Bonavia. Former and current Garvey associates Harvey Childers, Gary Bengochea, Bob White, Todd Connell and Brad Smisor were generous with their time.

For all those who sat to tell me their stories of Willard, it was a sincere pleasure to know you. A special thanks goes to the late Craig Miner, whose notes were invaluable.

My sweet, beautiful Belle (2000-2012): I stole you and you stole me back.

Finally, my beloved husband, proofer, researcher and copy editor Ken Krause walked the journey with me until 11:25 p.m. on New Year's Eve, 2011. This kind and patient man must love me very much. I can only hope to love him back half as much.

ABOUT THE AUTHOR

MAURA MCENANEY has more than 30 years of experience as an award-winning business writer and editor. She is a former journalist at *Bloomberg News*, the *Akron Beacon Journal* and other regional daily and weekly newspapers and trade publications.

Her work has appeared in the *Washington Post, Denver Post, Boston Globe, New York Daily News* and *BusinessWeek* online, among others. Maura was a staff writer on the Akron Beacon Journal's "A Question of Color," a year-long project examining race relations in Akron, which won the Pulitzer Prize Gold Medal for Meritorious Public Service in 1994.

Several months after graduating from Syracuse University, Maura met Willard Garvey in Paradise Valley, Nevada. She has been a close friend of his family for more than two decades. Maura now works in the financial services industry and lives in Medford, Massachusetts with her husband Ken Krause.